AMERICAN SCIEN

AMERICAN SCIENCE FICTION TV

STAR TREK, STARGATE AND BEYOND

JAN JOHNSON-SMITH

WESLEYAN UNIVERSITY PRESS
MIDDLETOWN, CONNECTICUT

Published by Wesleyan University Press
Middletown, CT 06549
www.wesleyan.edu/wespress

First published in 2005 by I.B.Tauris & Co Ltd

ISBN 0-8195-6738-8

Cataloging information for this book is available from the Library of
Congress

Typeset in Melior LT Std by Steve Tribe, Andover
Printed and bound in Great Britain by MPG Books Ltd, Bodmin

5 4 3 2 1

CONTENTS

ACKNOWLEDGEMENTS

My thanks to everyone who has helped me to write this book. Particular thanks go to John Ellis and Andy Medhurst, who offered advice when part of this was a doctoral thesis, and I am especially grateful to Eric Chauvin and James Morrison for their time and candour in interview.

As is customary to note, the ideas here are mine – and any mistakes are also entirely mine.

***

Part of this book is drawn from work in my Ph.D., 'Between the Candle and the Star' (2001). Some of the material in Chapter Four, 'The Sacrifice of Angels', appeared as 'Of Warrior Poetics and Redemption – *Space: Above and Beyond*'s TC McQueen' and was originally published in *The Journal of American Culture* (Vol. 21, No. 3, Fall 1998), 47–62.

In memory of
Mariko Hosono
and
George Johnson-Smith

INTRODUCTION

The history of science fiction television in the USA is almost as old as the medium itself. From *Captain Video and His Video Rangers* in 1949, the speculative extrapolations of science fiction (henceforth 'sf') have had a remarkably powerful presence, paradoxically in a medium associated strongly with the secure, the familiar and the domestic. From the mid 1980s, the number of science fiction and fantasy shows skyrocketed. As the elegiac Western genre rides into the sunset, science fiction is proving a seductive replacement. A handful of individual series have received detailed critical attention, in particular *The X-Files* and *Star Trek* in its various guises, and a multitude of on-line or published programme guides, technical files, encyclopaedia, alien-English dictionaries and recipe books provide an embarrassment of riches for fans of many series. Yet curiously little has been written about the collective television genre or its recent narrative, aesthetic and ideological trends – particularly its remarkable visual imagery. *American Science Fiction Television: 'Star Trek', 'Stargate' and Beyond* offers a starting point for the correction of this extraordinary oversight.

SCIENCE FICTION

In 1948, the famous sf author and pulp fiction editor John W. Campbell Jr. called for sf to be 'an effort to predict the future on the basis of known facts, culled largely from present-day laboratories'.[1] Almost thirty years later, Reginald Bretnor described sf as 'fiction based on rational speculation regarding the human experience of science and its resultant technologies'.[2] Modern American sf television undeniably offers considerably more than Campbell and Bretnor hoped for. It is individualistic, progressive, technically and aesthetically innovative, scientifically secular, potent, humanist, democratic – even egalitarian: it is the quintessential American Dream. Yet this era of technological advance is an awkward time for sf: many of its staple themes are now science, not fiction. The once immense and uncommon computer is portable and commonplace; through chat rooms and game zones we are in contact with people from around the world whom we have never met – and probably will never meet. With space travel also stretching tentatively beyond its infancy and the first tourists returned from the International Space Station, part of sf's once unique appeal has become a tangible reality. Today, we are familiar with pictures of the earth from space, yet it was only during the 1968 Apollo 8 mission that William Anders took the first pictures of the earth from the moon. Orbiting telescopes like Hubble afford us magnificent and mesmerising glimpses of far-flung galaxies, whilst NASA's website offers APOD (the Astronomical Picture of the Day): at the click of a button astounding images of distant nebulae unfold before our eyes.[3] Although the UK's mission to Mars, poor Beagle 2, failed to bark, NASA has enjoyed success with its own Rovers, Spirit and Opportunity, and the USA and Russia have again mooted manned excursions to the red planet in the future. Once we watched with fascination and awe as mighty Saturn V rockets erupted from their launch pads at Cape Kennedy/Canaveral, but today space stories no longer command the top news slot. If not exactly commonplace, they have become an accepted part of life.

Alongside travel in real space has come the advent of the voyage through virtual space: the infinite digital realm of cyberspace is ripe for exploration. With special effects (sfx) and computer generated imagery (cgi), television of all genres can seamlessly combine the analogue and the real with the digital and imaginary; it can 'photograph the impossible',[4] in what J.P. Telotte suggests are 'the greatest imaginative capacities of the film medium'.[5] However, science documentaries such as *The Planets*, *Walking With Dinosaurs* and *Space* also indulge in astounding feats of cgi. These not only open up vast new areas of study to their audiences but, despite the empty coffers of the European Space Agency and NASA, they help make scientific exploration sexy once more. This means that visually, as well as speculatively, science fiction has a lot more to compete with, since science 'fact' is fast catching up in popular discourse.

TELEVISION

Since the mid 1980s, sf television has risen to the challenge, not always successfully, but generally in a manner that has already delivered much and promises even more. One particular phenomenon has made modern sf television possible: the emergence in the mid 1980s of what John Thornton Caldwell calls 'televisuality'.[6] From the murky, low-quality black and white images of the 1950s, where static backgrounds/excessive wordiness dominated, through the action-packed but blurry and anodyne images of the 1970s, we have arrived in an era where far-seeing 'tele-vision' can finally live up to its name. Caldwell's theory of the televisual offers a crucial combination of causes and effects specific to the 1980s; he identifies a crisis in American television production, citing authorial, industrial and technical contexts amongst others. New cable and satellite systems mean that general 'broadcasting' is not the norm, now we also have niche service 'narrowcasting', with special interest groups served by specialist channels. Most important for this book is the technical, which impacts significantly upon the means by which narratives (in both drama and *mise-en-scène*) may be presented. Television pictures are now clear, sharp and crisp. They offer brilliant colours and dynamic motion to enhance their narratives: finally each picture can speak a thousand words. During the past twenty years in television there has been a general shift away from dim nondescript backgrounds and wordy expositional scripts to idealised locations and carefully designed composites of iconic images. The new, sharply defined *mise-en-scène* (set design, costume/makeup, movement and lighting) articulates crucial aspects of the narrative and renders excess verbosity redundant. In an era where we readily condemn films and television programmes as 'all style and no substance' perhaps it is time for us to consider that stories can emerge from more than the plotted action-narrative: *mise-en-scène* has its own narrative too, and in sf it enjoys a particularly powerful function.

Science fiction offers novel concepts for consideration – alien life forms, time travel, warp drives. Visual sf needs to manifest images of those concepts convincingly, and at some level sf television narratives must compete with the immense pyrotechnics of cinema and the often less immediately gratifying realities of prosaic scientific experimentation. The magnificent film *The Andromeda Strain* (1970) pays lengthy attention to time-consuming routine technological and scientific methodologies, and whenever I screen it to my undergraduates a majority complain bitterly that it takes ages for anything to happen – before conceding somewhat grudgingly that perhaps (just maybe) it was 'quite interesting' in the end. As a result, perhaps predictably, *Strange Days* (1995) receives far more appreciation from my endearing but impatient tutees, because its plotting doesn't exactly hang about and an interest in the scientific process has little to do with its enjoyable technological shenanigans. Actually both films offer that which sf relies upon: an inversion of what Samuel Delany calls the 'mundane' (that which we would consider everyday, routine and normal within our experience) through the foregrounding of the background – psychological, physical or geographical.[7] They provide what Darko Suvin calls a 'novum' (usually a novel scientific premise) in a context and language that challenges our everyday experience.[8] It thereby makes the unfamiliar known and the known eerily unfamiliar. Television sf hovered in the wings for so long whilst its big screen relation took both commendation and criticism. From the mid 1980s, with innovations in narrative strategies, a new clarity to its visual imagery and cgi sfx creating a remarkable interaction between the tactile and physical world of the analogue and the intangible realm of the digital, science fiction on television has truly come into its own.

MYTHO-HISTORY

This book explores the development of sf television over the last two decades, focusing upon narrative, imagery and ideology. It also makes a connection between the epic journeys that blend together to form what we recognise as ancient mytho-history and the more recent dominant mytho-history of the USA – the story of the frontier, the 'Wild West'. Records of epic journeys, part genuine exploration and part flamboyant speculation, are central to the development of a national character and psyche. Repeated explorations of these adjusted, amended and renovated journeys litter the arts of every continent – often transcending modern political boundaries and sometimes explaining them. Just as the quest for eternal life in *The Epic of Gilgamesh*[9] underpins Babylonian tales, so Scandinavians stir to oohooo of Viking voyages across the perilous Atlantic to Vinland the Good, and the Dreaming creates a profound communal and spiritual link for the Australian Aboriginal peoples.

In the case of the USA, from the time of white European migration the emergent tales depict not only a fascination with exploration, but also articulate a sense of wonder, an encounter with the Sublime, which we can locate in the classical tales. The sublime, that extraordinary sight which incapacitates our mental faculties through a combination of pleasure and fear, is closely associated with Immanuel Kant and Edmund Burke, and served as a major criterion of the Romantic period.[10] Yet it is also described in less terrifying terms by authors like Blaise Pascal and Pierre Teilhard de Chardin who consider such an awe-inspiring encounter as a remarkable opportunity for complex human beings to contemplate the minute and immense universe around us.[11] Splendid examples of the American sublime occur from the mid 1800s in literature, painting and film representations of the western frontier: aspects of these are examined here briefly as context and precursors to preoccupations prevalent in sf television narratives. Science fiction and the 'final frontier' of space offer an alternative progression to a potentially utopian future, one that has been firmly grasped by the numerous American film and television companies since the 1970s. Visions of the Wild West and the archetypal characters associated with it have much in common with those prevalent in the first few decades of American sf television, but more promisingly for both society and for storytelling, alternative ideologies and cultural discourses in both narrative-drama and narrative-imagery have begun to appear in recent series. This narrative imagery tells its own, sometimes discordant, story and is a strong feature in sf television today.

NEW IMAGES

John Hellman has argued convincingly that writers and artists have found a new location for a free re-working of the frontier myth in science fiction. He uses the original *Star Wars* trilogy as his focus,[12] but the television series *Wild, Wild West* had already made a provisional connection in the 1960s. However, convincing though Hellman's argument has proved in film and literary theory, it is seldom applied to television. I wish to redress that imbalance now and extend it into the visual manifestations through *mise-en-scène*. In space, in the future or in parallel worlds, the old binary oppositions can be challenged; their impossible positioning of civilisation against wilderness and of what 'culture' deems as 'nature' can be rejected. Revolutionary ideas and experiences can be offered, and a new element to television's storytelling repertoire has emerged in the shape of a dynamic and powerful *mise-en-scène*. In art and photography this visual narrative is accepted without question; bizarrely, in film and television – also visual media – it is still the action-narrative with which we are primarily concerned. Cinema offers spectacular *mise-en-scène*, but as we gaze mesmerised at that massive silver screen it is hard for us to work beyond the narrative: we are drawn into the diegesis and become too enveloped to question it easily or willingly.

Television offers an alternative, but not the glance encouraged by an acknowledged segmentation of programming: in the digital age, our viewing habits have changed.[13] Rather, television allows a more detached and observational mode of viewing; this facilitates philosophical interrogation of the texts and allows us to work through them as well as within them. Much like the perspectival air of quiet observation provided by the 'staffage' figures of nineteenth-century American landscape painting, as we watch we become part of a contemplative framework – complex beings suspended between the minute and the immense of the universe. The best sf seeks to provide just such thought-provoking scenarios, and instead of offering spectacle only as a delusional or phenomenological experience sf television uses it to provide a location for interrogation and analysis. The clearest examples of this televisual experience have occurred in series such as *Babylon 5*, *Stargate SG-1* and *Farscape*, where the use of real space imagery is combined with imagination to create a universe of majesty and awe – curiously alien and yet simultaneously reassuringly familiar. The very nature of sf demands that we renegotiate at every step; in doing so, we are made aware of our own inconsistencies as well as those of the creative process itself. The achievements and potential of science fiction television are immense, and this book is an attempt to record just some of what has occurred thus far.

CONTENT

There are diverse opinions as to what or what does not constitute sf; a general summary is therefore a useful starting point. Chapter One offers a broad exploration of what we mean by 'genre' and considers the unique combination of linguistic and narrative strategies that comprise sf texts. I have tried to be inclusive rather than exclusive, and the works of Darko Suvin, Patrick Parrinder, Eric Rabkin and Damien Broderick are helpful, especially regarding the language and content of sf. Useful too are the approaches to genre epitomised by Fredric Jameson, Steve Neale, Robin Wood and Claudio Guillen.[14] Chapter Two is essentially about history. It explores sf's connections with the Sublime and the parallels of artistic representation in epic speculative fictions of old with the ideas of scale and perspective offered by Pascal and de Chardin. It also considers images of America's own dominant mytho-historical epic: the concept of the frontier, the role of the Sublime and the forging of a national ideological identity in literature, art and moving images.

Switching to the medium of television, it explores television's common narrative structures and its visual strategies. The vast changes in technology have changed the face of television forever, and in thirty years we will doubtless laugh at 1990s cgi effects in the same way as we mock the rubber monsters, polystyrene rocks and 'red shirt' alerts of 1960s *Star Trek*. What occurred in television during the 1980s may impress us less, but perhaps we would do well to remember how much it impressed us at the time. The phenomenon of televisuality reaches across all of television: it changed things forever. The forensic scenarios of *CSI: Crime Scene Investigation*, the slow motion of *Witchblade* and the split-screen and self-contained detailed narrative of *24* are all heirs to Caldwell's theory of the televisual. None of them could exist today were it not for the advances he documents from the late 1980s and early 1990s in programmes like *Moonlighting*, *Twin Peaks* and *Wild Palms*. Therefore, although sf series from the 1950s offer much for study and perhaps deserve their own book, I explore them only briefly in order to provide an historical context for both sf itself and for television narrative. It is the series produced from the televisual revolution in the mid 1980s onwards upon which this book concentrates.

The four chapters in Part Two offer detailed case studies of several series, exploring the generic and ideological themes shared with other programmes and considering dominant forms and trends in narrative and narrative-imagery. No story of American sf would be complete without due reference to *Star Trek*, but as there are many excellent books delving into origins of 'the franchise', really only the later series are considered here, along with the development and direction of this remarkable franchise. The interconnected universe of the various *Star Trek* series serves as a sort of benchmark (for good or for bad) against which other series are judged and its use of verbal language, particularly in *The Next Generation*, is an area of considerable interest.

The question of our future and of untapped human potential is a continual fascination for us. We need not leave the earth to explore this area and there has long been a fascination with 'super' powers. Series like *The New Adventures of Superman/Lois and Clark*, *Mutant X* and *Witchblade* demonstrate this continued interest, whilst *Hercules: The Legendary Journeys*, *Xena: Warrior Princess* and *Young Hercules* are jovial reminders of its classical origins. However, the masks and costumes of latter-day American superheroes have more in common with the inversions of Bakhtin's medieval *carnivalesque* than with modern science fiction,[15] and the history and development of the superhero has been explored in detail elsewhere. Nevertheless, mainstream sf does draw from this line of interest: *Now and Again* offers a genteel representation in the superbody of Michael Wiseman, *The Sentinel* uses his specially honed senses to detect crime, while the body armour and cyborg implants of *Robocop, Earth: Final Conflict* and *Babylon 5* epitomise the drive for advantage, protection and perfection. More limited forms of remarkable human prowess – in the shape of heightened senses, psychic and telekinetic powers and genetically advanced abilities – are investigated in borderline sf series like *Psi Factor: Chronicles of the Paranormal, Poltergeist: The Legacy, The X-Files* and *The Dead Zone*. Whilst these programmes linger mostly in the area of the paranormal, and thus distance themselves from mainstream sf, others like *Dark Angel, The Visitor, The Sentinel* and *Prey* tackle the issue of what it is to be human through the question of special/advanced abilities. These programmes deal with the associated ideas of identity, representation and questions of 'otherness' – all issues common to science fiction. Certainly in the new context of alien encounters, humanity can pull together against a common enemy, our shallow prejudices rendered obsolete – we can even offer sanctuary to others, as *Alien Nation* demonstrates. A trend noticeable in more recent *Star Trek* series is for aliens to be portrayed by actors from ethnic groups: the question of difference is therefore highlighted both internally and externally to the story.

The question of difference is considered most fully through the intense and enigmatic character of Lt. Colonel T.C. McQueen in *Space: Above and Beyond*, a series whose investigations also touch upon a somewhat more thorny issue. Since the withdrawal of troops from Vietnam, the portrayal of the US military officer has been fraught with difficulty, yet many sf series use the military as a basis for their explorations – the *Star Trek* series claim a non-militaristic stance but they clearly draw from naval traditions,[16] while *Seaquest DSV* (and *Seaquest 2032*), *Seven Days, Freedom, War of the Worlds, Stargate SG-1* and *Andromeda* etc., all have clear militaristic leanings. For many white inhabitants of the USA, the military generally stands as no threat, it is seen as a loyal and protective force. For Native Americans and the diverse ethnic peoples who share a role in the history of the USA, the long-standing institutions of the political establishment and its military forces represent something other than the honourable protection of land and liberty. The sinister narrative of *Space: Above and Beyond* makes a considerable effort to interrogate the standing of the military and its relationship to the political and public sphere. It also considers the questions of human expansion and colonialism, issues that are explored in only a handful of others series, such as *Earth 2* and *Firefly*.

A theme common to recent series like *Star Trek: Voyager* and *Star Trek: Enterprise* is a tendency not only to draw on the past and present for inspiration, but also to look backwards with a desire to rewrite the past – not unlike the Western. There is a clear fascination with those staples of sf: time travel, wormholes and parallel universes, subjects that predominate in the longer sf stories reaching our screen and new means of creating sfx and cgi allow them to be manifested with remarkable detail and plausibility. The most famous early episodic series is perhaps *Quantum Leap*, which failed to follow sf's common law of *not* changing the past – far from it, Dr Sam Beckett and his sidekick Al positively relished tweaking it at every opportunity, aided and abetted by their computer, Ziggy. The underlying premise of *Enterprise*, with its temporal 'cold war', demonstrates this continued interest; the finale of *Voyager* offers the clearest example of the desire to rewrite history, but it played fast and loose with temporal physics on many occasions. *Seven Days* and *Odyssey 5* are both utterly dedicated to the changing of the past events via time travel, while *Early Edition* offers its protagonist the following day's newspaper headlines, thus affording him the opportunity to 'change' the future. At odds with this are series such as *Time Trax*, *Babylon 5* and most significantly *Farscape* which articulate very clearly that whilst travel forwards in time is not dangerous since it merely offers possible futures or 'unrealised' realities, *backward* time travel is inherently disastrous, regardless of good intentions. Perhaps this is why poor Dr Beckett never quite made it home.

The case studies culminate in a detailed study of all of these aspects of modern television sf in one of the most innovative and consistently challenging sf television series ever produced: *Babylon 5*. The issues so clearly articulated by the warrior poetics of *Space*'s McQueen reach an apotheosis in Commander Sinclair, Ambassador Delenn and Captain John Sheridan, and the final section of this book is devoted to this remarkable, ground-breaking series. Perhaps the only programme to have ever truly competed with *Star Trek* in the creation of a sustainable and plausible future universe, *Babylon 5* is a television epic offering a powerful future history and political intrigue by the bucketful. Its five-year, pre-planned closed story arc challenges traditional television narrative structures and binary ideologies, its stunning use of sfx and space imagery is unsurpassed for its era, and it provides a shining example of the possibilities of sf at the level of domestic television as well as the potential for television narrative itself.

However, whilst *Babylon 5* epitomises the remarkable combination of visual and verbal artistry in television sf, paradoxically, after such a rush of futuristic sf series in the mid to late 1980s through to the millennium, many of the series discussed here have either concluded or are approaching their end; others will undoubtedly step in to take their place. Precisely what will emerge next can only be eagerly anticipated, but whatever it may be, television drama can truly lay claim to a distinguished history in the visually thought-provoking adventure that is science fiction.

PART ONE

SCIENCE FICTION IN CONTEXT

1. KA D'ARGO IN *FARSCAPE*.

ONE

SCIENCE
FICTION

Before exploring sf television it may help to consider what we generally mean by 'science fiction' – how it functions as a genre, how it has developed over time and its major identifiable themes. The genre gained its popular designation in April 1926 from Hugo Gernsback, the editor of *Amazing Stories*. He described it as 'a charming romance intermingled with scientific fact and prophetic vision'[1] and cited Jules Verne, H.G. Wells and Edgar Allan Poe amongst its numerous authors. A variety of terms have since been used, but 'science fiction' remains the dominant one, often abbreviated to 'sf' and appearing sometimes in upper case as 'SF'. The mass media has adapted it into 'sci-fi', a term that Arthur C. Clarke feels has 'the advantage of being instantly understandable to everyone'[2] and one that certainly seems good enough for the popular cable/satellite 'Sci-Fi' television channels.

The 1993 *Encyclopaedia of Science Fiction* includes around twenty descriptions of sf, and lists many of the theories attempting to define it.[3] The letters 'sf' may also function as a convenient catch-all, as author and theorist Damien Broderick (1989) warns, because these 'initials are the accepted abbreviation of a whole sheaf of classificatory

terms applied to texts produced and received in ways marked only
… by certain generic, modal or strategic family resemblances'.[4] So
we run into immediate difficulty because science fiction clearly does
not lend itself to easy definition. As Vivian Sobchack notes in her
seminal book on American sf cinema *Screening Space* (1987), its very
rationale seems to work against the 'tyrannical' academic demand of
defining terms.[5] The content of a story is in itself little help, either.
Just as the Western need not contain beleaguered pioneers in wagon
trains, Apaches and the Seventh Cavalry, gunfighters and saloons, it
may do so: *Little House on the Prairie* (1974–1983) is superficially
quite unlike *Alias Smith and Jones* (1971–1973) and yet they share
enough ideologically, geographically and temporally to be quickly
recognised as Westerns. Equally, a science fiction story need not
be set in the future as *Dark Skies* (1996–1997) demonstrates, nor
must it include spaceships and alien invaders as *Prey* (1998) proves
– yet along with *Earth: Final Conflict* (1997–2002) and *The War of
the Worlds* (1988–1990), these television series are unquestionably
science fiction.

When and where embryonic or proto-generic sf began is even more
difficult to locate. Broderick's argument suggests that it is a modern
genre, since the technologies with which it is chiefly preoccupied
are relatively new, whilst publisher and author Lester del Rey
illuminates a direct lineage springing from ancient Mesopotamian
texts and includes myths and legends in his list.[6] It is not difficult
to make linkages to the epic, fable and romance – indeed by default
every story we have today must in some way be connected to ancient
early stories.[7] Nor is it hard to draw from the shadows of the gothic,
fantasy and the land of Faerie. Broderick sees sf as 'a diachronic
medium – that is, a medium of historical, cumulative change, in
which each step is unlike the last'. By contrast, he suggests that
myth is synchronic, offering 'a "timeless" dimension', whilst fairy
tales, legends and archaic mytho-history follow 'the "cyclical" time
of individual psychic and social development'.[8] Yet this is a narrow
view of sf, implying that only in an era of advanced technology can
stories of future development emerge. Science fiction is 'often' but not
always concerned with technological advances, and this approach is
essentially rooted in the technological preoccupations and prejudices
of the twentieth and early twenty-first centuries. In *The Ascent of*

Wonder (1994), Kathryn Cramer suggests that (along with utopian fiction), gadget-orientated sf originated in a:

> desire to create and predict the possibility of a better world. In sf, this better world will be created and predicted though science and technology; scientific exploration and technological innovations are political acts leading to world salvation. But without the tradition of the folk-tale, sf, if it existed at all, would be a literature of didactic tracts, blueprints for 'utopia'. Fortunately, the enlightened, rationalistic, utopian impulse collided with the irrational, romantic, fanciful folk storytelling tradition.[9]

So, if we consider a broader spectrum and include early speculative fictions and fantasies, such as the tales of Gilgamesh or Odysseus – all of which include discoveries and advances of knowledge – we find ourselves in worlds of myth, magic and non-technological possibilities. It seems that the science of today is the magic of yesterday, the magic of today is the science of tomorrow.

QUESTIONS OF GENRE

So the question remains – what do we actually mean when we call something 'sf'? The problem lies with genre theory in general, and in how we group texts together, whether capriciously or with empirical pragmatism. Since the 1071 publication of Claudio Guillen's *Literature as System*, the approach to literary genre study has evolved considerably, and his approach is equally helpful in the visual arts. For decades the pursuit of genre studies meant a search for the 'purest' example of a type – as Fredric Jameson suggests, it was a quest to 'unveil, surprise and possess the ultimate "secret" of the thing itself (a passion with a long history of its own *within* SF)'.[10] Guillen argues that pure manifestations of genre cannot be found, and that all texts emerge at the intersection of several genres from the tensions created by their very position and existence.[11] Tzvetan Todorov also puts forward a compelling case against purely empirical research in genre theory in his structuralist study of *The Fantastic* (1975), suggesting that 'it is not the quantity of the observations, but the logical coherence of a theory that finally matters.'[12] Todorov's study concerns nineteenth-century novels, so it does not initially appear relevant to a modern novel like Jeff Noon's nightmare of Mancunian life, *Vurt* (1993), and still less relevant to modern sf television series such as *The Visitor* (1997–1998) or *Firefly* (2002). However, the psychology behind Todorov's conclusion is useful because ultimately, as Broderick notes, he locates sf's zone of influence within the individual reader and the reader's subconscious rather than within the text.[13]

In his 1989 study *Fantasy and the Cinema*, James Donald argues that genre involves:

> not just the obvious iconographic and narrative conventions ... but also 'systems of orientations, expectations and conventions that circulate between industry, text and subject.' What distinguishes one genre from another are not so much particular formal elements as the way such elements – which may be common to a number of genres – are combined so as to produce particular narrative structures and modes of address.[14]

Fredric Jameson takes this further, suggesting that we should not simply 'drop [generic] specimens into the box bearing those labels, but ... [also] map our co-ordinates on the basis of those fixed stars and triangulate this specific given textual movement'.[15] Genre theory is therefore more useful for co-ordination and location rather than as a means of pure delineation, inclusion and exclusion. Television theorist John Caughie follows a similar path, suggesting that we need to be sensitive 'to generic difference as much as to repetition, and, in particular, to generic difference which cannot simply be assigned to the magical agency of authorship'.[16] In doing so, we see that 'genres are used for specific purposes, address specific problems, provide specific pleasures, produce specific types of insights and experiences.'[17] The question of what comprises any genre demands continual reassessment and reconsideration in the context of its era, ideology and culture, all of which impact upon it in the past, present and future. Just as a self-reflexive text must refer by default to its conservative ancestry, so the most conservative text must also contain the capacity for self-reflexivity and ironic critique: the capacity is only recognised through the act of reading – the power of individual realisation which lies within the reader. This provides an antidote to what Robin Wood calls 'the tendency to treat the genres as discrete. An ideological approach might suggest why they can't be, however hard they may appear to try: at best, they represent different strategies for dealing with the same ideological tensions.'[18] This offers the possibility of a comparison between, for example, a Western and a science fiction text, demonstrating the communality between apparently disparate genres and removing a huge obstacle to progress within genre theory.

CREATING WORLDS

A more practical approach is to simply ask what it is that helps us identify a story as 'science fiction'. Every text has a fundamental need: regardless of its medium, it must quickly and efficiently establish a convincing and sustainable reality. Science fiction's alternative realities are created both in and through visual or verbal language: its imaginary worlds are initially formed in a manner identical to those of other genres. The difference is that in sf these worlds must also distinguish themselves from the realities of our everyday world by creating new or different rules by which their realities function. As Broderick reminds us, at the heart of reading is an act that helps to:

> create a world, built out of words and memories and the fruitfulness of the imagination. Usually, we miss the complexity of this process. Like poetry and postmodern fiction, sf tests the textual transparency we take for granted, contorting habits of grammar and lexicon with unexpected words strung together in strange ways.[19]

This process is normally missed because the artifice involved in the means of relaying the message is concealed in many texts: the story takes priority over the style of the telling; the realist tendency means that the signifier is effectively effaced. The ambitions and lexicon of sf are in contrast with the central objectives of most other genres. For Delany, 'mundane' fiction generally proceeds:

> as a series of selections from a theoretically fixed, societally extant lexicon of objects, actions and incidents. In the s-f tale, a series of possible objects, possible actions, possible

incidents (whose possibility is limited, finally, only by what is sayable, rather than what is societal) fixes a more or less probable range of contexts for a new lexicon.[20]

So, despite similarities, there are important differences immediately isolating the sf text from even the experimental poem or the postmodernist text.

A remarkably high degree of plausibility is vital to science fiction. One manner in which sf stories vary from the mundane is through their methods of highlighting difference at multiple levels, and the necessity of doing this both rapidly and convincingly for the reader or viewer is paramount. There are several key underlying conventions of realism, but fundamentally we expect a story to create a world. According to literary critic Jonathan Culler, our reading creates a 'model of the social world, models of the individual personality, of the relations between the individual and society, and perhaps most important, of the kind of significance which these aspects of the world can bear'.[21] Readers identify specific components in a text and in doing so they 'naturalize the details of the text by relating them to some kind of natural order or pattern already existing in our physical or cultural environment'.[22] In effect, these component elements enable readers to construct the story world in a fashion plausible to them. However, for a genre like sf, not only must the world be plausible, but a strong degree of estrangement from the mundane world is also vital. Whether in verbal or visual form, sf must break with everyday reality.

This is achieved in several ways. It occurs through the form and style of the textual presentation and its utilisation of various linguistic strategies – poetic phrasing, arcane juxtapositions, neologisms and transformed language, for example. In addition, we are forced to pay attention to elements normally taken for granted because the background location of a scenario is foregrounded – which is particularly important for sf film and television. This is in itself an estranging experience, particularly in plays, films and television drama, as it prioritises the visual over the narrative – whereas we have been trained throughout our lives to prioritise the narrative experience over the visual (somewhat strange in visual arts). Replacing the dominance of the narrative story with the parity or dominance of the visual experience creates the pleasures and awe of spectacle.

Unusual experiences and extraordinary encounters can provoke either a sense of wonder, or if pushed further, an almost irrational fear, one often associated with the Sublime. This in turn further challenges our cognitive capacity, sometimes stalling it completely. Science fiction relies upon a careful combination of these practices to achieve its break with mundane reality and in doing so creates a sense of cognitive estrangement. The following sections explore how each of these elements contributes towards achieving this break with mundane reality.

FORMALISM AND REALISM

In *Metamorphoses of a Literary Genre* (1979), Darko Suvin identifies sf's break with the real world as the condition of 'cognitive estrangement', a feature common to sf in all forms. He describes sf as a genre 'whose necessary and sufficient conditions are the presence and interaction of estrangement and cognition, and whose main formal device is an imaginative alternative to the author's empirical experience'.[23] Audience estrangement was a practice favoured in the 1920s onwards by Russian Formalists such as Viktor Shklovsky and Jurji Tynjanov and by the German dramatist Brecht. They claim their works offer something radically different from the normal experience of the audience, and the main method by which a change in perception is achieved occurs through a process of defamiliarisation and estrangement – in Russian, *zatrudnenie*, 'making difficult', and *ostraneniye*, 'making strange'.[24] For Shklovsky, the role of poetic art is to 'explode the encrustations of customary, routinized perception by making forms difficult',[25] and a variety of methods can be utilised to achieve this, including the roughening of poetic language, wordplay and/or arcane figures of speech.[26] Much as Delany observes differences between 'mundane' fiction and 'science' fiction, the Formalists differentiated between the text that repeats recognisable and conventional rhetorical forms of reality, and those that in some manner attempt to break with them.[27]

Importantly for sf television, the Formalists were the first to explore the analogy between film (visual) and language (verbal). Drawing on the work of the Swiss linguist Ferdinand de Saussure, Tynjanov compared montage to prosody (the study of versification) and argued that just as 'plot is subordinate to rhythm in poetry, so plot is subordinate to style in cinema'.[28] This is not the same as postmodernism, which is concerned with style, simulacra and the absence of meaning rather than its presence, but theorists of Fredric Jameson's ilk demonstrate their Formalist heritage in their preoccupations with style over substance in late twentieth-century capitalism.[29] Formalist theory emerges in direct opposition to the representational sign of Realism 'which effaces its own status as a sign in order to foster the illusion that we are perceiving reality without its intervention'.[30] In his seminal studies of linguistics, *S/Z* (1975), Roland Barthes developed the notion of a double sign, one that gestures 'to its own material existence at the same time as it conveys a meaning' and, according to Eagleton, can therefore be identified as 'the grandchild of the "estranged" language of the Formalists and Czech Structuralists, of the Jakobsonian poetic word which flaunts its own palpable linguistic being'.[31] Texts are therefore no longer seen as stable or delineated as structures, and the apparently scientific objectivity of the critic is relinquished. For Barthes and Eagleton this means that:

> [The] most intriguing texts for criticism are not those which can be *read*, but those which are writable (*scriptible*) – texts which encourage the critic to carve them up, transpose them into different discourses, produce his or her semi-arbitrary play of meaning athwart the work itself.[32]

In effect, the reader becomes a producer, not a consumer.

Roman Jakobson continues with this line of enquiry, suggesting that 'in poetry any verbal element is converted into a figure of poetic speech.'[33] Christian Metz took it to a comparable level in visual arts, arguing that any element in cinema could be turned to expressive purposes, i.e., into Jakobson's poetic speech. Prior to their arguments, reflectionism had been the accepted approach – that is, a text was assessed against some mutually accepted monolithic and eternal concept of the 'real'. With reflectionism under assault, realism in general, and cinematic (or visual) realism in particular, could be considered as 'an effect produced by certain kinds of texts'.[34] Just as sf cannot belong to an existing textual version of reality because its entire *raison d'être* is to speculate and encourage speculation about other potential and plausible realities, so a more practical starting point is to consider that realism in any genre is wholly internal and produced anew in every discourse. For science fiction, forever seeking to create new realities, this is a distinct advantage.

DEFAMILIARISATION AND ESTRANGEMENT

What then is sf doing when it uses estrangement to create its new worlds? Three authors offer slightly differing conclusions, but ultimately all confirm the importance of defamiliarisation and estrangement in the process of creating sf scenarios. Writing of Philip K. Dick's *Time Out of Joint* (1959), Fredric Jameson follows in the rich Formalist tradition, suggesting that what sf offers is simply 'the estrangement and renewal of our own reading present'.[35] In *Terminal Identity* (1993), Scott Bukatman suggests that sf primarily 'narrates the dissolution of the very ontological structures that we usually take for granted', and argues that the '"multiple mock futures" of science fiction work by transforming our own present into the determinate past of something yet to come.'[36] Consequently, sf defamiliarises our lives and with them the sf lives we read about, and reflects them back to us in an extravagant, extrapolated fashion. For Larry McCaffrey, in a 1990 collection of interviews with famous sf authors, this means places composed of 'cognitive distortions and poetic figurations of our own social relations – as these are constructed and altered by new technologies',[37] are temporarily experienced by the sf reader. Reality is thus in a state of near-constant flux.

This returns us to sf's tendency to foreground the background in a manner seldom found in other genres. Information that the reader of a mundane novel may take for granted – the opening of a door, or the turning on of a tap – must be specified and explained in sf stories. Samuel Delany asks in what other genre would a door not *open*, but *dilate* – much to fellow author Harlan Ellison's joy. Certainly as a naturalistic piece of fiction, Delany agrees the phrase 'the door dilated' is meaningless, but 'as sf – as an event that hasn't happened, yet still must be interpreted in terms of the physically explainable – it is quite as wondrous as Ellison feels it.'[38] In television, we have the iris shielding the gate in *Stargate SG-1* (1997–), the event horizon itself, and the wormholes of *Farscape* (1999–2003), *Sliders* (1995–2000) and *Star Trek: Deep Space Nine* (1993–1999). They are not 'doorways' as we recognise the everyday concept, yet we accept them within the sf context. Delany calls this shift between foreground and background 'the deposition of weight between landscape and psychology',[39] which is why only in sf can a phrase such as 'her world exploded' be taken legitimately as anything other than metaphor.[40] This frequently means that the information required by the reader or viewer is dispersed by oblique or implicit means, which requires more concentration and thus automatically engages them in a manner different to that required by a story of the everyday world.

As a result, sf texts spend far more time on background information than do mundane stories, which often leads to the complaint that sf is all style and no substance – there is neither characterisation nor plot development. In fact, the development is often in the background – in the setting and location. This technique invites criticism about a lack of symbolism in sf texts, but science fiction largely 'does not have time for symbolism (in the accepted sense of the word); its aesthetic framework, when richly filled out, is just too complex.'[41] Nevertheless, it is fair to say that on first appearances in sf stories just about everything is foreground and, as such, provides another means of creating the estrangement associated with the genre.[42] Jameson's discussions of postmodernism and cognitive mapping can be helpful in explaining why this is so; where the cultural symbols and icons of our world have become simulacra, empty and meaningless they are therefore of little use to us as means of locating ourselves either culturally and socially. Equally, in the more alien worlds of sf, it is hard to insist upon symbols and icons because nothing is recognisable until the new world has been established within which readers might begin to locate themselves. Nevertheless, after a prolonged period of immersion in an unfamiliar world which does have specific rules by which it functions, some icons may become established, such as the mysterious 'Triluminary' in *Babylon 5* (1994–1998) or the concept of the Force in the *Star Wars* films (1977–1983, 1999–). Conversely, a perverted form of recognisable mundane cultural iconography can be used to shock just as effectively, since in an sf landscape it also becomes a form of estrangement. Little would work as effectively in the *Planet of the Apes* (1974) as those final scenes where Taylor

(Charlton Heston) gazes up at a half-buried and derelict Statue of Liberty, and realises that he was 'home all the time'. Through this 'thematic and stylistic estrangement', the most challenging science fiction thus allows 'that renewal (and cognitive mapping) of the reader's present'[43] and, in doing so, negates the effect of classical realism.

THE NOVUM

Alongside cognitive estrangement, Suvin identifies one other major structural component of sf: the narrative hegemony of a fictional innovation or novelty, the novum, where the narrative is determined by a change/changes to the mundane experience based upon some scientific or logical innovations. This idea can be simplified to suggest that most science fiction stories are based upon the premise 'what if...?' Science fiction creates new histories or new futures and examines their impact upon societies and individuals.[44] Philip K. Dick's 'Breakfast at Twilight' (1954), for example, asks how a family would react if it were sucked temporarily into some dreadful apocalyptic future just eight years away and then sent back to the present to finish breakfast. In Ray Bradbury's 1952 short story 'A Sound of Thunder', also filmed as an episode for *The Ray Bradbury Theatre* (1985–1992), a group of time-travelling hunters journey into the past in search of dinosaurs. One traveller accidentally slips from the safe path and treads on a butterfly, inexorably altering the pattern of evolution on the planet and thus the very future to which he must return. Both stories demonstrate Suvin's novum – an idea, a technological breakthrough – that allows the central question, often moral or philosophical, to be addressed. In this case, it is an ability to travel through time. Having provided and demanded centrality to this novum, the sf story extrapolates to their logical conclusions the cultural, social and technological ramifications, and they take effect upon the world we know from empirical experience. The result is the creation of a 'reality sufficiently autonomous and intransitive to be explored at length as to its properties and the human condition it implies'.[45]

This capability is unique and vital to sf; it cannot take over an existing textual production of reality, because its entire *raison d'être* is to speculate about *other* possible realities. Essentially, the novum functions as a specific device whose ramifications for existing reality are then explored in combination with the Formalist-based method of foregrounding the background.[46] Cognitive estrangement can therefore be seen as defining the textual effects of such work: the text faces its audience with something that will not fit into the existing patterns of verisimilitude, yet is being asserted and explored as fact.[47] Science fiction narratives explore what this break in reality means for the remainder of reality.

There are limitations to the degree of estrangement that sf can achieve successfully. Regardless of its medium, the sf diegesis 'must stand in some kind of cognitively discoverable relation to our own empirical experiences'.[48] Therefore, not only are we thrown into new worlds by sf, but to ensure that we appreciate the vulnerability of our situation, it also carefully 'specifies how we got there'.[49] This encourages interrogation of ideas, cognitive estrangement means that we must question and challenge what we see in order to comprehend it. This is not to say that other genres cannot also encourage such a process, but it is a fundamental principle within sf, and Suvin's model thus stands in opposition to a passive or submissively uncritical acceptance of any ideology, religious or secular. The 'idea of cognitive estrangement takes its stand in the ongoing battle between agnostic materialism and mystical idealism'.[50] This critical and exacting process means that science fiction does not often appeal to the higher or intuitive logic of the occult, but is distinguished by cognition as a correlative, which Suvin considers 'identical to that of a modern philosophy of science'.[51] In this way it is also distinguished from fantasy and supernatural genres.

Suvin's definition of sf as a genre of cognitive estrangement is useful for film and television as much as for literature. Firstly, it offers us a sense of the loci of sf, and secondly it seeks neither to include nor exclude. Instead, it takes into account the fact that any generic model is at the mercy of endless qualification and that, in common with any paradigm, the organising perspective is the issue of primary significance.[52] Suvin's approach is chiefly structural and therefore he defines sf by its clearest patterned content: science. In English the word 'science' is strongly biased towards natural sciences rather than technology, whereas the French word *science*, like its German counterpart *Wissenschaft*, is better translated as 'knowledge'.[53] This subtle difference in meaning suggests that in broader cultural terms we may wish to include speculative fictions, tales of ancient and fabulous journeys and adventure – such as *Gilgamesh*, Sinbad's voyages in *The Arabian Nights*, or Odysseus' superhuman quests in *The Odyssey* – within the framework of the genre. Certainly, these tales function as informing predecessors, providing sf with a heritage as rich as any genre, and it seems reasonable to suggest that sf extends its roots and claims a birthright from a deeper time line than the limits of our modern technology.

Parrinder suggests that:

> the criterion of proto-science fiction in earlier periods, all the way to the Greek legends, must be not so much its anticipation of the specific themes of later SF (such as the journey to other worlds) as its relationship to the body of cognitions in its own day.[54]

Most narrative structures in sf create 'a base from which the reader can reason about the ways in which the world of the text differs from our world, whilst simultaneously justifying the ways in which the two worlds are similar'.[55] The accompanying sense of cognition allows for authorial explanations of any technological advances, so there is no need for sf to limit scientific awareness by our own current scientific or technical abilities. If this were not the case, the spice merchants of Herbert's *Dune* books (1963–1985) could not 'fold space' and Reese could not travel back in time to rescue Sarah Connor in *The Terminator* (1984). The sf author has to create a kind of scientific/common sense explanation for actions, one that is 'based upon reasoning from natural laws, whether those happen to be empirically true or not'.[56] Therefore, sf narratives notably create their own limitations; for instance, Federation vessels in the various *Star Trek* series cannot exceed Warp 9.9. There are theories of how the barrier can be broken, of course, but any attempt at experimentation invariably ends in disaster, involves dubious alien technologies, or demands an unacceptable ethical and moral position. *Star Trek: Voyager* (1995–2001) demonstrates this in the seasons 5 and 6 bridging episode 'Equinox'. Here, the crew of another Federation ship lost in the Delta Quadrant is draining aliens of their life force to create a faster means of reaching home, but Janeway and her colleagues rapidly remind them of the importance of Federation values even – especially – so far from home.

The values implicit in much science fiction are those of our own culture, sometimes idealised, sometimes extrapolated, but firmly recognisable: honour, duty, loyalty, all those things which create integrity are illuminated as the aspects of humanity most valued even in future societies. J.G. Ballard points out that although at its worst sf film 'offers the sheer exhilaration of the roller-coaster', it has another, more valuable contribution to make. 'At its best, and to its credit,' says Ballard, 'it tries to deal with the largest issues facing us today, and attempts, however naively, to place some sort of philosophical framework around man's place in the universe.'[57] Actor Ben Browder makes a similar point in a *Farscape* interview for the Sci-Fi Channel, noting how 'good' sf is often concerned with ethical and moral issues.[58] The issues themselves are quite literally cast in an alien light: stripped of their everyday context they invite fresh consideration from a different perspective.

In fantasy, the same moral values we prize in life mark out Frodo, Sam and Aragorn in J.R.R. Tolkien's *The Lord of the Rings* (1954–1955): their selflessness, their sense of duty and sense of honour shine through. Fantasy offers magic instead of technology – mysterious far-seeing palantír orbs, flying carpets, the gift of second sight – none of which is explained to us. In contrast, the sf reader is likely to be given a spaceship or a 'portable anti-gravity' device, together with details of their development.[59] Science fiction's explanatory nature – one of the elements of Suvin's term 'cognition' – is 'an identifying characteristic of the genre, distinguishing it categorically from fantasy'.[60]

Yet there is also the central issue of evolution through time; any reasonably advanced technological system would be inseparable from magic for a lesser mortal. Ursula K. Le Guin's novels of *Earthsea* (from 1971) and series like *The Adventures of Sinbad* (1996) and *Witchblade* (2001–2002) provide magical worlds where so commonplace are the miracles of the mystical ancient arts that they are governed by the same inevitability as scientific experimentation and its resultant technology. Magic is not magic if it is everyday. In *Babylon 5*, both fantasy and scientific extrapolation are utilised. The Techno-mages in 'The Geometry of Shadows' are an intelligent reminder of this juxtaposition. To the Techno-mages of 2259, the combination of technology and alchemy is a learned skill: to the uninitiated observer, their works are acts of magic. Here science and magic collide, and are revealed to have the same function, united by artistry. They are only confused or obscured through time and the limits of individual perception.

POSTMODERNISM

This brings us to an important cultural phenomenon – postmodernism. In the 1930s and 1940s, pulp magazines like *Astounding* were predicting the very future in which we now find ourselves living, demanding a re-examination of 'central narrative assumptions and metaphorical frameworks'.[61] During the 1950s and 1960s, authors like Ballard and Dick were respectively providing postmodernism in the shape of condensed novels and stories of simulacra before the phrase 'postmodernism' was ever coined or applied: Ballard was arguably the first to have isolated what Bukatman calls 'the death of affect'.[62] Theorist Jean-François Lyotard suggests that we rely upon an uncritical and unquestioned foundation for our understanding of our cultural location and the location of cultural institutions in the world today, categorising it as 'incredulity towards meta-narratives'.[63] This is yet another challenge to the manifestation of the 'real' as a monolithic definitive absolute. In *Crash* (1973), Ballard wrote of the end of modernism in literature, characterising its 'sense of individual isolation, its mood of introspection and alienation'. He describes a new cultural dominant, that which we now recognise as postmodern, one defined by rapid technological change busy at work in a landscape of extremes:

> Across the communications landscape move the spectres of sinister technologies and the dreams that money can buy. Thermonuclear weapons systems and soft drink commercials co-exist in an overlit realm ruled by advertising and pseudoevents, science and pornography.[64]

This is postmodernism made manifest; the concept of 'cognitive mapping'[65] has been in some ways anticipated. In sf, as in postmodernism, it is the loci provided by such mapping that is often destroyed in the drive to subvert and challenge our sense of reality.[66] Nevertheless, unlike postmodernism's iconoclastic drive, sf still generally creates a concrete reality in which alternative rules function.

METALINGUISTICS AND NEOLOGISMS

Just as attitudes differ regarding what comprises sf, there are a variety of approaches to it – satire in *Brazil* (1985), parody in *Galaxy Quest* (1999) or romance in *Somewhere in Time* (1980). The stories nevertheless share one common factor: they offer comment upon our own world through metaphor and extrapolation, with utopian or dystopian visions of alternative realities.[67] Essentially, these approaches are concerned with creation and exploration – they make the unknown known and the known unrecognisable, and achieve this by sending us on magical, mythical and technological journeys of human (self-)discovery. The corollary of these journeys is that various representations of ritual and convention from our own world can be seen through new eyes. Author Sarah Lefanu notes that unlike 'other forms of genre writing, such as detective stories and romance, which demand the reinstatement of order ... science fiction is by its nature interrogative, open'.[68] The possibilities for open, radical, questioning texts in sf appear to be endless.

Ursula K. Le Guin's society of hermaphrodites in *The Left Hand of Darkness* (1969) and Joanna Russ's tales of *Alyx* and *The Female Man* in the 1970s clearly out set their authors' agenda for equality. Russ says that one of the best things about science fiction is that:

> at least theoretically – it is a place where the ancient dualities disappear. Day and night, up and down, 'masculine' and 'feminine' are purely specific, limited phenomena which have been mythologised by people. They are man-made (not woman-made) ... Out in space there is no up and down, no day and night, and in the point of view that space can give us, I think there is no 'opposite' sex – what a word! Opposite what? The Eternal Feminine and the Eternal Masculine become the poetic fancies of a weakly diamorphic species trying to imitate every other species in a vain search for what is 'natural'.[69]

Russ's condemnation of these binary 'poetic fancies' not only points out our near-constant cultural reliance upon binary oppositions, it also brings us to the final element that distinguishes sf from even postmodernist mundane texts: its unique use of language.

The language of sf is one of its distinguishing features. A particular discourse or lexicon is essential to genre, but the sense of wonder in the vocabulary of sf is paramount. It is a call to the fears and pleasures we find in the unknown, in the alien and in the Sublime, an experience facilitated and amplified by the break in reality which demands that we renegotiate our location and its significance at every step. However, the imaginary worlds of sf must still stand in 'some kind of cognitively discoverable relation to our own empirical situation'.[70] The purpose of descriptive residues – objects with no apparent role in character/plot development – is to:

> denote the *thereness* of the world. SF writers also include such items in their texts, but now the items do more than denote the simple *thereness* of the world they belong to; they also tell us – again, usually in oblique ways – something about the nature of the world we find them in.[71]

Eric S. Rabkin has identified three main functions of metalinguistics – the relationship of language to meaning – in his work on sf literature. He suggests that:

> the text can at points take language as its subject; the text can use language as the material it cuts and patterns and sews into new creations not necessarily having anything overtly to do with the linguistic materials; and the text can remind us that language itself forms part of the context determining our understanding of the particular language we are reading.[72]

Most interesting for visual sf are the first two categories.[73] Science fiction uses language as a subject because sf writers are aware that they must explain how communication is achieved for characters from different cultures, eras and planets. *Star Trek* series generally avoid this problem by employing a 'universal translator', even *Enterprise* (2001–) relies upon this, only half-heartedly charting the problems in its database development. The opening credits in *Farscape*'s later seasons are initially presented in an alien language before morphing into English, whilst the entire series relies upon translator microbes for Crichton (and the audience) to comprehend the multitude of alien languages. *Babylon 5* stresses both communalities and differences in communication, often using subtitles for alien languages. The second category, the transformation of language, is a more subtle approach as its gradual creation has a longer lasting but less immediate effect upon the reader.[74] Le Guin's *The Left Hand of Darkness* is a clear example of this. The location for this story is the planet Winter, where the extreme climate means that even volcanoes are frozen in ice. Familiar phrases are transformed: 'Rome wasn't built in a day' becomes 'The Glaciers didn't freeze overnight', while 'Mountains should be seen and not heard' clearly originates in 'Children should be seen and not heard'.[75] Rabkin describes this as:

> [a] shift of consciousness away from the human and towards the environmental. Thus, by a metalinguistic engagement with something we might call an ecological code, Le Guin subtly and implicitly claims a special kind of reality for certain aspects of her science fictional world.[76]

The transformation creates something new, but also illuminates and enforces a shared educational heritage, a linguistic connection with something old and/or mythological, thereby ensuring that the text can safely make its claim to reality.[77]

An alternative course for sf is the use of new or alien words. Like all fiction, sf is a semiotic practice, and its specific genre can be recognised by the reader because of the individual characteristics described above. In a study of the differences between 'realist' and 'sf' discourse, Marc Angenot argues that realist mundane texts offer 'allusive linguistic detail which serves not to conjure a visual image but to establish the concrete nature of the world'.[78] In fact, they do of course create a visual image, but it is mundane and, in that sense, unremarkable. However, neologisms in sf remind us that we must repeatedly renegotiate our relationship with the reality of the sf textual world. Angenot argues that the 'truthfulness of language is two-fold: external (in its reference to the empirical world), and internal (in the operative character of its code)'; sf uses the schism between 'the signified and the referent, concepts which are incompatible yet necessarily linked and taken for each other'. This produces 'a paradigmatic mirage', which demands that the act of reading is also an act of conjecture.[79] Essentially Angenot's claim is that concepts or acts taken for granted in our everyday world can mean something entirely new when used within the sf text. Consequently, we do not necessarily grasp the significance of what is actually there, and in order to comprehend the text we must accept that we are only guessing its 'meaning'. In sf texts, this is sometimes complicated by the inclusion of what Myra Barnes (1975) designates as 'exolinguistics' – the lexicon of alien worlds.[80] The Minbari and Narn languages of *Babylon 5* offer examples of this, and whereas they are usually translated for us by means of subtitles, words are sometimes used in the midst of English sentences as a powerful means of contrast and we are told that there is no accurate translation.

Whilst sf is replete with transformed language, neologisms and exolinguistics, the majority of words within any kind of tale must still be recognisable – otherwise the reader is truly alienated. When we encounter new situations in reality our initial vocabulary is frequently inadequate – we struggle to find an appropriate phrase and are rendered speechless. Caught halfway up a mountain during a thunderstorm, artist Thomas Cole wrote of the experience in his journal, saying: 'Man may seek such scenes and find pleasure in the discovery, but there is a mysterious fear [that] comes over him and hurries him away. The sublime features of nature are too severe for a lone man to look upon and be happy.'[81] Cole's experience makes clear that in such a situation the landscape becomes totally incomprehensible, the human eye longing for something other than the frightening challenge of uninhibited elemental forces and the chaos of the wilderness. He also makes clear that we can only describe with confidence what we see and what we know – or what we can imagine based on an extrapolation of what we know. Our seeing is a discursive act, and by extrapolation we imagine our future with our current ability, and an adorned or embellished vocabulary. We build on what we know, advancing as far as common sense and imagination dictate, but in mundane fiction our vocabulary and patterns of syntax limit us, whereas in sf neologisms can be employed. Unlike literature, visual sf also allows us to concretise futuristic visions, a 'wormhole' can be manifested for our benefit – thus, although both words and images are abstractions, visual sf offers other potentials and faces different challenges to those confronting its literary counterpart.

THEMES

So much for the form and language of sf: what of its themes and narrative preoccupations? Stories of heroic quests, epic explorations and the ongoing search for knowledge can be traced through the ages, narrating the development of civilisations. Many early speculative fictions (stories combining historical events with extravagant imaginings), provide parallels with modern fictions of exploration and discovery and thus can perhaps help us towards a clearer delineation of sf's generic themes. The structures and syntax of early speculative fictions such as *Gilgamesh* and *The Iliad* are often similar to the linguistic juxtapositions discussed previously. Just as modern sf demands we map ourselves anew in a cognitive sense, so the use of ancient and elusive forms of language allows us to experience manifestations of an elusive and shifting mytho-historical past. This technique effectively (re)creates old worlds for us to explore as if for the first time, yet simultaneously offers some familiarity. In sf, this paradoxical combination is highly potent, permitting us to explore new worlds without losing the vital link between these worlds and the world we inhabit. Moreover, we constantly return to these patterns in modern storytelling.

Lester del Rey argues that at least some of the roots of sf storytelling can be traced to the most ancient examples of literature:[82] clearly this is true of all modern stories. Nevertheless, there are particular comparisons to be made here regarding sf. Just as many sf novels draw from mythology for their foundation, several major sf television series also make significant use of ancient mythology. *Babylon 5* borrows from Babylonian legends of chaos and order and from the remarkable alliances forged by Gilgamesh; *Stargate SG-1* predominantly uses Egyptian/Norse legends (although its seventh season shifts slightly, concluding as the fabled Atlantis rises). Along with *Farscape* and *Star Trek: The Next Generation* (1987–1994), these series all refer at some stage to the 'Ancients' or the 'First Ones',[83] while *Earth: Final Conflict* introduces us to the Atavus, a pre-human earth race. The light-hearted *Special Unit 2* (2001–2003) and *The Chronicle* (2001–2002) steal from every folk tale and myth they can find, with Bigfoot, the Sandman, deadly spider-women, dwarves and goblins littering their quirky stories. *The X-Files* (1993–2002) also draws upon urban legends, the gothic, alien abduction and anything else vaguely unsettling to our impressionable minds for its Machiavellian narratives.

The mytho-histories to which sf programmes refer are not in any way sf as we know it today, but their fabulous quests and sublime speculations are paralleled in the genre. So, as del Rey suggests, this means that modern sf can claim a partial heritage 'precisely as old as the first recorded fiction. This is the *Epic of Gilgamesh*.'[84] The heroic or epic narrative generally follows the pattern of a quest and the emphasis lies upon encounter and illumination. Often an incredible journey or voyage is part of the tale (Gilgamesh, Odysseus), emphasising not only the experiences of the journey (Jason and the Argonauts, Sinbad), but the splendour and awe of remote, unknown places (Hercules, Aeneas). One need only look at the immense success of the *Indiana Jones* films (1981–1989) to recognise the enduring potency of this combination. The epic has other important elements: geographic locations are a prime concern, but more important is the historically contextualised location of the narrative.[85] *Gilgamesh*, *The Iliad*, *Beowulf* and *Sir Gawain and the Green Knight* create plausible alternative realities, parallel universes of meta-mythologies into which we will happily transport ourselves at any time. Key words – locations, names – are used, and because they have no definitive meaning, they are easily accepted into new contexts – Atlantis, the Elysian Fields, Camelot. Their exoticism is memorable, and they contribute to the catalogue of evocative mytho-history to which adults refer when they enjoy the cultural arts. More importantly, our myths are not set. There is no single legend of King Arthur, nor a definitive *Arabian Nights*, nor *Gilgamesh*, etc., and because these stories originate in the flexible oral tradition, we have no difficulty in accepting minor alterations. They are simply another manifestation of an old friend, and we incorporate them into a familiar, growing, mytho-historical meta-narrative.[86] For modern stories the use of a language poetic and arcane to us, but in keeping with another era, signals difference, whilst more familiar aspects simultaneously reassure us. As we hear stories of the fabled Atlantis, we maintain the desire for digging up new histories and with them, new futures, and potentially astounding discoveries. Missions to the Moon and Mars, whilst gathering scientific knowledge about the origins of the universe and life in our solar system are simultaneously quests for and explorations of possible ancient and fallen civilisations. They fulfil much the same function as their ancient progenitors.

THE GOTHIC AND THE SUBLIME

The epic is not the only mode utilised and honoured by sf narrative. The rise of modern science fiction can be broadly defined as a 'response to the rise of modern science'.[87] Robert Scholes believes that speculative fiction 'returns deliberately to confront reality' in the form of allegory, satire, fable or parable.[88] Following the scientific discoveries of the nineteenth century, humanity was able to speculate and contemplate as never before. A story generally considered the first post-industrialist sf work is *Frankenstein* (1818). Mary Shelley's book owes much of its atmosphere and gloomy *mise-en-scène* to the Gothic, and provides two links: one is with the ancient tales of gods and humankind with its sub-title reference to Prometheus; the second leads to more modern concerns. Its framework and its themes still operate significantly today within sf, connecting us with more traditional literary pleasures of the past.

In the Gothic mode, as Brian Aldiss and Brian Wingrove suggest:

> emphasis was placed on the distant and unearthly … Brooding landscapes, isolated castles, dismal old towns, and mysterious figures … carry us into an entranced world from which horrid revelations state … Terror, mystery and that delightful horror which Burke connected with the Sublime, may be discovered … in science fiction to this day.[89]

The more psychological aspects of the Gothic can be located in much American literature, and in turn this has informed American science fiction. The film *Blade Runner* (1982) offers a neo-Gothic Los Angeles; John W. Campbell's novella 'Who Goes There?' (1938) was re-worked in film form as *The Thing (From Another World)* (1951) and as *The Thing* (1982) and the series *American Gothic* (1995–1996) provides a television version. However, we can draw more than the ghostly and shadowy sense of the Gothic from this.

Aldiss and Wingrove mention the Sublime, a major Romantic concept and criterion which links us back to the ancient epics and their sense of wonder, a facet vital to science fiction. Burke's *Philosophical Enquiry into the Origin of our Ideas of the Sublime and Beautiful* (1757) creates an important category in the Sublime; to him it reveals the overlap between pain and pleasure. He places terror at its heart, but points out that it produces delight when it does not pose too close a threat to us. 'When danger or pain press too nearly, they are incapable of giving any delight, and are simply terrible; but at certain distances, and with certain modifications, they may be, and they are delightful, as we every day experience.'[90] Burke counts artistic representations, tragedy, for example, within the Sublime. Immanuel Kant's *Analytic of the Sublime* (1790) rather overshadows Burke's earlier writings, defining the Sublime's psychological effect as:

> at once a feeling of displeasure, arising from the inadequacy of the imagination in the aesthetic estimation of magnitude to attain to its estimation by reason, and a simultaneously awakened pleasure arising from this very judgement of the inadequacy of the greatest faculty of sense being in accord with ideas of reason.[91]

Kant felt that we are unable to comprehend what we see at such a time, a state of mind that arouses both pleasure (excitement) and fear.

In sf, the Sublime is often manifested as a mere plot device for introducing something alien, or something 'very, very big'.[92] However, the sense of wonder drawn from the Sublime can offer much more. For 'twentieth century sf, man is no longer sustained "between two infinities" but "between three infinities"'. Drawing upon the seventeenth-century belief that the 'human condition is sustained between two abysses', Cornel Robu quotes Blaise Pascal, who argues that:

> he who regards himself in this light will be afraid of himself, and observing himself sustained in the body given him by nature between those two abysses of the Infinite and Nothing, will tremble at the sight of these marvels; and I think that, as his curiosity changes into admiration, he wil[l] be more disposed to contemplate them in silence than to examine them with presumption. For, in fact, what is man in nature? A Nothing

in comparison with the Infinite, an All in comparison with the Nothing, a mean between nothing and everything. Since he is infinitely removed from comprehending the extremes, the end of things and their beginning are hopelessly hidden from him in an impenetrable secret; he is equally incapable of seeing the Nothing from which he was made, and the Infinite in which he is swallowed up.[93]

Science fiction offers this third infinity, a new perspective, one afforded by the juxtaposition of scale – 'the infinity of inexhaustible complexity and variety at the "average" level, at the level of "human" size and common macroscopic perception'.[94] So there is not just the Nothing and the Infinite, there is also the Complex. According to Pierre Teilhard de Chardin, each infinity is characterised by its own effects 'not in the sense that they belong to it alone – but in the sense that it is on its particular scale that these effects become sensible or even dominant. Like the Quanta in the Minute. Like Relativity in the Immense.'[95] Robu takes this further, suggesting that if this third infinity is 'acknowledged in the field of literature, the aesthetic concept of the Sublime may operate ... in [practically] all major sf topics and motifs'.[96] Although the Sublime is not a key to the essence of sf it is helpful in locating its influences and vital to visual sf's later aesthetic stylistic tendencies, particularly in television. Much of sf's appeal lies 'in its combination of the rational, the believable, with the miraculous. It is an appeal to the sense of wonder.'[97] As a result, as Nicholls and Robu suggest, 'the concept of the sense of wonder may be necessary if we are to understand the essence of sf that distinguishes it from other forms of fiction, including most fantasy.'[98] It is an exploration of the very schism created by the name 'science fiction', and reaches its apotheosis in sf film, television and art. The sense of wonder also connects us immediately with the experience of the heroic epic and the creation of a national mythology.

H I S T O R I E S

T H E   A M E R I C A N   W E S T ,
T E L E V I S I O N   A N D   T E L E V I S U A L I T Y

For over a century, the creation and perpetuation of the frontier, the epic story of the forging of a new nation in the sublime western landscape, was central to the American arts. Jorge Luis Borges notes that whilst 'literary men seem to have neglected their epic duties, the epic has been saved for us, strangely enough, by the Western ... saved for the world, by of all places, Hollywood'.[1] The Western remains uniquely American, recreating a romantic, idealised version of the frontier, an area markedly responsible for creating the national character. Ironically, for a nostalgic genre, it seldom spoke of its present but of the future – of what would happen when the wilderness became a garden. The myths of any culture often offer keys to decoding elements of what can be perceived as a national identity, a collective psyche. The vast West seemed to 'test the will of the nation's new citizens, and the emerging technologies of industrial capitalism were extraordinarily suited to the colonization and economic exploitation of these territories'.[2] Popular tales of the American West chiefly project the image of an independent frontiersman, situating such individuals within an intensely masculine narrative dependent upon an incredible human confrontation with implacable elements. The myth provides a 'shifting ideological play', with a clearly identifiable common dialectic.[3]

As cinema-history, the Western suggests a unified culture where people pull together, and it does so to a greater extent than any other genre. Hollywood's sustained commitment to genre film-making spanned the Depression to the cold war, a time when Americans had to pull together against a clearly defined common enemy, be it economic, military or political. In the early 1960s, the influence and input of film-makers working outside the Hollywood system brought about a new vitality and commercial viability to genre film, but they also took advantage of the growing tension between classical myth-making and the modernist impulse for demystification. Classical forms were pushed to the limits of narrative logic and ideological coherence, and these new films contained subtexts which openly questioned the very basis of the homogeneity of their generic values. With economic prosperity and world superpower status following the Second World War, American society became increasingly factionalised: people continued pulling, but no longer in the same direction. Racial unrest, the sexual revolution, the Vietnam War and a growing cynicism towards politicians after Watergate could only ever eventually surface in Hollywood, and the Western, the apparently collective fundamental ideology of the USA made manifest, was a prime candidate for the articulation of such concerns. *The Green Berets* (1968), *The Deer Hunter* (1978) and *Apocalypse Now* (1979) all demonstrated, intentionally or otherwise, precisely how inappropriate it was to hold on to an anachronistic ideal of American history.

During the 1970s, Hollywood's output of Westerns dwindled significantly. Many Westerns from the late 1960s onwards, like *Ulzana's Raid* (1968) and *Soldier Blue* (1970), could more easily be seen as commentaries on the tragedy of Vietnam, the wanton destruction of the Native American civilisation and the fraudulent mythology of the American frontier, rather than elegiac or nostalgic remembrances of a glorious pioneering past. Since then, the demise has been almost complete: there are only occasional revisionist Westerns, such as *Young Guns* (1988), *Dances With Wolves* (1990) or *Unforgiven* (1992). Taking over from cinema in the 1960s as the purveyor of a unified culture, television's output of Westerns was initially high, with series like *Rawhide* (1958–1965), *Gunsmoke*

(1955–1975) and *The Virginian* (1962–1969). Some series survived briefly into the 1970s, but there were few compared to the 1950s. At the start of the twenty-first century, apart from occasional mini-series like *Lonesome Dove* (1989, 1993) and the saccharine medical drama *Dr Quinn: Medicine Woman* (1993–1998) the Western has all but vanished.

THE FINAL FRONTIER

Between the 1820s and the Civil War, Congressman and Senator Thomas Hart Benton encouraged the push away from Europe towards a destiny in the West, not just to California, but across the Pacific Ocean to Asia. Benton was not alone. Less than fifty years after dispatching the British from New Orleans in the overlooked 1812–1814 war, the Union was torn asunder by the secession of the Southern States. In his 1863 'Gettysburg Address', Lincoln referred to America as a 'nation, under God', which would 'have a new birth of freedom'.[4] A reinvigorated sense of purpose and national destiny found its home in the West, and a new unifying enemy was identified in the indigenous Americans, notably the Plains Indian nations, who fought desperately against the rapid white settlement and increased industrialisation of their lands. In 1871, Walt Whitman's 'Passage to India' prophesied the 'culmination of American westward progress in regaining of civilized man's lost harmony with nature',[5] and portrayed America's 'purpose vast' as being fulfilled in 'the rondure of the world at last accomplish'd'. This was not just for the purposes of trade and exploration, but for the completion of 'God's purpose from the first'.[6]

John Hellman suggests that 'springing from shared cultural impulses, Whitman's poetic vision, like Benton's political one, articulates aspects of the mystical and millennial significance East Asia early held in American myth.'[7] He also notes that the progress of the once more *United* States of America is beautifully articulated by the building of the Union Pacific Railway, which, in 1869, provided the long-awaited highway to the Pacific later eulogised by Whitman's poem. After the frontier's closure in the 1890s, Americans sought to vicariously re-attain the spiritual essence of this short-lived version of their early society. In the Western, they recreate a mythical narrative

2. ALBERT BIERSTADT, 'YOSEMITE VALLEY' (1868).

existing beyond a real time and place, where there are few social restraints, and where society can reinvent itself in a democratic or egalitarian form, in the broad terms of the prevalent Judaeo-Christian ethos. The Wild West holds a definite appeal, and:

> from time immemorial [it] has beckoned to statesmen and poets, existing as both a direction and a place, an imperialist theme and a pastoral utopia. Great empires developed ever westward; from Greece to Rome, from Rome to Britain, from Britain to America. It was in the West as well that the fabled lands lay, the Elysian fields, Atlantis, El Dorado.[8]

As the newspaper editor says, in John Ford's 1962 film *The Man Who Shot Liberty Valance* – 'When the legend becomes fact, print the legend.'

CREATING A DESTINY

The writings and lectures of Frederick Jackson Turner in the late 1880s and 1890s rearticulated the thoughts of Benton and Lincoln but, more importantly, they enthusiastically associated the wilderness with the development of desirable 'American' qualities. 'Out of his wilderness experience,' Turner suggested, the American man 'fashioned a formula for social regeneration – the freedom of the individual to seek his own.'[9] At the turn of the century, Theodore Roosevelt spoke of the necessity not only to remember pioneering values, but also to develop them as fundamentals of American history. In short, the combination of nostalgia and political propaganda ensured that the wilderness became fashionable. In *The Incorporation of America* (1982), Alan Trachtenberg observes that as:

> an invention of the cultural myth, the word 'West' embraced an astonishing variety of surfaces and practices, of physiognomic difference and sundry exploitations ... Land and minerals served economic and ideological purposes, the two merging into a single, complex image of the West; a temporal site of the route from past to future, and the spatial site for revitalizing national energies. As myth and as economic entity, the West proved indispensable to the formation of a national society and a cultural mission: to fill the vacancy of the Western spaces with civilization, by means of incorporation (political as well as economic) and violence. Myth and exploitation, incorporation and violence: the process went hand and hand.[10]

The conquest of the West explored so powerfully by Richard Slotkin in his seminal book *Regeneration Through Violence*,[11] was gradually shaped into an idealised, custom-made mythology, which Turner and Roosevelt (and his Harvard associates: Owen Wister, author of *The Virginian* [1902] and the artist/sculptor Frederic Remington) found infinitely preferable to the somewhat more inglorious reality. The three Ivy League friends all headed west in the late 1800s – Remington for his health, the other two as ranchers.[12] Perhaps above all others they are responsible for reshaping the visual ideological and literary history of America, creating the 'Wild West' frontier and using it to reinvigorate an insipid *fin-de-siècle* urban-based population.

The process of transforming the American landscape from a dark and uncharted wilderness (the 'devil's territories') – thus making it ripe for charting, clearing and infusing with light – creates a semi-surreal landscape scattered with symbols and icons representative of both nature and culture or, more complexly, both. *Bend of the River* (1952) typifies this kind of representation in its scenes with pioneer wagons and settlers clearing the land to a stirring, quasi-religious voice-over. Here only a drastic alteration to the *eco*-culture facilitates new *agri*-culture, a process paralleling the symbolic conflict between non-domesticated and domesticated men, permitting the completion of the new agricultural civilisation. At this time the western landscape ceases to be one of reality: it is instead a composite of what the West as symbol has come to represent. In art, what John Conron has called a 'composite vista'[13] is not a landscape painting of an actual place, but instead a collection of images and narratives, gathered and relocated into a single picture, carefully balanced with a false but strong sense of human perspective. It is as if key components of Monument Valley, Yosemite and Yellowstone, the Catskills and the Rocky Mountains co-exist in one location: the sublime wonders of the Wild West are framed and tamed.

MISE-EN-SCÈNE AND SPECIAL EFFECTS

Intrinsic to these compositions is the process of *mise-en-scène*. Within the *mise-en-scène* of American art there is a gradual desertion of realism for idealism and mythicism, best illustrated by artists emerging from the Hudson River School – the likes of Thomas Cole and Frederick Church. Post-Civil War American landscape painters (notably those of the Hudson River School) were responsible for 'a body of work which lent to the American terrain an almost mystical power. These post-bellum works depict nature as the stage of dramas of growth and decay, or aspiration and defeat – and invested it with emotions appropriate to visions of national destiny.'[14] By the 1900s, a growing cult was echoing the murmurings of Thoreau, Emerson and Crèvecoeur, believing the frontier and the pioneer past to be:

> responsible for unique and desirable national characteristics. Wilderness acquired importance as a source of virility, toughness and savagery – qualities that defined fitness in Darwinian terms. Finally, an increasing number of Americans invested wild places with aesthetic and ethical values,

emphasizing the opportunity they afforded for contemplation and worship.[15]

There is also a psychological link between the use of 'effects' in American frontier art of the mid to late 1800s and the 'special effects' utilised in American film and television sf: a call to the Sublime – to the sense of wonder. The natural American landscape is one notably lacking in the comforting, enclosed and secure Claudian vista so familiar to European eyes. American landscape artists were fond of allowing some kind of context, often in the shape of a solitary observer or 'staffage' figure, one utterly absorbed in contemplation of the wondrous landscape. As de Chardin and Pascal argue, relative scale is of great importance in such compositions. Essentially, nineteenth-century American painting became 'immersed in nature'.[16] According to Earl Powell, 'the sublime experience was transformed into a new mode of landscape expression: the transcendental sublime setting was augmented by the transcendental sublime sensibility, a sensibility that founds its roots in man's internal perception of time and space.'[17] The work of Thomas Cole and the Hudson River School was contemplative, silent, philosophical, an artist's rendition of Emerson's words:

> Standing on the bare ground – my head bathed by blithe air and uplifted into infinite space – all mean egotism vanishes ... In the wilderness I find something more clear and connate than in streets or villages. In the tranquil landscape, and especially in the distant line of the horizon, man beholds somewhat as beautiful as his own nature.[18]

The aspirations associated with the West are represented through an elevation of landscape, while a sense of divine destiny and potential glory is symbolised in quasi-religious splendour by the beckoning golden glow of distant, often snow-capped peaks. The narratives are not only of subdued conflict within nature, but also of survival: the pastoral warmth in which the landscape basks attests to the security and serenity of this 'wilderness' scene. Observation and meditation on nature was 'considered virtuous because nature conveyed a "thought" which was considered good. The very act of looking was considered by some to be an act of devotion.'[19] The elevated point of view creates what Albert Boime has called the 'magisterial gaze', significant in sf television – particularly in the *Star Trek* series. This viewpoint embodies 'the exaltation of the nineteenth century American cultural elite before an unlimited horizon that they identified with the destiny of the American nation'.[20] It offers a 'commanding view', which is 'the perspective of the American on the heights searching for new worlds to conquer'.[21] It is the opposite of the common upward European reverential gaze and by 'always projecting the vision across the valley as a step ahead of the point where the viewer is located at any given time',[22] it supports the expansionist desires of the nation.

A transcendental use of diffuse light as religious rhetoric is common to these pictures. The God-given garden of the American West became not only an ideal but also the acceptable image of the West. These landscapes were seldom pictures of the wilderness in any real sense, but representative of the 'myth of a bigger America'.[23] The 'mobilization of the gaze promises nothing less than the mobilization of the self, the transformation of seemingly fixed positions of social identity. This mobilization, however, is promise and delusion in one.'[24] The composite vista is the perfection of this promise and delusion.

Having aided in turning the West into an ideological destiny, and Yosemite into a magnificent picnic garden, artists like Albert Bierstadt and Frederick Church commenced 'redrawing' history. The massive works of artists emerging from the Rocky Mountain School offered landscapes of dazzling immediacy. More importantly, they offered landscapes of *effects*[25] and, as Bukatman notes:

> [While much of this] immediacy was achieved through the hyperbolized detail of the rendering, the scale of the works was also meant to overwhelm the sensibility of the spectator. These representations of exotic landscapes in the American West or South America were too large and too detailed to be 'taken in' with a single glance: the spectator's gaze had to be put into motion in order to assimilate the work.[26]

Such pictures were often put on show like fairground attractions, and the idea behind this was not new. Moving panoramic 'rolls' of western landscape had been created before: a fine example is Henry Lewis' *Mammoth Panorama of the Mississippi River*, on 45,000 square feet of canvas. These panoramic spectacles were often accompanied by a commentary and music and they were, in effect, ancestors of the film travelogue.[27] They were garish and brilliant studies of American progress, comparable to 'the diorama and magic lantern show', testament to a certain unwillingness to constrain their reverence for the 'essence of natural wonders'.[28]

Advances in paint technologies paralleled the technology-based expansion of America. As new means of transportation and communication allowed an ever-expanding and more secure frontier, new cadmium-based pigment production permitted artists to unleash 'astonishing, bold colour experiments (special effects) ... in depicting his twilight skies and volcanic eruptions'.[29] There is a sense of revelation in these pictures, a combination of luminism and phantasmagoric kineticism. Church's *Twilight in the Wilderness* (1860) literally takes American Light as its subject matter, 'symbolic of the new world Apocalypse. It is a compelling work of art which combines two aspects of the new Sublime, the traditional interest in nature as object and the transcendental concern for nature as experience, through color, space, and silence.'[30] Barbara Novak suggests that:

> [these] overtures to sublimity in America's early history paintings were readily transferred to the landscape, and lead to a study of artistic rhetoric, that style or formal declamation which is the appropriate mode for public utterance. Such a study also involves a consideration of art as spectacle. Persisting late into the nineteenth century, this art has a clear twentieth century heir in film, which rehearsed many of the nineteenth century's concerns.[31]

Today, this art also has an heir in television.

LOOKING FORWARDS

The story of the frontier is American mytho-history. It is a primary epic – the struggles of an immigrant people to create a future and a nation for themselves in the hostile New World. Repeatedly in Westerns the representative of the domestic, of culture and civilisation – the woman – says that one day this new land will be a fine place for a home. Even in the desolate Monument Valley of *The Searchers* (1956), some day the wilderness will be a garden. In 1862, as the American Civil War tore into the Union, Abraham Lincoln made his second Address to Congress and remarked that the 'dogmas of the quiet past are inadequate to the stormy present'.[32] Equally, it can be said that many of the icons and ideologies of the Western are inadequate to the concerns of the late 1900s and early 2000s. Nevertheless, the legacy of the Western lives on, both in its sense of destiny and in the Sublime. With the *western* frontier closed, 'Space, the *final* frontier'[33] offers an alternative, or perhaps a mutation, with which to inspire the collective American psyche. Kennedy followed Roosevelt's example and tried it with his technology drive in the 1960s: the 'New Frontier'. There can be little doubt that the magnificent Saturn V rockets which blasted into space during the 1960s and 70s played no small part in expressing America's determination to resurrect its pioneering spirit and national pride after Sputnik sped across the night sky in 1957, shattering the USA's post-war complacency.[34]

In the nineteenth century, 'America revealed its obsession with the relation between nature and human power and human destiny in prose, paint and politics.'[35] In American science fiction, 'nature' is replaced with the universe, but the remainder of the relationship is the same. The location of the story is perhaps less important than the perception of that location. So it was not without reason that Kennedy turned to the next frontier, space, in order to revitalise American spirits in the cold war. It follows too that *Star Trek* would be promoted as a 'Wagon Train to the stars'.[36] Perhaps it is most appropriate that in drawing upon the Sublime, or the sense of wonder and the voyaging traditions of the heroic epic, sf should find some of its most potent visual manifestations in the spectacular cinematic art of the USA. In modern America, that same magisterial gaze and promise of destiny which infuses the work of the Hudson River and Rocky Mountain Schools and Hollywood film and television finds a natural home in visual science fiction.

TELEVISION

Television has long been associated with the domestic, the mundane and the secure. The little box sitting in our lounge or den is seen as a friend, an entertainment and a pleasingly familiar diversion. In form, sf television must adhere to many of the same institutional rules as any other programmes. It must identify itself with recognisable and consistent programme titles and credits; fill specific time slots and be of a specific length; and is subject to commercial breaks on most channels and to voiceover adverts for forthcoming programmes. In contrast to mundane drama, sf also needs to formulate strategies within its narratives that challenge the domestic and familiar framework associated with television.[37] For long-running mundane generic drama that can be an advantage; for long-running series sf stories like *Star Trek*, too much familiarity is problematic.[38]

With the rapid advent of new technologies in the 1980s, the ability to create high-quality visuals and more complex scenarios within television texts has changed. This requires a different reading of television narratives and, with the arrival of VCR, DVD and TIVO technologies, our ability to read them has also changed. More experimental television drama shows, many influenced by cinema and made by film directors, were developed in the USA during the 1980s. Caldwell identifies a particular moment in television aesthetics and a distinctive movement in prime-time television practice, one that plays with the limits of what can be done 'within the constraints and confines of the limited television frame'.[39] Grouping these factors together as the phenomenon of 'televisuality', he explains how they challenge television's 'existing formal and presentational hierarchies. Many shows evidenced a structural inversion between narrative and discourse, form and content, style and subject. What had always been relegated to the background now frequently became the foreground.'[40] This is not unlike the function and operation of the science fiction narratives explored previously.

In the 1980s, television programmes became more complex, more demanding of their audiences, and developed particular styles, not only through the increasingly graphic nature of the modern medium (as opposed to the staunchly cinematographic nature of film), but also through badges of individuality. Programmes were marketed as distinctive cult and/or boutique productions and the new narrative strategies facilitated by technological advances were offered with a visual flourish. The successful production of programmes with long, complex narrative threads and the greater use of visual imagery facilitated the development of sf television as we see it today. However, before we explore the influences of televisuality, it may be helpful to consider the television medium *before* new production technologies affected it. In this way we can establish an idea of the general and historical aesthetics of television drama in contrast to the opportunities afforded to science fiction by these technical advances.

LOCATING TELEVISION

Broadcast television's most obvious feature, and thus the easiest to overlook, is its everyday nature. Ubiquitous and intricately interwoven with the lives of almost everyone[41] television is often considered an inferior pulp medium lacking the critical cultural status shared by other art forms – something it shares with sf, often regarded as 'just' fantasy and therefore for children. Television occupies a major space in our domestic lives,[42] which places it in direct contrast to the non-domestic moving images of cinema – frequently and falsely considered television's close relative.[43] The high-quality images of cinema are larger and more detailed than those of television and aid the process of an almost complete submersion in narrative. The immediate knowledge of having paid for a ticket is also a good reason for paying attention! Television is also paid for, but the payment seldom occurs at the same time as the viewing, so the effect is diminished, although Pay-Per-View and rental videos are closer to the cinematic experience in this respect. However, these are usually one-off experiences (feature films or major sporting events) and thus they are visitors *to* television rather than being *of* television.

Television's immediacy and apparent intimacy create a sense of what Stephen Heath calls a 'seamless equivalence with social life'.[44] This does not make it a private or limited experience. It is often shared, and the ability of its audience to concentrate is potentially diminished by the doorbell, the telephone or the sudden yearning for a drink, all of which create interruptions to viewing and to the impact of a discrete, coherent narrative. Combined with television's historically poor technical visual aesthetics, these factors create a tendency to *glance* at television rather than *gaze* at it – a more sustained attention mode associated with cinema.[45] The remote control allows a different sort of interruption, the possibility of surfing between channels. This potential interruption combines with the idea of flow, which John Ellis believes 'severely compromises, and alters the separate texts that TV has manufactured',[46] suggesting a kind of segmentation in television formats at odds with the idea of a single text. This is in direct contrast to the uninterrupted, separate and progressive narrative nature of film. The block advertisements of commercial television seem particularly to endorse and encourage this appearance of segmentation.[47] Consequently, television tends to be a 'segmented narrative form built upon the principle of interruption, organising expectation and attention into segments and a multiplicity of plot lines as a way of compensating for interruptability'.[48] This is as true for the public service broadcasters as it is for commercial stations.

REPETITION

The reproductive and repetitive nature of genre suggests that there is a finite amount of expansion, transformation and subversion available to us – particularly within the confines of one television series. We certainly seem to enjoy repeated visitations to familiar scenarios – hence the enduring popularity of genre as a concept. This is partly dependent upon how we 'read' pieces of series, both episodic and sequential. For western culture, repetition and modulation have mattered at least as much as, if not more than, innovation, and Umberto Eco suggests it is 'not by chance that modern aesthetics and theories of art ... have frequently identified the artistic message with metaphor ...'[49] The defining features of the mass media, such as television, rely upon repetition – particularly obedience to pre-established schemes – and redundancy as opposed to information. Genre supplies much of this, but the characteristics, vices, gestures and habits of the individual protagonists allow us to recognise more precisely Columbo (his cigar and scruffy raincoat, his tenacity, the tardy and incisive final question) or Inspector Morse (his vintage Jaguar, his erudite nature, the love of classical music and good ale) and to consider them as our old friends. We are safe in the hands of the characters and their creators. Similarly, a traditional story of detection 'presumes the enjoyment of a scheme, the scheme is so important that the most famous authors have founded their fortune on its very immutability'.[50] Part of the attraction of an Ed McBain *87th Precinct* novel or an episode from *Star Trek* is rooted in the gradual, continuous rediscovery of things that the readers/viewers already know and wish to know again.

This creates another problem for science fiction series if it is not limited to one or two aspects of the story. The Betaville setting and introductory set in *Welcome to Paradox* (1998) or the characters and crew of *Star Trek: The Next Generation*'s Enterprise may be welcome consistent elements, but other components within the narrative must create new challenges, otherwise it fails as sf. Nevertheless, much of the pleasure in television drama comes from 'the non-story ... the distraction consists in the refutation of a development of events, in a withdrawal from the tension of past-present-future to the focus of an instant, which is loved precisely because it is recurrent.'[51] In contemporary society, with its constant change in standards and traditions, these narratives of redundancy offer a necessary or useful 'indulgent invitation to repose, a chance of relaxing'.[52] If we extrapolate, we can consider film and television as modern extensions of a similar 'novelistic discourse into new media, new technologies, and new forms of transmission and reception'.[53] Therefore, when we watch them, part of us is seeking an opportunity to rest, to relax – again, not a psychological state to which sf aspires.

NARRATIVE FORMS

In *Doctor Who: The Unfolding Text* (1983), John Tulloch and Manuel Alvarado attempted to locate the long-running BBC science fiction series within traditional narrative formats. Faced with the realisation that *Doctor Who* (1963–1989) actually overlapped existing categories, they went on to create a new typology, identifying four major types of television narrative: the continuous serial, the episodic serial, the sequential series and the episodic series.[54] For a considerable period of time, the episodic series has been the mainstay of television, each episode consisting of discrete narratives but continuity provided by a use of the same locations and/or protagonists. Science fiction programmes made in the 1960s onwards, such as *The Twilight Zone* (1959–1965), *Land of the Giants* (1968–1970) and *Voyage to the Bottom of the Sea* (1964–1968) all demonstrate this provision. The continuity in *The Twilight Zone* comes not only from the opening sequence, but also from Rod Serling's introductory narration during the title sequence, although each episode remains discrete. In the other series it also emerges from a continuity of location (i.e., the tiny 'Spindrift' spaceship in *Land of the Giants*, the submarine 'Seaview' in *Voyage to the Bottom of the Sea*). Just as cinema uses typecasting as a short cut to character exposition, so the episodic series uses audience identification with protagonists/stars to maintain high viewing ratings. *Lost in Space* (1965–1968) and *Time Tunnel* (1966–1968) also fulfil the requirements of this category; although they use new incidents to draw back their audiences, but these act more like a trailer for the next episode than a continuous thread. Episodes may therefore be missed or seen out of context without any damage to the narrative coherence, and although there are occasionally double episodes, they are essentially just feature-length stories and do not readily refer back to previous episodes.

The other three categories of television narrative (the continuous or episodic serial and the sequential series) all pose 'an enigma at the end of most episodes (with a consequential lack of narrative closure), thereby using narrative structure to draw an audience back for the next episode'.[55] The episodic serial generally has a limited run of episodes – at the end of *V* (1983), *Taken* (2002) or *24* (2001), the story is complete – although a subsequent discrete run of episodes is not ruled out, as evidenced by *V: The Final Battle* (1984) and the second and third series of *24* (2002, 2003).

In contrast, the continuous serial is capable of running infinitely, and possessing 'multiple narrative strands which are introduced and concluded in different temporal periods. There are therefore multi-layered narrative overlaps.'[56] This format is generally associated with soap operas, so programmes such as *EastEnders* (1985–) and *Days of Our Lives* (1965–) fit this pattern, series appearing as both prime-time television and morning or afternoon shows, and forming a mainstay of television schedules today. It is unusual for sf series to develop along the same lines, although the follow-up to the two self-contained series of *V* demonstrated this potential in 1984–1985, losing sight of its powerful sf origins and allegorical narrative in a plethora of romances and stunt pieces. The sequential series is slightly different, its narrative developing from episode to episode, requiring the audience to have viewed earlier episodes in order to understand the narrative – it may be short or long in duration.

SUSPENSE

If television uses common and recognisable patterns, how does it maintain its audience's interest? The chief means is the same necessary means of creating interest in the development of any story: suspense. In drama, suspense is created when the order of the narrative is switched around by plotting to delay the receipt of information. David Bordwell and Kristin Thompson suggest that instead of stories progressing alphabetically from A to F, plotting means that we may find ourselves watching D–F, which in turn reveal A–C.[57]

	(	A	Crime conceived	
	(	B	Crime planned	
Story	(	C	Crime committed	
	(	D	Crime discovered	)
	(	E	Detective investigates	) Plot
	(	F	Detective reveals A, B and C	)

This is a common enough feature of detective stories, but the act of investigation is a vital motivational plot device in all genres.[58] Clues must be located so that the protagonists may discover who wants what and why, or to discover how the technology works, etc. The typical crime narrative has two component stories: that of the investigation and that of the crime that created the investigation, but the act of detection works in reverse, with what Tzvetan Todorov calls 'prospection' replacing 'retrospection'. The reader/viewer is motivated by curiosity and suspense, not just 'by what has happened, but also by what will happen next; he wonders about the future as about the past'. Therefore, there is 'the curiosity to learn how past events are to be explained; and there is also the suspense: what will happen to the main characters?'[59] This exerts a powerful effect upon audiences, repeatedly drawing them back – and, for series like *Twin Peaks* (1990–1991) or *Space: Above and Beyond* (1995–1996), this is crucial to their appeal.

The latter series rely upon audience identification with their storylines or protagonists to retain viewers; indeed, audience figures of any kind demonstrate that a considerable rapport develops between the viewing public and the characters of long-running series like soap operas. The cliffhanger question of 'Who shot JR?' in *Dallas* (1978–1991) occupied considerable tabloid newspaper space, running neck and neck with the current affairs of the period. So entrenched was *Dallas* in its audience's lives that eventually it became part of a social ritual in which 'our culture engages in order to communicate with its collective self'.[60] Like Western archetypes, the characters in *Dallas* became an articulation of national characteristics, good and bad. Since the 1950s, television has provided a modern version of the oral tradition. This relationship brings us back to the bardic storytellers of ancient times, who provided a vital communicative link, passing on not just tales but also news and information. The bard operates as:

> a mediator of language, one who composes out of the available linguistic resources of the culture a series of consciously structured messages which serve to communicate to members of that culture a confirming, reinforcing version of themselves. The traditional bard rendered the concerns of his day into verse. We must remember that television renders our everyday perceptions into an equally specialised, but less formal, language system ...[61]

Long-running television series with socially immediate contortions of continually developing plot lines are therefore effectively reproducing an ancient process. They reassure us of our collective moral values, but alongside this offer imaginary and heroic scenarios, drama and comedy, tragedy and melodrama. In *The Medium Is the Message* (1967), Marshall McLuhan and Quentin Fiore suggest that television confers 'a mythic dimension on our ordinary individual and group actions. Our technology forces us to live mythically.'[62] Comparing television with ancient oral tribal traditions, McLuhan and Fiore suggest that 'we are back in an acoustic space. We have begun again to structure the primordial feeling, the tribal emotions from which a few centuries of literacy have divorced us.'[63]

Notably, it is a science fiction series, *Steven Spielberg's Amazing Stories* (1985–1987), which articulates this link more clearly than any other television programme. The title sequence begins with a cave-dwelling family sitting around a fire, listening to a storyteller. As he speaks, images of action swirl around, whisking us through time and space, until the sequence ends. We are now facing a television set surrounded by a contemporary family, on which we see the cave-family listening avidly to their storyteller.

How then, can an aesthetic of television be summarised? Broadcast television is certainly no different to other media in its dependence upon an established series of components, genres, and formats. Its segmentation and active use of narrative redundancy is a means of compensating for any potential distraction. It relies upon the pleasure of repeated textual encounters, using minute variations in repetition and multiplicities of infinite storylines or unchanging situations to entrance its audience. In the past it has mostly relied upon static formulae where action and words matter more than the *mise-en-scène*, because the quality and definition of the television image has been its weakest element. Its natural tendency is to provide secure and familiar scenarios in its dominant dramatic forms, the sitcom and soap opera. It wants to entertain its audience because in order to exist, it needs to maintain its audience.

S F O N T E L E V I S I O N

Science fiction is intent not only upon fracturing our sense of reality and creating a degree of cognitive estrangement, but also in tipping the balance between foreground and background in a manner alien to mundane texts. It would seem to do the very thing most television refutes and to require the very thing that television has traditionally lacked – probably why television executive Scott Siegler claims 'science fiction doesn't work on TV.'[64] Given the domestic and repetitive nature of television, this would appear true. However, science fiction has always maintained a presence on television, which suggests that Siegler is incorrect. What then of science fiction on the small screen? As Todorov suggests:

> [like] any other institution, genres bring to light the constitutive features of the society to which they belong ... the existence of certain genres in one society, their absence in another, are revelatory of that [society's] ideology and allow us to establish it more or less confidently.[65]

The notion that the popularity of a genre holds clues to the ideological and cultural preoccupations of its producing society is useful. During the 1970s, when the Western was in rapid demise, films like *Star Wars* (1977) offered the USA a new way forward, a new sense of destiny. It was a way of rearranging, if not rewriting, its national mythology in the same forward-looking way as the Western, but in a new arena, one not tied by historical detail. The cultural earthquakes of the 1960s reverberated through sf as much as any other genre, but not to the same destructive degree as in the Western. So, while the Western collapsed in the 1970s, science fiction inspired the big screen, mostly shunning alien monsters and space exploration for societal and environmental concerns in films like *Planet of the Apes*, *THX 1138* (1971) and *Soylent Green* (1973).

The big-screen success of sf was quickly taken up on the small screen, in series like: *Kolchak: The Night Stalker* (1974); *Planet of the Apes* (1974); *The Six Million Dollar Man* (1974); *The Invisible Man* (1975); *The Bionic Woman* (1976): *The Gemini Man* (1976); *The Man From Atlantis* (1977); *The Fantastic Journey* (1977); *Logan's Run* (1977); *Project UFO* (1978); *Buck Rogers in the 25ᵗʰ Century* (1979) – and so on. Sufficient series lasted for more than one season to suggest that the broad scope of sf was a subject inviting creativity and audience interest. However, while film and literature explored ecological and social issues, television programmes remained closer to adventure and technology in theme. Other than those drawn from film or literature (like *Planet of the Apes*) they were mostly concerned with space/time travel, alien invasion, new technologies, etc. The Earth-bound series preferred to bombard their audiences with a lot of 'secret', brand new technology – *The Six Million Dollar Man*'s slow-motion bionics, or *Time Tunnel*'s massive whirring computers nursed through problems by grey-haired, bespectacled scientists in lab coats. Unable to offer visual displays equal to cinema at that time, they eschewed a challenging *mise-en-scène* and followed instead Horace Newcomb's 'static formula – dynamic situation',[66] concentrating upon plenty of formulaic action set against starry backdrops with lots of flashing lights.[67] The difference between the representations of Steve Austin (Lee Majors) in *The Six Million Dollar Man* and Superman (Dean Cain) in *The New Adventures of Superman/Lois and Clark* (1993–1997) highlights the remarkable advances made between the

1970s and 1990s. Austin's bionic cyborg-hero is able to run at 60mph and has super strength, but the technology of the time limited the repertoire of sfx at the show's disposal. Majors is filmed in real time and the image replayed in slow motion, impressing power upon us rather than speed. In contrast, more recent sfx technology permits Dean Cain to be filmed either in purely analogue (real) time or for the analogue to be supplemented by cgi sfx. The overall image can then be digitally remastered and perfected so that in an apparently analogue setting, Cain's Superman demonstrates both speed and power.

Science fiction has therefore enjoyed a continual presence as episodic television, despite the medium's apparent resistance to the inherent non-domesticity of the genre. The more daring shows grasped the potential for social commentary. The long-running episodic tales of the first *Twilight Zone* (1959–1964) and *Outer Limits* (1963–1965) series were, at their best, thoughtful and provocative tales of alternative perspectives, and no discussion of the 1960s would be complete without mentioning the first series of *Star Trek*, which ran for three seasons,[68] with its now-famous split infinitive. The voiceover introduction announced its rationale in each episode:

Space: the final frontier.

These are the voyages of the Starship Enterprise.

Its five-year mission: to explore strange new worlds, to seek out new life, and new civilisations – to boldly go where no man has gone before.

The driving force behind the series, Gene Roddenberry, believes it was 'probably the only show on American television that said there is a tomorrow, that all the excitement and adventures and discoveries were not behind us'.[69] Each story was a morality tale, and the series maintained 'an indomitable faith in man as an essentially noble animal'.[70] The major characters, Captain James T. Kirk, First Officer Mr Spock, the ship's doctor, Leonard 'Bones' McCoy, and Chief Engineer Montgomery Scott transported down to various planets, weekly encountering strange new worlds and a variety of alien life forms. The show generally closed with a didactic message from Kirk to the aliens/planetary residents about the mistakes they had made and the errors of their ways, or an old-fashioned military victory over either of the long-standing galactic enemies, the Klingons and the Romulans. Nevertheless, Kirk and his crew also learned lessons, and showed their audience new ways of seeing.

Star Trek certainly broke with tradition: the pointed-eared half Vulcan-half human Mr Spock was Kirk's right-hand man; Communications Officer Lt. Uhura was a Bantu woman; and the helmsman, Mr Sulu, was Japanese. In the second season, the Russian Mr Chekov joined the bridge crew, allegedly when a Pravda critic noted frostily that the first nation to have a man in space was not represented.[71] At the height of the cold war, this was forward-looking indeed, and the ambitions of the series were equally bold. The pilot episode was rejected by network chiefs for being 'too cerebral'. Although Star Trek was cancelled at the end of the 1960s, its popularity amongst its fans remained undiminished[72] and Paramount negotiated with Roddenberry for its return (in some form) from 1975.[73] Following the success of Star Wars, the original crew made a bold return to the big screen in 1979, with Star Trek: The Motion Picture proving popular with new and old audiences.

Roddenberry points out that by creating 'a new world with new rules, I could make statements about sex, religion, Vietnam, unions, politics and intercontinental missiles. Indeed, we did make them on Star Trek: we were sending messages, and fortunately they all got by the network.'[74] By taking the contemporary issues (of war, racism, sexism, and ecology, etc.) outside of their own society, they could be examined with less prejudice and subjectivity. As Roger Fulton says 'its heart was in the right place'[75] and without a doubt, the best of Star Trek was a high spot in 1960s sf television. Series emerging later gradually began to draw on a variety of social issues of their time. Perhaps naturally, Star Trek: The Next Generation was particularly keen on this, addressing racism, sexism, sexual orientation, arranged marriages, genetic engineering, even the guilt over the treatment of Native Americans in a variety of episodes, as we will explore in the following chapter. The trend perhaps culminated in the first season of Seaquest (1993–1995) whose end titles included cast and crew introducing the audience to a form of marine life, or noting an ecological issue related to the ocean – another form of narrative disruption: the injection of the real into the story world.

Generically speaking, sf television of the 1960s and 1970s is in keeping with Isaac Asimov's stages of American sf literature: adventure dominant (1926–1938); technology dominant (1938–1950); sociology dominant (1950–?), and to borrow from Fredric Jameson's extrapolation, from the mid 1960s, 'aesthetics dominant'.[76] With less history than literature (or film) the television medium required a little more time to work through the process, social interests only replaced by aesthetic concerns in the 1980s. American sf series in the 1970s demonstrate a growing preoccupation with ingenuity and technological advantages. In the era of the cold war, the necessity of such advantage was played to great effect, and there was generally a constant military presence within series such as *The Six Million Dollar Man*, *Time Tunnel* and *Project: UFO*. Many of these programmes articulate a steady underlying narrative of pride in American scientific and technological achievement, often underlining intellectual capability through fastidious detective work and logical deduction. However, the period with which we are concerned runs after this, from the mid 1980s, a time when the nature of the television text and the potential for sf on television was changed forever. Caldwell's study of 1980s American television explains how new technologies and a new ability to offer clearer resolution (and thus immensely powerful images) meant that something quite remarkable was happening to television: style was coming to the foreground.

TELEVISUALITY

Televisuality manifests itself in a variety of fashions, most importantly for this argument are technological developments and the use of imagery in *mise-en-scène*. George Spiro Dibie, President of the American Society of Lighting Directors, worked on many 1980s series like *Growing Pains* (1985–1992) and *The Ellen Burstyn Show* (1986–1987); he considers that whether 'lighting for features, [or] lighting for television, the light is identical'. Oliver Wood, the director of photography (DP) for *Miami Vice* (1984–1989) suggests that in television 'you can't be [cinematographer] Vittorio Storaro. But what you can do is like music.'[77] In the 1980s, lighting and photography for television finally came of creative age; thanks to new technical processes, which facilitated new narrative approaches, television shifted from a predominantly verbal medium into a predominantly visual medium. The new film stocks and transfer technologies created 'film-style video – programming practice, acting, and promotional considerations encouraged a second industrial mythology: program individuation'.[78] Television programmes claimed individual identities and idiosyncratic styles for the very reason previously used against excessive style in television: the lack of good visual clarity. Steve Larner worked as photographer on one of the early televisual series, *Beauty and the Beast* (1987–1990), and points out that the team was proud because 'the cinematography is really very important to it. The producers feel strongly enough to give the director of photography a credit at the beginning of the show rather than at the end – and *Beauty* is the only episodic TV show that does it that way.'[79]

The improvements in lenses and changes in the video and recording processes made during the 1980s challenged the accepted murky and 'weakened' visual style of television. They suggested instead that 'precisely because the TV screen is smaller than that of film, *producers need stronger stylisation*', and *Beauty and the Beast* was not only stylish, it was also self-aware. As Larner reminds us, the DP is given visible credit for creativity and placed on the same level as the writers, actors and other 'above the line' personnel. The show has a unique visual style, located around fog and halo-effect filters, coloured gels, heavy use of smoke and directional lighting. At the same time, a 'reduction in script verbiage challenges the most conventional wisdom about television style' – *Beauty and the Beast* scripts tended towards under thirty pages of dialogue for the one hour of drama (including commercial breaks) rather than the more typical fifty or sixty.[80] This shatters the traditionally wordy nature of television scripts, their sometimes painfully expository nature and overtly redundant dialogue, methods through which pre-1980s television frequently rearticulated what could now be articulated solely by the *mise-en-scène*. The former strategy was based upon the belief that low resolution image of television was 'unable *by itself* to communicate essential narrative detail'.[81]

STYLE

There are other televisual features in production values of the 1980s, and Caldwell notes that if some 'recent programmes work by selectively intensifying their *mise-en-scène* around an identifiable look, others depend upon ... a more eclectic and selective use of visual codes better termed "masquerade".' In effect, other shows were parodying or 'playing off' cinematic styles.[82] *Moonlighting* (1985–1989) was the keenest perpetrator of this 'retrostyling'. Stylistic references came to be an audience expectation, with the 'dramatic content of an individual episode' in the later series 'frequently tied to a specific visual style' – Greg Toland/Orson Welles deep focus, MTV, or film noir, etc'.[83] These references did not just pay homage to mass film or television culture, but also to styles associated with 'more marginal taste cultures, like independent film'.[84] Caldwell notes how Horace Newcomb's theory drew upon 'the tension between the static formula and the need for some generic change as a partial basis for his proposal that continuity is one of the chief aspects of a television aesthetic'.[85] Now, television began to challenge this, adapting and/or aping the 'mythology of cinema's visual prowess' to the extent that even noise and poor or grainy docu-film quality could be adopted into these new televisual codes:

> [T]he stylistic and presentational aspects are the very elements that change on a weekly basis, whilst characterization becomes the medium's static and repetitious given from episode to episode. With *China Beach*, *thirtysomething*, *The Wonder Years*, *Quantum Leap*, *Northern Exposure* ... even less prestigious shows like *McGuyver*, the viewer is now encouraged to speculate before each episode about what the program might aesthetically transform itself into this week: documentary, dreamstate, oral history, music video, homage to Hollywood or expressionist fantasy.[86]

There is another element here which helps to create television where 'style' could be bought into. For fans of *Doctor Who*, those despotic silver pepperpots, the Daleks, will be forever associated with their creator, Terry Nation. Similarly, *Star Trek* will be forever associated with Gene Roddenberry[87] and the posthumous *Earth: Final Conflict* is seldom known just as that, but rather as *Gene Roddenberry's Earth: Final Conflict*. Similarly titled is *Gene Roddenberry's Andromeda* (2000–). The cult marketing power of the Roddenberry name as a signal of production values, ideology, and association overrides the name of the series. This is another feature of televisual programming, which can be located 'along an axis formed by relative degrees of authorial intent and manufactured notoriety'. In the 1980s, the emergence of a popular culture myth about 'quality' television was based upon the premise that television was not anonymous: it too had famous names – just like film. As a result:

> [Although] Aaron Spelling and Norman Lear were already household names, other producer-creators like Michael Mann and Stephen Bochco began to be discussed alongside their actors and series in popular magazines and newspapers. As with American film in the 1960s, authorial intent played an important role as an indicator and guarantor of aesthetic quality in primetime programming of the 1980s.[88]

Actually, television has seldom been anonymous, vocalised credit references to producers like Quinn Martin and Mark Goodson-Bill Todson leaving no 'doubt in the viewers' minds about where their shows came from'. By the 1980s, producers like Stephen J. Cannell appeared in 'dramatized filmed I.D.s tagged on to each of their episodes'. Today, series like *Babylon 5* and *Andromeda* share the identifying tag with these series – in this case the coveted 'created by' included in the opening titles. The expansion of television to a twenty-four hour multi-channel flood has created a potential monotony in the experience of viewing. A means of countering this emerges through boutique programming, which:

> constructs for itself an air of selectivity, refinement, uniqueness and privilege. The televisual excess operative in boutique programming then, has less to do with an overload of visual form than with two other products: *excessive intentionality* and *sensitivity* ... subtle orchestrations of televisual form that create the defining illusion of a *personal touch*.[89]

Andrew Darley suggests that 'conceptions of genre (and

authorship) are anyway being radically affected – outstripped, even – by the prevailing trends in contemporary visual culture.' Darley is predominantly interested in film, music videos and computer games, but given the dependence modern sf television has upon digital visual effects, it seems useful to consider applying some of his conclusions about film to television. He suggests that in 'many of the visual cultural practices of present day mass culture – long since saturated with (visual) mediation – intertextuality has become institutionalised as an aesthetic norm'.[90] The marketing and financial aspect of this is most notably apparent with blockbuster movies. They are designed as 'multi-purpose entertainment machines that breed music videos and soundtrack albums, TV series and video cassettes, video games and theme park rides, novelizations and comic books'.[91] Therefore, various fragments, styles and techniques are 'constantly migrating between each of these and the other forms at play (i.e. TV series)'.[92] For Darley:

> when such texts are *already* – in the first instance – themselves thoroughly intertextual in character, then one begins to grasp something of the extent and structural reach of this new condition. A *familiarity* on the part of the spectator with previous texts, their styles, generic features, character tropes, and so forth, becomes a central feature of spectator involvement in current ones. Extra-textual reference recedes as such convolution and the complex circularity it involves takes over spheres of mediation.[93]

BOUTIQUE PRODUCTIONS

With the advent of increasingly complex digital techniques, there is a growing tendency to create sharper images, more 'outlandish and yet more realistic by the same turn – impossible yet photographic (spectacle cinema, computer animation)'. Authorship and genre would thus appear to be displaced by other aesthetic concerns – 'the adjuster and the renovator'.[94] J.M. Straczynski explains that his series *Babylon 5* was 'perhaps the first series produced entirely as a slightly more advanced form of desktop television' and, although this is now more common practice, *Babylon 5* was certainly in the vanguard.[95] The filmed episode is transferred to videotape, and then each take of each scene is digitised and edited on an Avid. When this is complete, the data is taken to post-production. The special effects are also produced through desktop work, and yet more pioneering work has taken place with the sets – many of which are virtual. The result of this is not just impressive science fiction scenarios and plentiful, convincing space battles, but also cheaper television. An hour of serial television such as *Space: Above and Beyond* or *Voyager* costs on average between $1,000,000 and $1,900,000. In contrast, *Babylon 5* costs considerably less than the licensed network-to-studio allowance of $800,000 and, according to Straczynski, was the first science fiction show to ever come in under budget during its first two seasons.[96] Comparing this 'budget tv' to desktop publishing, Straczynski suggests that 'instead of having a handful of monolithic studios, you may very well end up with dozens of boutique production companies capable of buying, selling and producing TV series.'[97]

For programmes demanding a specific and challenging alternative reality such as the surreal *Twin Peaks* or the postmodern television future of *Wild Palms* (1993), and especially for sf television, this kind of boutique production may simply be another way of describing the 'personal touch'. The special effects co-ordinators, the matte artists, set and costume designers have as much to do with bringing the worlds of *Voyager* or *Babylon 5* to fruition as do the writers, actors and producers. Straczynski may well have been the driving force behind the series,[98] but he also worked with a team of writers, directors, cast and crew, many of whom he knew from previous collaborations.[99] He was available to discuss the work with fans on the internet, named ships and transient personnel after those same fans and posted countless messages with his responses to alternately inane and in-depth questions on internet message boards. It was an extraordinary marketing strategy and exemplified the personal and sensitive element Caldwell identifies – the fan/cast message board on Paramount's *Star Trek* website could not compete with this. Put simply, this is not so very far from the system that enabled directors like Hawks and Ford to use a stable of actors and crew and could only contribute to the sense of personal ideological and visual continuity within their films.

The association with fandom drawn upon by Straczynski is a powerful one. Continuity and repetition are as much part of the phenomenon of fandom as they are an aesthetic of television. Fans relate to repetition and to a sense of the secure, the familiar and the everyday – things which encourage a feeling of ownership. This a major feature of cult television and, due to the open nature of its texts and its strong reliance upon potential rather than reality, sf seems to attract something akin to McLuhan's tribal following. Prime-time televisual shows also attract cult followings: *Moonlighting*, *Miami Vice* (1984–1989), *Twin Peaks* and *The X-Files* are clear examples. They gained the appreciation of a dedicated fan following not just because they were strongly visual, but 'because they also utilized self-contained and volatile narrative and fantasy worlds, imaginary constructs *more typical of science fiction*', as Caldwell points, out. Like science fiction:

> televisuality developed a system/genre of alternative worlds that tolerated and expected both visual flourishes – special effects, graphics, acute cinematography and editing – and narrative embellishments – time travel, diegetic masquerades, and out of body experiences. Such forms, simultaneously embellished and open, invite viewer conjecture.[100]

This means that even in mundane television, the limits of plausibility are being stretched; by default this legitimises or normalises some aspects of sf's 'fantasy' realms, as well as challenging sf to do more to maintain the chasm between it and mundane narrative.

During the middle years of the twentieth century, the purchase of certain commodities 'connoted difference in class, in social position, and in cultural aspiration'.[101] At the turn of the twentieth century, commodity comes 'in an increasing number of different guises: in special editions; different packaging; decorated with logos; or with subtly differentiated design. What matters now is "style".'[102] Cable/satellite television offers 'packages' to suit image-conscious 'lifestyles' in the form of grouped, themed channels. These in turn provide identifiable 'boutique' productions, programmes aimed at specific audiences, and creating specific worlds, like *The X-Files*, *Beauty and the Beast*, even *Frasier* (1993–2004) etc. The existence of a dedicated fan audience allows considerably more flexibility with narrative strands, thus bringing us to the increasing narrative complexity of the mid 1980s onwards. Series like *Twin Peaks* and *The X-Files* heralded more than just a new style of cult television imagery; they introduced us to more sustained alternative worlds. Programmes experimented with a new kind of narrative, one demonstrating complex long-term threads, some of which may lie dormant over a period but which can be drawn together at various points within the series/seasons.

NARRATIVE PATTERNS

These narrative patterns originated in mundane drama, in shows like *NYPD Blue* (1993–) and *Hill Street Blues* (1981–1987). In the 1990s, science fiction took up this trend in a major way. However, unlike the occasional single-season mundane dramas, which are at least sketchily plotted-out in advance – *Murder One* (1995–1997) and *24* are prime examples – the earlier sf series' *lack* of pre-planning can lead to narrative inconsistencies. This creates a need for rather extraordinary twists in plot and narrative in order to justify/explain previous occurrences. They also moved a small distance away from the redundancy of soap opera dialogue and the continual one-liners of the unchanging sitcom. *Dark Skies* (1996–1997), *Space: Above and Beyond* and, to a lesser extent, *The X-Files* all provide demonstrations of this penchant for threads and mini-arcs. The former two programmes also demonstrate the dangers of remaining too much of a cult show rather than entering into the mainstream's more accessible programming schedules. The long-running *X-Files* was far more episodic in nature, with the background story building occasionally and implicitly rather than consistently and explicitly.

The insertion of long narrative threads within a series places a different demand upon the audience. Episodic series offer recognisable scenarios and continuity through their crews and vessels, but seldom demand knowledge of past episodes. *Stargate SG-1* possesses continuing themes (such as the battle against the Gou'ald System Lords, the quest for the Ancients). Regardless of these threads, like *The X-Files*, *Stargate SG-1* still relies mostly upon the weekly episodic adventure, with occasional double episodes, and the option to return intermittently to a previous theme by introducing it as 'Previously on *Stargate SG-1* ...' Too long a gap can, however, be confusing, as the general reliance upon the episodic narrative can lull the viewer into a false sense of security. This demands a different audience commitment to the episodic serial, the soap or the mini-series, which offer frequent reminders via character discussions, expositional scenes or introductory visual flashbacks. A series with longer narrative ambitions like *Space: Above and Beyond* expects still more commitment: the story and its complexities evolve slowly – and this is the risk: if it is inadequately pitched, its audience may have turned off before the story truly begins. The final few episodes of its brief season demonstrated a remarkably complex narrative philosophy, but it was too late: the initial dominant tale of lost love in space had already turned off viewers in their droves.

All of these series are less explicit than older shows; they expect more attention from their viewers and are perceived as more rewarding and more complex – indicative of television's potential for intellectual challenge. As Caldwell suggests:

> the morasslike flow of television may be more difficult for the TV viewer to wade through than film, but television rewards discrimination, style consciousness, and viewer loyalty in ways that counteract the clutter ... spectatorship in television can be quite intense and ingrained over time.[103]

Lacking in overt redundancy – but brimming with clues and signposts to future events, and thus constantly hooking and re-hooking its audience's attention – *Babylon 5* is the epitome of the kind of sf television we can now enjoy. It rewards the careful, committed viewer who watches it just once and positively indulges those who enjoy repeated viewings.

In *Television Drama*, John Caughie notes that:

> in non-classical television drama which is accorded the status of art and which has an investment in the creativity and inventiveness of its authors – whether they be writers, directors, or producers – the unexpected comes to be expected: originality carries a higher premium within the system than conventionality.[104]

Caughie proposes a new mode of authorship for television, one perhaps implicitly identified by Caldwell's study. He suggests an author who can make:

> conscious choices of form and meaning, aware of the limits of the system, the institution, and the language; who is invested with freedom and honoured for creativity, but whose freedom is constantly qualified by calculation: how much or how little difference can the system take in this context and at this time?[105]

This is what Struczynski did, and his major selling point was indeed that he did what no one else had ever tried, thus bringing novelty to the sf genre on television in the form of a pre-determined epic story arc.[106] *Babylon 5* truly broke with tradition.

THE CRITICAL SPECTATOR

In cult television, there is more potential for a relaxed detachment and the possibility of 'a space of engagement which is also a critical one'.[107] Walter Benjamin's 'absent minded' spectator/examiner applies to television as well as cinema in the new millennium,[108] and is echoed in Brecht's desire for a spectator who watches and yet can still be critical – a critical detached engagement:

> The time and space of television seem to provide the conditions for the existence for such an engagement ... the 'everydayness' of space works against the fantasmatic identification with the narrative space which one experiences in the cinema. While neither may produce precisely the estrangement effect which Brecht promoted in the theatre, they seem to me to produce the conditions for the detached engagement of irony.[109]

Art television suggests an intelligent, critical and aware audience, cognisant of the potential creativity of an authored text.[110] This is another important feature of the epic, of course: a sense of detached objectivity, and an awareness of this potential within television opens up new areas for dramatisation.

Caughie's argument produces two results. Firstly, like art cinema, it suggests that art television is less bound by generic convention and relies 'less on an iconography of meaning which is already in place and which has become meaningful through repetition, and more on the articulation of meanings whose force lies in their difference and originality'. This Formalist estrangement and distanciation is 'central to the basic functioning of art', a process which allows us to see reality (whatever that reality may be) as if for the first time. The second result is a problem for sf: shown week after week at the same time, with the same theme tune and mostly the same programme preceding it to set the mood – any 'difference is absorbed with astonishing rapidity'.[111] Thus, it is hard for a radical series to continue weekly and still provide what sf claims to offer. As we established at the beginning, science fiction creates imaginary worlds where the very ontological structures we take for granted are challenged at every step through the process of cognitive estrangement, metalinguistics and the foregrounding of the background – whether on the level of the minute or immense. Even to argue that the unexpected is expected is to argue that conventionality has set in. After a while, *NYPD Blue*'s zip pans are not as flamboyant and not as disorientating, the extraordinary is ordinary in *The X-Files* and the bizarre is quite routine in *Twin Peaks*. The exotic becomes insipid, mundane – the very antithesis of science fiction.[112] The nature of these television models nudges us towards concluding that science fiction can work well on television in episodic form, like the original *The Outer Limits* and its subsequent incarnation (1995–2002), or *Perversions of Science* (1997), but that it is rather more difficult to sustain over a longer term.

More recent commodity forms, such as video recording technology – which stands in contrast to the traditional association of television as a disposable commodity – and other new technologies facilitating more complex visuals have allowed television to take the graphic route. It can layer its images, create composites and use painterly effects (akin to those of the American landscapists) – essentially it can do everything possible to dismiss the accusation of shallowness made by 'critics, detractors, and film production people because it is flat'.[113] Caldwell makes the connection between the worlds of his televisual texts and sf and, as I have argued in previous chapters, the foregrounding of the background and inversion of everyday discourse is precisely what is attempted by sf narrative. Given the visual repertoire of new technologies flourished by television producers in even mundane texts, it seems that rather than readily accepting Siegler's negative axiom, we would in fact be wise to regard television as a potentially ideal location for science fiction. Finally, it has come of age: not only can it tell stories of cognitive estrangement, it can also deliver them with persuasively 'realistic' visuals.

NEW WAYS OF VIEWING NEW NARRATIVE FORMS

Caldwell's arguments identify a major shift in the way the television audience is perceived. Earlier writings about the nature of broadcast television and its potentially distracted viewers emerged before the time of pre-recorded and iconoclastic, stylised video-television. These programmes drastically changed the nature of television, and they occurred during a period when American society was moving away from general terrestrial broadcast channels to selective non-terrestrial narrowcasting. There is an increased opportunity to offer texts demanding more attention because the audiences have selected the kinds of texts they wish to view. Their interest is not guaranteed, but it is far more assured. Added to this, video technologies afford more opportunity to record the programme and watch it at leisure and with full attention. Cult television is the order of the day: television itself has changed. In an era dependent ever more upon narrowcast television, we have video – we have the opportunity to watch and watch again. We select from the constant stream of trash and tabloid television the programmes that, as individuals, we believe overtly address us – those that ask us to be motivated and selective in our viewing.[114] It is unlikely that we have, *en masse*, more time for television viewing. We do, however, have far more from which we can select, and of necessity that requires more discrimination. Watching television today is not inherently about distraction: it is about the *choice* to pay painstaking attention.

It would seem that the *Farscape* or *Deep Space Nine* addict and the videophile cannot exist if we merely offer a casual glance at television, but the glance and the segment relate to each other: the segment is necessary if the audience's attention is even possibly divided. Information comes in small pieces, easily digestible and until recently, oft repeated in- and ex-diegesis. The feature of television differentiating it most strongly from film is its narrative segmentation and repetition. Series like *The X-Files* and *Babylon 5* may have created a new form of complete narrative for television but, like other series emerging from the period of televisual experimentation, importantly they do not change the use of the segment. Each episode has six acts, including the trailer and tag, although they may be of varying lengths, and the episodic narrative rises intermittently to strong suspense to permit the commercial interruptions of American television.

Many of the programmes created since the 1980s are not examples of Caldwell's televisual products; many of his criteria for televisuality would not sit easily with its production and his discussion concerns particular programmes made at a particular moment in time. Most of the series under discussion here are heir to the televisual phenomenon, and were certainly made possible by its innovations. A finite series like *Babylon 5* could not have been made prior to the period of televisual narrative experimentation of the mid 1980s/early 1990s. *Babylon 5*'s narrative structure makes it the first series to physically show what will or may happen in later seasons. It does not just fall back on the past as detection in the form of a flashback, but also uses predictions – in the form of seers, visions or flash-forwards. Previously, not only was there no technological ability to facilitate this kind of narrative, but nor would the creation of a sustained alternative world be attempted outside of mundane narratives like soap operas and sitcoms. The advent of the mini-series, like *Centennial* (1978), *Roots* (1977) and *North and South* (1985) offered harbingers of what was to come. *Twin Peaks* and *Wild Palms* offered more, but not even in postmodern or surreal fiction has a finite, epic series of such complexity ever been attempted before on American television. A science fiction narrative such as *Babylon 5* was made possible because of the changes Caldwell identifies, and perhaps because we constantly seek something which straddles that fine line between innovation and repetition. For an evolutionary and enigmatic series like *Babylon 5*, the careful construction of a specific scenario from the start is akin to the putting together of a jigsaw puzzle. A hitherto unprecedented degree of audience loyalty is required, but its possibility is the result of a trend that has now been in existence for almost twenty years. The existence of such complex narratives is facilitated by highly 'informed and motivated' viewers willing to 'buy into' Caldwell's 'boutique' productions.[115]

PART TWO

THE SERIES

3. *STAR TREK: THE NEXT GENERATION* — THE USS ENTERPRISE.

THREE

YESTERDAY'S ENTERPRISE

REPRESENTATION, IDEOLOGY AND LANGUAGE IN *STAR TREK*

Nothing has dominated American sf television for as long as the various incarnations of *Star Trek*. The series are primarily episodic in nature, although from *The Next Generation* onwards they reference earlier adventures and *Deep Space Nine* develops a strong story arc. The later series also demonstrate continuity via either character or mini-story arcs in keeping with the televisual era's narrative trends. This chapter considers the changes within the *Star Trek* universe (which overlaps Caldwell's pre- and post-televisual eras), as well as exploring the ideology and imagery of the various series. The newer series remain mostly true to the aspirations of the original programme, but thus also risk the charge of being anachronistic. Exploring this, this chapter considers representations of humanity and alien life in contrast with other programmes and examines the series' use of heightened or alien language.

THE SERIES

The original *Star Trek* series lasted only three seasons and was cancelled in 1969. An animated series featuring the voices of the original cast ran from 1973 to 1975, but fans, stations and producers fought to get the live-action show back on the airwaves, finally achieving success in 1987 with *The Next Generation*, one of the earlier televisual series to which Caldwell makes reference. Since then, the various series have enjoyed an almost constant presence on television, even excluding repeats. *The Next Generation*'s seven-year narrative is set some 78 years after Kirk's twenty-third-century missions. *Deep Space Nine* follows seven years later, and the Enterprise 'D' stops at the station to drop off some crew in the show's pilot episode 'Emissary' (1993). Picard's former transporter chief, Miles O'Brien, is welcomed aboard Deep Space Nine as Chief Engineer, but Picard's own arrival prompts a somewhat frosty reception. Benjamin Sisko, newly appointed to the station, is still grieving after the loss of his wife, Jennifer, and blames Picard for her death. In a neat example of continuity, it is revealed that Jennifer died three years ago at Wolf 359, an encounter with the Borg shown in the *Next Generation* season three/four bridging episodes 'The Best of Both Worlds' Parts 1 and 2. Picard is assimilated and temporarily becomes 'Locutus of Borg', a sort of Borg spokes-drone. The assimilation process allows the Borg to instantly share all Picard's knowledge concerning the Federation and its defensive capabilities, and thus he is unwittingly associated with the tragedy of Wolf 359.

The sense of continuity is again articulated two years later (temporally both in- and ex-diegesis), as *Voyager* departs from the Deep Space Nine station in its own pilot episode 'Caretaker' (1995). The ship is in pursuit of Maquis rebels, whose existence is indicated by several of the final-season *Next Generation* episodes and who are encountered in a variety of *Deep Space Nine* episodes, notably 'Defiant' and 'For the Cause'. *Enterprise* is a prequel, set in the year 2151, well before the time of Kirk and Spock, yet also links itself to other series, encountering not only Klingons and Vulcans, but also Andorians, a race introduced in the original series, and the Borg. Transporters and replicators are not in common usage, human outposts do not yet litter the galaxy, there are only the forerunners of phasers and photon torpedoes, and the famed 'universal translator' is being compiled via the linguistic expertise of Lt. Sato Hoshi. The near twenty-year gap between the televised adventures of Kirk and Picard notwithstanding, *Star Trek*'s universe has maintained a remarkable dominance over our ideas of future space exploration and civilisation. *Babylon 5*'s creator,

4. *STAR TREK: THE NEXT GENERATION* — RIKER AND WORF.

J.M. Straczynski, recalls an extraordinary interchange with a viewer who demanded to know why hand-links were used in his series when 'it's been established that in the future chest communicator-pins will be the accepted technology.'[1] Even in such small matters, the *Star Trek* heritage shows its cultural potency.

Contemporary social and cultural issues have always been at the heart of *Star Trek*: this is true of most sf. A clear indication of this linkage between our future imaginings and our current fears occurred around the turn of the twentieth century – the end of the millennium. Not content to ponder the millennium fear of a world-wide computer failure, a plethora of stories in the sf and horror genres emerged from more sinister origins, warning of an impending Armageddon. Their depiction of the forces of darkness moving to control/destroy the world is testament to our extrapolated depiction of present-day concerns in sf and other fantastic genres. The dark mindscapes encountered by the psychic Frank Black in *Millennium* (1996–1999) and the post-apocalyptic world of *Jeremiah* (2002) confront the idea head-on. *First Wave* (1998–2001) draws on Nostradamus' prophecies of the earth's destruction in three 'waves', and the very title of *Earth: Final Conflict* explains its premise. Equally, non-sf series *American Gothic*,

Witchblade, *Brimstone* (1998–1999), *Buffy: The Vampire Slayer* (1997–2003) and *Angel* (1999–2004) all echo these concerns in the horror and gothic genres. However, the dominant cultural question of recent decades has been that of representation and, since the original *Star Trek* series began in the 1960s, a revolutionary period for concepts of ethnicity, gender and sexuality, it announced its aspirations in just such areas quite clearly via Roddenberry et al. Naturally, the later *Star Trek* franchises also fall under the representational spotlight.

GENDER IN SPACE

A desire for equality was clearly integrated within *Star Trek* from Roddenberry's pilot episode, although representations of gender do not always fare particularly well – in the first instance because of network and audience objections. *Star Trek*'s pilot episode, 'The Cage', offered a cool and efficient woman (Majel Barrett) as second-in-command to a character called Captain Pike (Jeffrey Hunter). Barrett's role as 'Number One' was rejected by NBC, which felt that the public of 1966 was unprepared to see a woman in such a position of authority. Feedback from test audiences was ambiguous; the reactions had 'ranged from resentment to disbelief. Yet audience questionnaires stated they liked the actress.'[2] As a result, Kirk arrived as Captain, Mr Spock's character became the executive/science officer and second-in-command, whilst Barrett was given the role of Nurse Chapel, a women condemned to forever lust after the elusive Vulcan (and doubtless his rank) from the safety of sickbay. Footage from 'The Cage' was later incorporated into the double episode 'The Menagerie', but it seems that audiences could cope with an alien man as a second-in-command more readily than a human woman. For the most part, human women in the original series are depicted as recognisable stereotypes. They offer a romantic interest, particularly in the case of Kirk's blonde and blue-eyed Yeoman, Janice Rand, or as the means of communications, Uhura, or as healers and comforters – Nurse Chapel. 'Turnabout Intruder', the final episode of the original series, is a sad exit point for gender issues, markedly telling us that Dr Janice Lester was so consumed by her jealousy of Kirk's captaincy that it drove her mad. She could not just love James T. Kirk, she wanted to command a starship – she wanted to be Kirk. As a result, she was unable to enjoy a fulfilling life like that of 'any other woman', and in her rage she steals Kirk's body, simultaneously rendering him 'impotent' in her own. It could perhaps be read as a commentary on issues of equality, but the emotional basis of her behaviour whilst Captain and the 'cool' logic of Kirk whilst trapped in her body suggest a more sexist thrust to the narrative.

For a time, women did not enjoy many primary roles in *Star Trek*, other than as Kirk's numerous soft-focus alien love interests. Despite lots of brief video appearances by women admirals and other high officials, the only other Federation female captain we encounter in depth during *The Next Generation* is Rachel Garrett – Captain of the Enterprise 'C' in 'Yesterday's Enterprise' – and even she needs to be gently reminded of her duty by Picard. The two most prominent women aboard the Enterprise 'D' are involved with traditional female roles: they are communicators and healers. Deanna Troi is a counsellor and Beverley Crusher a doctor, and there was only a brief role in the first season for Lt. Tasha Yar as a rather over-zealous security officer. Worf's memorable half-Klingon, half-human partner K'Ehleyr adds dignity, strength and humour in two *Next Generation* episodes, 'The Emissary' and 'Reunion', challenging Worf's 'warrior' code and his rigid insistence on tradition, whilst mocking her own warrior tendencies. *Deep Space Nine*'s Jadzia Dax and Colonel Kira are also more rounded characters, but it is not until *Voyager* that a strong human female role arises in the form of Janeway, ably supported by her half-Klingon, half-human chief engineer, B'Elanna Torres, and the ex-Borg Seven of Nine.[3] Kate Mulgrew's Janeway is clearly based on a detailed study of Katharine Hepburn, and she:

> raises her eyes, sighs, weeps and comforts in the most classic registers of Hollywood femininity ... The image is that of a woman who has sacrificed not one iota of her femininity in the accomplishment of her job as military leader ... Women's advancement need not be at the expense of compassion, emotional literacy and a very feminine conception of self.[4]

Indeed, Janeway is a highly plausible character, perhaps precisely because of the very clear linkage to the late, legendary and very real Katharine Hepburn.

RACE IN SPACE

Many critics, including Daniel Bernardi and Mia Consalio, have condemned *Star Trek* for its (at best) naïve or (at worst) racist approach to anything other than a 'white' and American-led future. Brave though the inter-racial kiss was between Uhura and Kirk in 'Plato's Stepchildren', it was forced upon them by an alien power, so it can be viewed alternatively as a clever plot device with positive intentions, or as a less constructive expression of inter-racial relations, and a myriad of positions in between. In *Star Trek and History: Racing Towards a White Future* (1998), Bernardi argues at length about racism in the various series,[5] whilst Consalio (1996) explores the discourses of race in science fiction narratives and finds *Star Trek* guilty of normalising 'whiteness' in society and using it as an ideal.[6]

Certainly, it is sometimes hard to disagree with Bernardi or Consalio regarding the original series, although an episode like 'Let That Be Your Last Battlefield', with its black/white and white/black combatants, presents both explicit and subtle points about our attitudes to race and the cultures supporting them. In doing so, it creates an uneasy confrontation of stereotypes and, as Samuel Delany argues, often something more positive can be achieved by stories which dramatise difference in terms of conflict, forcing us not just to watch, but to actually 'think through the situation'.[7] *Star Trek*'s position on slavery is also clarified in 'The Cage', which has the Talosians note, through the reaction of Captain Pike, that humans have such a hatred of captivity that they would prefer death. *The Next Generation* episode 'Code of Honor' is amongst the worst in its tribal representation of the Ligonians, as is 'Skin of Evil', where the oily 'black' alien Armos kills the very 'white' Tasha Yar. This blatant use of archaic racist stereotypes may cause considerable discomfort for many of its audience, regardless of their own ethnicity and it is clear, as discussed by Consalio et al, that questions of ethnic representation sadly remain unresolved.

Nevertheless, the worlds of *Star Trek* mostly try to suggest equality by inclusion and collaboration, rather than exclusion and conflict. *The Next Generation*'s Commander Geordi LaForge is a respected and wholly three-dimensional senior officer who is black and visually impaired. Adam Roberts suggests that Geordi is not the cool, sexually self-assured stereotyped black man, he is essentially a super-competent computer nerd, unable to communicate well with women, shy in social gatherings and 'his best friend is a robot.'[8] The only blatant bigotry Geordi suffers concerns his reliance upon a VISOR (Visual, Instrument and Sight Organ Replacement), commented upon in depth, and notably by aliens, in 'The Masterpiece Society'. Geordi's lack of coolness could certainly be seen as a negative portrayal, of course, but his nerdy tendencies are well balanced by his warm and generous nature and by the wise and enigmatic Guinan (Whoopi Goldberg), Ten-Forward's sometime bartender. She plays the traditional bar tender role of confidante, dispensing warm and witty pearls of wisdom to her Federation flock; she also offers a sense of awareness and intuition lacking elsewhere on the ship, save from the Betazoid empath Troi.

Deep Space Nine provides us with a *Star Trek* series' first black commanding officer and, despite Consalio's pertinent criticisms, it is also perhaps fair to remark that out of five series, three captains have been white (two American and one French), one black and one a woman: as an ensemble cast this could be considered reasonably balanced.[9] Captain Sisko makes his own stand on race, and for a long time refuses to frequent Vic's 1950s bar in the holodeck for the very good reason that 'our people' were not allowed entrance in the historical reality. Ultimately, Sisko relents, but only to save the uniquely programmed Vic in 'Badda Bing, Badda Bang' – the moral of the story firmly based around the strength and need for a unified action. 'Far Beyond the Stars' offers a more poignant tale: in a dream state, Sisko imagines that he is Benny Russell, an sf writer in 1950s America – again a period significantly removed from the actual era of the production. All of his colleagues appear as characters in his dream, as workmates or as people he encounters. Russell/Sisko is unable to have his photograph taken as part of the writing team of *Incredible Tales* magazine, and so is the white woman author K.C. Hunter, as it would be unacceptable for either of them to be seen as part of the magazine's creative team. Russell/Sisko's story is actually the *Deep Space Nine* diegesis, the story of Bajor's religion and of Sisko's encounters with the Prophets, but Russell's 'Negro' Captain protagonist is unacceptable in the 1950s American diegesis, and the only compromise his editor can offer is to have it as a dream – which of course it is. When the story is finally published in *Incredible Tales*, the magazine proprietor has the entire issue pulped, and Russell is fired. The episode confronts America's history of bigotry and the dreams of its population for equality by contrasting it with the equality of the 'real' *Deep Space Nine* diegesis and characters with which we are familiar. The significance of Russell/Sisko being 'the dreamer and the dream', and the parallels with the famous 'I have a Dream' speech of Martin Luther King in January 1963 are hard to miss. The episode also confronts its own series' history, the dream of equality and the dream of the future; as Michèle and Duncan Barrett say, 'the dream is the dream of science fiction: it is an analogy for *Star Trek* itself.'[10] The concern is whether the dream is aspirational or delusional.

ECHOES OF THE WEST: NATIVE AMERICANS

Despite lapses in rational ethnic representation, for the most part senior figures – doctors, admirals, political leaders – throughout the later series are drawn from a variety of ethnic groupings and are shown as respected equals. Ironically, there is one ethnic background by which *Star Trek* is rendered utterly bewildered. Ambivalence and ambiguities run riot in *The Next Generation* episode 'Journey's End', where Picard is faced with ghastly echoes of American history and given the unpalatable task of relocating a group of Native Americans from their planet, which has been recently ceded to Cardassia under a new treaty. The treaty with Cardassia is the starting point for what becomes known as the Maquis rebellion, a topic pursued in 'Pre-emptive Strike' and more consistently in subsequent series. Here, events unfold disastrously with the Native American settlers refusing to be moved – their leader referring openly and unromantically to the history of lies between the white man and his people. The ultimate route is for the Native Americans to move on to another plane of existence, driven from their land yet again, with only their 'mystical' faith to aid them. The only gesture of hope comes from Wesley Crusher. Contemplating his career in Starfleet, he resigns and elects to join the Traveller, whom we've met in the earlier episodes 'Where No Man Has Gone Before' and 'Remember Me', and who appears here as a Native American mystic. Together they embark upon an exploration of the universe from this other 'plane'. Significantly, *Voyager*'s second in command is a Native American, Chakotay. A former Maquis rebel who joins Janeway and her crew in the Delta Quadrant, he brings little more to the mix than a neatly wrapped piece of fur with which to access his spiritual 'animal guide' and a striking tattoo. In seven seasons, the character seldom leads an episode, although the episodes chiefly concerning him are of interest. In 'Cathexis' it is Chakotay's spirit that saves the crew; in 'Tattoo' he is forced to confront his own ambivalent attitudes to his hereditary cultural values in order to save the ship; and in 'Manoeuvres' his warrior's pride is given as the natural rationale for his direct defiance of Janeway's orders. In 'Nemesis' a Vietnam-like battle scenario is played out, as human-like aliens capture and brainwash Chakotay into hatred of another, outwardly very *in*human race. At the episode's conclusion, he is left unable to look at them without revulsion, despite their collaborative effort with the crew of *Voyager* to rescue him. The rest of the crew seem shocked by Chakotay's hatred, despite his attempt to interrogate the emotions involved, and he is seen as perhaps weaker, rather than desirable. The audience is forced to confront its own preconceptions about appearance and difference, but the representation is uneven and confusing, oscillating between depicting Chakotay shallowly as a noble and enigmatic warrior and a more three-dimensional approach which allows his character to interrogate his identity and the impact of white civilisation upon his ancestors.

Despite their ambiguity, these representations are still more positive than the idealised pastoral approximation of Native Americans in the *Star Trek* episode 'The Paradise Syndrome', a scenario which would suit Bierstadt's idyllic frontier composites, associating Native Americans with nature, not culture. Suffering from amnesia, Kirk is found emerging from inside a religious obelisk. Mistaken for a god or a messenger of the gods he is made Medicine Man to the tribe, an appointment understandably resented by the previous incumbent. The episode suggests that the indigenous people cannot tell the difference between aliens and gods, and Bernardi suggests that the 'knowing' audience is therefore encouraged to construct them as foolish and primitive.[11]

ALIENS

It is equally easy to see other aliens in the various series as national stereotypes. The Klingons were originally represented as cold-war warriors, but the collapse of the Soviet bloc and the return of Russia to the capitalist fold is paralleled in the film *Star Trek: The Undiscovered Country* (1991), where a catastrophic explosion on the Klingon moon, Praxis, forces the High Council to seek an Alliance with the Federation. In later series, the Klingons in particular – now often played by actors of ethnic backgrounds, a significant statement on difference both in- and ex-diegesis – have been portrayed mostly as valiant heroes and their warrior code identified less with bushido, but rather as a strange mixture of Sioux and Viking. 'Today is a good day to die,' drawn from Sioux tradition, becomes the Klingon approach to battle,[12] whilst honourable death means a place in Sto'vo'kor, a sort of Klingon Valhalla. This is explored in detail in *Deep Space Nine*'s 'Shadows and Symbols', as Worf seeks a place for his dead wife, Jadzia, in the hallowed halls, and in *Voyager*'s 'Barge of the Dead', where Torres tries to save her mother's soul. Otherness is thus incorporated into the Federation's honourable intentions throughout the series.

Other aliens remain chiefly as antagonists, plumbing the depths of villainy. The Ferengi are capitalists to the core, with a quasi-religious litany of 'Rules of Acquisition'. But they are despised: capitalism has no place in the egalitarian and secure Federation society of *Star Trek*. The Romulans live up to their nomenclature, but their society shares the fascism of Cardassia, with the terrifying secret service the Tal Shiar (although Vulcan longevity allows now-Ambassador Spock to work for peace between the Federation and Romulus in *The Next Generation*'s 'Unification'). Vulcans themselves are continuously portrayed as logical and enigmatic, with a nod to a more complex past, especially where sex is concerned: 'Amok Time' in the original series and *Voyager*'s 'Blood Fever' both explore aspects of 'Pon Farr', the seven-yearly requirement to mate. Despite the premise of emotionless Vulcans, the original *Star Trek* episodes invariably ended in some sharp interplay between the emotional 'Bones' McCoy and the calm Spock. *Voyager*'s Tuvok had great difficulties in accepting the demands of logic as a child, and *Enterprise* suggests that Vulcans are not always so logical. T'Pol is a notably arch science officer, and in 'Fusion' the Enterprise encounters the initially endearing cult 'V'tosh Ka'tur', or 'Vulcans Without Logic', who sound more like a rock band and positively revel in any experience possible.

One of the most fascinating and deadly aliens has already been mentioned: the Borg, first introduced by the petty trickster Q in 'Q Who'. Accusing Picard of arrogance, he suggests that the Enterprise's crew is not ready for what is 'out there' and flings the vessel deep into Borg space, light years from its former position. The Borg are actually cyborgs, seeking perfection through a hive-like unity, assimilating members for their collective from any species worth time and effort; they have repeated run-ins with the Federation in *The Next Generation* and *Voyager*. The cyborg, the human blended with the machine, is an enduring sf theme, and draws upon Freud's theory that any threat to the development of the ego might encourage the creation of some kind of defensive armour 'in which the subject attains invulnerability by aligning itself with the rationalistic predictability of the machine'.[13] Freud's theory of the ego creating 'a mental projection on the surface of the body' also touches upon Nietzsche's man and superman in its desire to supplement the human body.[14] These concepts manifest themselves in another Roddenberry series, with *Andromeda*'s Tyr Anasazi (of the Nietzschean race), while films such as *The Terminator*, *Aliens* and *Robocop* (and the 1994–1995 television series *Robocop)* all play on this idea and, given the increasing real symbiosis between the human body and machinery in modern mundane life, in the extreme worlds of sf the body becomes ever more heavily and visibly armoured.[15]

The fear of fascism, of external control, is underlined in a great many series, by the cyber-virus and implants the Taelons inflict upon their human associates in another Roddenberry's series, *Earth: Final Conflict*, and in *Babylon 5*, through the use of such technology by the Shadows and the Drakh. *Babylon 5* also demonstrates this on a minuscule level in the command staff's constant summons via their 'links': 'Never lets you finish a sentence, does it?' says Sinclair to Sheridan in 'War Without End'. The telepathic Psi-Corps is a more regimented, continued reminder of this, using drugs to repress those who will not join it (like Ivanova's mother). In other ways, the question of humanity (in the sense of freedom, individuality and personal control) is articulated early in episodes such as 'Infection' and 'The Quality of Mercy'. Both concern individual issues, yet relate historically to more grandiose concerns, whilst 'Mindwar' warns of a more devious use of technology against unaware humanity. In season four's 'Between the Darkness and the Light', the new Warlock class ships built for Clark with Shadow technology – a terrifying union of the bulky, rotating-hulled Earthforce destroyers and the obsidian, spidery Shadow vessels – warn of the perils of blind technological advance without thought of the consequences.

In *The Next Generation*, when Picard is transformed into Locutus of Borg in 'The Best of Both Worlds', a lingering shot shows the single tear forming in his eye as he is stripped of his humanity and the last vestiges of his spirit appear broken. In *Voyager*, the gradual humanisation of Seven of Nine creates a three-season narrative thread, starting with 'Scorpion' and highlighted in 'Dark Frontier', when the Borg queen attempts to re-assimilate Seven – an interesting battle for control between the co-operative human collective of Janeway's Voyager and the enforced Borg collective. The 'freedom with responsibility' concepts underpinning the Federation collective is cast against the uncompromising and unindividuated nature of the hive-like Borg collective, and the Federation's protective and nurturing nature is supplemented by the arrival on Voyager of several children who have also been assimilated by the Borg. Another balance to the fear of the man-machine hybrid occurs in *The Next Generation*, which replaced the logic of Spock with the android Data, a purely mechanical being with a highly complex 'positronic' brain who spends his time longing to experience and understand emotions, humour and human vulnerabilities, the chance for which is temporarily allowed him by an uncharacteristically generous Q in 'Deja-Q'.

Borg influence in *Star Trek* is finite, however, and in *Deep Space Nine* its threat is replaced by the grey, reptilian Cardassians and the shapeshifting 'Founders' of the Dominion. The grim, Stalinesque Cardassians are the former military occupiers of Bajor, their cynicism and lust for absolute power epitomised by the merciless Obsidian Order. The Founders' Dominion is supported by a horde of violent warriors, the Jem'Hadar. Travelling through the wormhole linking Deep Space Nine with their quadrant they set out to avenge their wronged ancestors by destroying 'solids' (non-shapeshifters). Forging a temporary alliance with the Cardassians, they infiltrate the Klingon empire in an effort to destroy both it and eventually the Federation. Akin to Loki, that other harbinger of Armageddon (the Shapeshifter of old Norse myth) – or perhaps Ares in Greek mythology – they are portrayed as devious tricksters, Jungian shadows leading us astray. Constable Odo, who maintains civilian order on Deep Space Nine, is also a shapeshifter, although he was lost as a child and thus has no knowledge of their plans and methods. Odo's upstanding character serves as a moral balance to the imperialist plans of the Dominion. Shapeshifting Odo is more rigid than most 'solids' in his morality and quest for justice.

Throughout all of the series, 'other' civilisations are frequently depicted as helpless and gullible, or sinister and murderous. Kirk's discovery of a Declaration of Independence in 'The Omega Glory', his negotiations in 'The Cloud Minders', and the Wild West aspect of his psyche developed in 'Spectre of the Gun', a reworking of the infamous gunfight at the OK Corral, all demonstrate his 'superior' American heritage, as do his moral speeches which generally close the episodes of the original *Star Trek*. Yet amongst these examples of an all-encompassing white American, heterosexual and patriarchal future, there are more than a few glimmers of hope. The apparently naïve Organians in 'Errand of Mercy' have a few gentle tricks up their sleeves, and the alien Horta creature in 'Devil in the Dark' is healed by the good McCoy (protesting that 'I'm a doctor, not a bricklayer'). In 'Day of the Dove', a remarkable if uneasy alliance is established between Kirk and his Klingon counterpart, Kang. In *The Next Generation*, Jean-Luc Picard takes the more politically aware and less confrontational route on many occasions – for instance, he refuses to destroy the crystalline entity in 'Silicon Avatar', wanting rather to learn about it; and in 'The Measure of a Man' he fights for Data's right to be recognised as a sentient being and not merely an android (this idea is repeated in *Voyager* with 'Author Author' and the holographic Doctor's rights regarding his novel).

Countering these examples is 'The Host', also a *Next Generation* episode. A Trill symbiont is a slug-like creature transplanted to live in the host's abdomen, an apparently beneficial process which means that not only does the host have his or her own memories, but can also access those of the previous host(s). Here the clumsy response of Beverley Crusher to the non-gendered Trill, whom she meets in the body of a man, only to find it then transplanted to the body of a woman, demonstrates more than a little nervousness about issues of sexuality and representation. Doubtless it also shows the network's reluctance to support what amounted to a lesbian kiss on prime-time television. By the time of *Deep Space Nine*, this was clearly less of a problem: in 'Rejoined', Trills Jadzia and Lenara indulge in a decidedly active and prolonged 'lesbian' kiss which made it to the screen. Nevertheless, the presentation is ambiguous. The kiss is between two aliens, and the narrative makes clear that Jadzia is actually kissing the symbiont who has the memories of the former host, her male lover, not the current female host. In 'The Outcast', Commander Riker, following with delight in the footsteps of Kirk in never missing a romantic opportunity, experiences a clear reversal of heterosexist discrimination when he falls for someone from an androgynous culture who expresses 'female' tendencies. The initial suggestion is rather worrying, that a good 'man' can turn the head of any 'woman', but there is a second and more complex commentary here. The J'naii ban heterosexual practices, considering them deviant, and re-educate the 'female' with whom Riker has developed a relationship – a clear critique of institutionalised anti-gay and lesbian cultural practices.

Issues of individual difference are also explored in many episodes. *Star Trek*'s 'The Enemy Within' depicts a transporter incident that splits Kirk; his associates are faced with two captains, one a strong but psychologically troubled man, the other a kindly but weak character. This is repeated in *Voyager*, with the half-Klingon half-human Torres split into two people, a timid human and an assertive Klingon, by the Vidiian aliens in 'Faces', and the situation reversed with Neelix and Tuvok in 'Tuvix' where, rather than being split, the effusive Talaxian and the restrained Vulcan discover the benefits and problems of being temporarily fused. In *Deep Space Nine*, we have a permanent example of the positive side of symbiosis in Trills Jadzia (and then Ezri) Dax. The host prior to Jadzia was Curzon, a friend of Sisko's, and his relationship with Curzon is underlined by his tendency to call the young woman who is the new host 'old man' and her ease in calling him 'Benjamin'. In all these examples, the narrative points towards the value of combined elements in each personality, the benefits of embracing difference and how much we need all of those different elements to exist. At times the expression of this superior and egalitarian future can be overwhelmingly smug: characters are prone to comment how they'd heard about such awful things in 'history' classes, or how (as Kirk frequently said at the end of an episode) 'we have learned' to do better. At times the crew are so dutiful, so patient, so nice it is almost a relief to witness aberrant behaviour, just to prove that the Federation does not brainwash its citizens into submission. Indeed, many of the more interesting characters in *Star Trek* are rebels – K'Ehleyr, Riker's 'twin' Tom, Ro Laren, Tom Paris, Quark and Seven of Nine. They challenge the Federation's values and thus also those of *Star Trek's* audience.

Nevertheless, individuals in *Star Trek* are seldom reduced to more stereotype – perhaps excepting Chakotay – and the power of the individual within society (in this case, the society of the Federation) to fight against excessively revisionist or denialist historians is not lost. If we consider sf author Gordon Dickson's thesis that only 'full spectrum humanity' can co-ordinate and preserve the 'Splinter Cultures', we can see that aliens are, almost inevitably, 'merely isolated aspects of our own humanity, in need of reconciliation'.[16] Dickson notes that various aspects of humanity are represented in 'Splinter Cultures', but reminds us that only the broadest range of humanity can offer real hope for the future.[17] Aliens invariably represent repressed or respected (but elusive) aspects of humanity, and only through total reconciliation can we achieve completeness. Dickson is not alone; much psychoanalytical theory argues that in sf the alien represents that to which we ascribe the abject, the disavowed, the other.[18] Perhaps the only conclusion to draw is that at least the sf of today is not afraid of articulating the preoccupations of the day – racial discourses are problematic within our society – and our readings of television representations, a discursive act in themselves, identify and highlight these problems. The result of this can actually be positive: as we praise or condemn various aspects of ourselves we also see human beings as a single united force. Concomitantly each aspect can be cherished for its diversity and uniqueness, for its frail, fallible and recognisable humanity.

Other contemporary shows also consider issues of representation but, aside from *Space: Above and Beyond*, discussed in the following chapter, they mostly dwell upon other concerns. Nevertheless, it is worth contrasting *Farscape*'s approach to that of *Star Trek*. In the opening episode, lost astronaut John Crichton finds himself aboard the Leviathan Moya amid a chaotic and diverse collection of alien species. This is not commented upon other than in his fear that, when they suggest it is 'time to eat', he may be the main course. Becoming part of the crew, Crichton finds himself working alongside Pa'u Zotoh Zhaan, a Delvian priestess who is a blue humanoid 'plant', Dominar Rygel XVI of the Hynerian Empire, a small grey-blue slug-like creature with several stomachs, who moves by means of a hover-chair, and the fearsome Ka D'Argo. A Luxan warrior, D'Argo has highly sensitive tentacles cascading from his head and a long, prehensile tongue which can incapacitate an enemy. While they battle to avoid recapture by the black leather-clad human-looking Peacekeepers, with whom Crichton is constantly confused, they are joined by the Officer Aeryn Sun, disgraced and irrevocably 'contaminated' because of her contact with alien species. In 'Won't Get Fooled Again', Crichton is drugged and wakes to finds himself apparently back on Earth after a failure of the Farscape test mission. His friends from Moya are present as part of his everyday Earth-life: Aeryn appears as the doctor who first treats him, Zhaan is a psychiatrist, D'Argo is an irritating jock and Rygel is cigar-smoking Chief Executive. Aware that he is not home, Crichton tries to point out to those around him why he knows it isn't really Earth. In session with Zhaan, he explains that part of the reason he can't take her seriously is because 'you're blue' – she calmly inquires whether he has 'a problem with people of colour' while he continues to point out that people 'don't come in blue' on Earth. When he calls Rygel a 'two-foot slug on a golf cart', his 'father' is disgusted: 'What does the man's disability have to do with it?' The apparently casual juxtapositions of Crichton's rationalised human reaction jar profoundly against the perspective of normality offered by the characters and the *mise-en-scène* on the fake Earth. As a result, every expectation and stereotype is challenged, every step forces Crichton, and therefore the audience, to renegotiate the environment in which he finds himself, and to interrogate the layers of cultural and social behaviour.

Stargate SG-1 spends less time concerning itself with representation, since most of the races it encounters are originally human, with the exception of the ancient races like the Asgard. Teal'c is a Jaffa warrior and carries a young Gou'ald within his stomach, but his difference is only remarked upon occasionally by O'Neill, who tends to inquire whether or not 'junior' (the larvae) is okay or to dismiss his more warrior-like actions as a 'Jaffa thing'. However, as with *The Next Generation*'s Klingons, Teal'c is played by an actor from an ethnic minority – his difference marked by his casting, but then denied by his humanised role. Equally, Daniel Jackson and (in season six) Jonas Quinn provide a counterpoint: within the SG-1 team, they, not Teal'c, are the odd men out. Along with the various *Star Trek* series, these programmes make an effort to 'displace' questions of sexual and racial difference onto the 'more remarkable difference between the human and the other'.[19] This is one of science fiction's promises for the future: it creates the potentially *scriptible* texts discussed earlier, allowing a fresh approach to that which we find abject in ourselves – they permit us to escape from the corresponding socio-cultural and psychological 'baggage'. At best, they provide fine social commentary and, like all sf, having cast our contemporary social divisions into a new light, encourage us to take a step further and interrogate them.

UTOPIAN FUTURES

The comfortable future of all the *Star Trek* series depicts an admirable, almost utopian society, but crucially we do not see how it has been achieved. One particular *Next Generation* episode demonstrates this problem most clearly. In 'The High Ground', Dr Crusher is confronted by the ideological and moral complexities of terrorism.[20] Seized from the Rutian capital by dissidents, Crusher discovers that they have been using a dangerous inter-dimensional transporter process to carry out their raids and are desperate for medical aid, but is upset and confused by the violent actions they carry out against their state. Accused of idealism by her captor, Finn, a man who demonstrates his nature to be both artistic and sensitive, she responds to his cynicism by saying: 'I come from an ideal culture.' Although she is sympathetic to him, her response is not to seek what drives him to such actions, but merely to comment on how she cannot understand them. In the parallel storyline, Commander Riker deals with Alexana, the official state representative, in an attempt to gain Crusher's release. He finds himself equally baffled by the firmly uncompromising attitude of the apparently friendly female government official. Ultimately, despite the Federation's official refusal to become involved but with the very real involvement of two of its people, both sides meet and the prospect of peace appears on the horizon.

This third-season episode was first screened in the USA in January 1990, and is perhaps more in tune with the USA's then apparent inability to comprehend what terror and terrorism is about. The disruption of everyday life and communications for ordinary people is the most obvious way for such strong expressions of subversion to be expressed by dissidents. Large-scale and international terrorism on the US mainland has only occurred in the very recent past. The episode demonstrates a pre-September 11th desire in the USA to avoid conflict with other warring parties and also to act on behalf of others as a force intended for good – so Riker and Crusher see the only way out for Finn, and the oppressive government emerges from trust through negotiation. The chasm between this neutral and satisfactory ideal of possible negotiation and the 'War Against Terror' that followed September 11th is remarkable: any substantial role for the Federation's equivalent, the United Nations, has been rejected and the sovereign right of the USA to pursue suspects rendered paramount.

The real power of 'The High Ground' lies in how it is critical of all parties concerned. With the use of dangerous technologies as a means of terrorism, and the utilisation of oppressive strategies by the government in power, it makes clear that the moral 'high ground' of the title, to which Crusher and Riker both cling, as well as the stance taken by both the opposing sides, is limiting and ultimately destructive – certainly a futuristic approach in comparison to current attitudes. Partly because of *The Next Generation*'s episodic nature, there is also no real sense of interrogating the reasons behind terrorism itself, which seems a very minor issue to the Federation of the twenty-fourth century, as it was to the USA in the 1980s and early 1990s. The notion of terrorism reared its head briefly in *Deep Space Nine* through the Maquis, but more so in the second season of *Enterprise*. Post-September 11th, the season two finale 'The Expanse' depicts the destruction of part of Florida and the Caribbean by an unknown race finally identified as the Xindi – underlining just how very much inspiration current issues provide for extrapolated futuristic speculation.

The moral dilemma in 'The High Ground' remains, for the most part, at a personal level rather than as a broader social issue: it is overcome relatively easily and the episode concluded. Yet, from *The Next Generation* onwards, a capitalist society apparently no longer exists and, given Tasha Yar's horror at an alien group's request for fresh meat in 'Lonely Among Us', everyone seems to be vegetarian, there is little or no religious conflict within the diverse membership of the Federation and equality and justice are frequently reassured. However, because this achievement has been established *a priori*, the struggles necessary to achieve such a remarkable state are used as a structuring absence: we are merely shown the flagship of the new regime.

In *The Next Generation, Deep Space Nine, Voyager* and *Enterprise*, from the late 1940s Roswell UFO incident parodied in 'Little Green Men' until the late twenty-third and early twenty-fourth centuries, Earth is neither seen nor discussed in detail – although, interestingly, the films do touch upon a variety of ecological and social issues. *Star Trek IV: The Voyage Home* (1986), for example, is concerned with the extinction of marine life. The television series generally distance themselves from any 'human' responsibility or take immediate narrative action to demonstrate good will. *The Next Generation* episode 'Force of Nature' parallels the dangers of vehicle and fossil fuel emissions when an alien race tries desperately to prove to Picard that warp travel is destroying the fabric of the universe. As a result, the Federation quickly agrees that Starfleet vessels will ordinarily proceed at no more than Warp 5. In turn, *Voyager* clashes with the environmentally reckless Malon in 'Juggernaut' and 'Extreme Risk'. The Malon are dumping toxic waste in an area of space far from their own planet; the waste emits deadly theta radiation which is destroying the environment for the local inhabitants, known only as 'Night' aliens. Janeway and her crew suggest they can find an alternative means of processing the waste, but the offer of assistance is rejected and so Voyager joins the Night aliens in their efforts to thwart the thoughtless Malons. It seems that at some stage 'we have learned' about the dangers of environmental contamination but, again, how this is achieved is not depicted.

Apart from Kirk's accidental encounter with the Earth of 1968 in 'Assignment Earth' and the *Voyager* episodes '11.59' and 'Future's End', both of which clearly mark the purely selfish financial aims of some within capitalist society, *Star Trek* series stay clearly in the distant future or in the pre-1960s past. When a transporter accident thrusts *Deep Space Nine*'s officers into the troubled San Francisco of 'Past Tense', the 'past' is the late twenty-first century, still firmly set in the viewers' future, so we can make no immediate connections. There has been some sort of nuclear holocaust (again mentioned from time to time by Kirk and co, but discussed in detail really only in *First Contact*); a lack of diplomacy has led to decades of conflict between the Klingons and the humans, but the Earth depicted is akin to an eco-friendly holiday haven with overtones of a pastoral and Edenic wilderness paradise very much along the lines of Bierstadt's Yosemite. We rarely see negative aspects of this 'present'. Perhaps the clearest examples occur in *Deep Space Nine*'s two paranoid episodes concerning a possible takeover of Starfleet by Dominion shapeshifters. Appropriately named 'Paradise Lost', witch-hunts paralleling those of McCarthy's anti-Communist trials in the 1950s begin to affect life on Earth, until Starfleet regains its sense of balance. Even when confronting Federation methodology, the basis for action is usually immediate need: the ends always justify the means and it is invariably an individual perversion that has precipitated the crisis, not a fault with the ideals themselves. Just as the problems reverberating from Vietnam were initially avoided by American television and film, so, with the exception of the original series, the *Star Trek* franchises generally avoid politics beyond their own diegesis.

STAR TREKKING: NARRATIVE

Star Trek is not a soap opera, but it has undeniably created a universe: with so many series, episodes and characters it would be impossible not to do so. *Deep Space Nine* aside, the series seldom offer a truly connected narrative, only the consistent and clever use of what has gone diegetically before by a team of dedicated writers and producers creates the sense of an uninterrupted progressional narrative. There is no reason why a series should be pre-planned or connected in any way, and the episodic nature of *Star Trek* allows for considerable flexibility. *Deep Space Nine* differs from the earlier series but, despite its early overtures to a prolonged storyline, it is not until the final two or three seasons that this asserts itself fully. A great deal of time is spent in individual, lightweight episodes, which detract from the overall narrative rather than embellishing it in any way. 'Badda Bing, Badda Bang' is set during the final days of war against the invading Dominion, yet the crew have time to depart to the ever-useful holodeck for a gambling escapade, helping out the holographic lounge singer, Vic Fontaine.[21] Even in the hands of the Dominion, Ezri Dax and Worf spend more time arguing about their relationship than they do in resisting their captors. Since the story was not pre-planned, elements occurring in earlier seasons jar with the conclusions reached. After seven seasons, and with intermittent contact with the non-linear and non-corporeal wormhole aliens, it transpires that Sisko is the child of one of them. Yet when Sisko first arrives, although the Bajorans quickly accept him as Emissary, the messenger of the Prophets, and as proved to be right, the wormhole aliens, who exist concurrently in all times, apparently have no knowledge of him or corporeal life forms, of Bajor – of anything outside their wormhole. Coincidences abound, and the story climaxes in a sudden, final feature-length episode rather than arcing gracefully to a conclusion.

This is not to detract from the power of episodic television, nor from *Deep Space Nine*'s latterly dark future vision, which offers a refreshing challenge to Starfleet hegemonic ideology. *Enterprise* also demonstrates this edgier attitude towards institutionalised command structures. However, *Deep Space Nine*'s critique is ill sustained and purely character-driven – and thus less effective. It gives an impression of complete continuity, but this is only an impression. *Deep Space Nine* is about a group of people living on a space station and places great emphasis on experiences and individual growth and achieving a sense of concreteness through their adventures. It relates the loves and losses of Jennifer and Sisko, Sisko and Kassidy, Bashir and Jadzia Dax, Jadzia Dax and Worf, Worf and Ezri Dax, Ezri Dax and Bashir, Odo and Kira, Kira and Vedek Bareil, Vedek Winn and Gul Dukat. The war against the Dominion and Cardassia is invariably seen only in the terms of individual protagonist/antagonist experiences, not of its greater impact. *Deep Space Nine* does not attempt to leave the personal or individual experiences of a small cohort of officers.

Despite there being no preordained story arc in the entirety of *Star Trek* series, there is a painless and natural expansion of the universe through the sheer volume of episodes. There are frequent references to the adventures of Kirk, Spock or Picard in the later series, and characters guest between series, adding to the sense of community, and to fan amusement. Mr Scott appears in *The Next Generation*'s 'Relics', an episode about a Dysonsphere, and a grumpy and elderly Dr McCoy appears in the pilot, 'Encounter at Farpoint', performing the role of a good champagne and blessing those who sail in the Enterprise 'D'. O'Brien, Keiko and eventually Worf moved to the former Cardassian station to become *Deep Space Nine* regulars. Troi, Barclay and Riker from *The Next Generation* have all appeared in *Voyager*, as has the intergalactic pest Q. Even characters/guest stars who have played key roles can be used as a source of amusement and in-jokes. In 'Q-less' (a first-season episode of *Deep Space Nine*), the omnipotent alien Q turns up to taunt Sisko, whose earnest and serious character he mocks, comparing him unfavourably with the more passionate Picard. He also makes repeated visits to *Voyager*, wooing Janeway, and creating havoc upon other occasions. More referentially, Suzi Plakson, who plays Worf's mate K'Ehleyr in the *Next Generation*, later guest-stars in *Voyager* as a member of the Q Continuum, in 'The Q and the Grey'. She emerges second best from an argument with B'Elanna Torres, *Voyager*'s half-Klingon/half-human engineer, and remarks archly how she truly admires Klingon women – 'They're so spunky.'

Special episodes, invariably created for some particular anniversary, reinforce this sense of continuity. The most notable and technically/aesthetically impressive example occurs in 'Trials and Tribble-ations', a *Deep Space Nine* episode celebrating *Star Trek*'s thirtieth birthday in 1996. Using the need for time travel to prevent an assassination attempt on the legendary Captain Kirk[22] as a plot device, it incorporates footage of a successful comic episode from the original series: 'The Trouble with Tribbles'. New computer processes allow the *Deep Space Nine* characters to interact with the original Enterprise crew in a televisual spectacular, with the result that the episode is not only technically impressive, but also manages to mock itself with in-jokes to which we, the (fan) audience, are privileged. We laugh at the intelligent and independent Lt. Dax's delight at the 'micro-skirt' she puts on, and the remarkable difference between the very human appearances of Klingons in the original series and the deeply ridged exo-skeletal brow of Worf and his *Next Generation*

Klingon compatriots. 'We do not discuss it with outsiders' says a deadpan Worf, already suffering from the presence of small, furry, trilling Tribbles, who dislike Klingons as much as Klingons dislike them. The episode also expresses a rare comment on its media peers and competitors, casting a saucy jibe at *The X-Files*. The time-travelling event (frowned upon by a Federation whose 1990s incarnation despairs of Kirk's 1960s maverick heroics) is investigated by two dour agents whose names are a play upon those of Scully and Mulder: Lucsly and Dulmer. Just to underline the point, 'Trials and Tribble-ations' immediately echoes *The X-Files'* graphic mission statement: 'The Truth is out there.' When Sisko asks if the investigators are sure they 'don't want anything' (to drink or eat), the reply is curt: 'Just the truth, Captain.'

The joke about *The X-Files* is unusual in *Star Trek* terms, as the series generally insist upon an isolated existence. They may be self-referential but they shirk from too much obvious external referencing, especially of current media and popular culture. Occasionally, and particularly in the original series, there are references to human history, even the arts, but very rarely to science fiction, and any degree of self-awareness seems mostly reserved for the more light-hearted films. *Voyager's* '11.59' has Janeway remembering her ancestor Shannon O'Donnel (also played by Kate Mulgrew) at the end of the twentieth century and, in 'The 37s', the mystery of lost pilot Amelia Earhart is solved: along with various other people from 1937, she is revealed to have been kidnapped by aliens. Janeway also consults Leonardo da Vinci when she is suffering from stress ('Scorpion') and during an attack by the Hirogen ('The Killing Game') the holodeck is transformed into a Second World War French village resistance scenario. However, the choices of scenario are substantially distanced through time and myth and, in the case of those involving the holodeck, yet again by their holographic status, so they remain intangible. Tom Paris' love of twentieth-century Americana asserts itself when he creates a black and white holodeck adventure program called 'Captain Proton' – clearly based upon popular 1940s/1950s sf strip adventures. Even here, rather than referring to an actual television series, like *Flash Gordon* or *Buck Rogers*, an 'unreal' series is created – thus stressing *Star Trek's* reluctance to really connect with its audience's own (science fiction) past.[23]

Enterprise makes some genteel references to classic twentieth-century European films, with its frequent 'film nights'; Captain Picard has a penchant for 1940s pulp detective stories; and Worf and his son play Clint Eastwood-type cowboys in 'A Fistful of Datas' in *The Next Generation*, but generally *Star Trek* shirks references to television, popular culture and science fiction in particular. The main area of interest is the holodeck, which underlines one of our current social fascinations and the very act we are indulging in when we watch *Star Trek*: the ability to interact and immerse oneself partially or totally within an entertainment scenario.[24] Science fiction promises to show us brave new worlds, so it is not surprising that Geoff King and Tanya Kryzwinska's study of sf finds it to be hugely 'prominent in new media forms such as virtual reality simulations and computer games that explore dimensions of immersion and interactivity'.[25] The holodeck concept of total immersion is still only a promise, but film and television are fascinated with the idea of inhabiting 'second-hand experiences – with all their transgressive, visceral and emotional sensations – but with the advantage of being able to switch off the technology'.[26] From attempts to visually record personal experiences in *Brainstorm* (1983) to the cyberspace hell of *The Lawnmower Man* (1992) to the computer-dominated un-reality of *The Matrix* and *The Matrix: Reloaded* (1999, 2003), cinema has explored this idea. The bewildering but stylish *VR5* (1995) offered a television version of virtual reality, and *The Lone Gunmen* (2001), in a spin-off series from *The X-Files*, touched upon it in their comedy clashes with evil. The holodeck offers *Star Trek*'s genteel version of this idea – with the 'computer: freeze program' instruction and 'safety protocols' as the cut-off switches, although when these go wrong with the Sherlock Holmes/Moriarty program in *The Next Generation*'s 'Elementary, Dear Data'/'Ship in a Bottle', or are affected by an external power such as we encounter in *Voyager*'s Beowulf-based 'Heroes and Villains', the potential dangers of a holoworld that has suddenly become real are explored.

In *The Next Generation*'s 'The Neutral Zone', Data tells us that television 'did not last much beyond 2040'; as 2040 approaches this becomes less likely, but the entertainment we see on the Enterprise and Voyager is notably live and collective – musical recitals, plays, poetry readings or individual and private holo-adventures. Picard likes to read actual books: he doesn't download texts from the computer, although, like Janeway after him, he frequents the holodecks, with a preference for film noir scenario and a detective called 'Dixon Hill'. Watching visual media, whether for entertainment or for news, is apparently almost a deviant activity – it is Tom Paris who adores late twentieth-century American popular culture and, significantly, he is *Voyager*'s semi-reformed rebel. This absence of recognisable and extrapolated popular culture can create a cultural desert for the viewer, because a context is so hard to come by – at its worst, *Star Trek* functions (quite literally) in a vacuum; at its best it is dependent upon a structuring absence.

By way of contrast, in *Babylon 5*'s opening episode, 'Midnight on the Firing Line', Security Chief Garibaldi spends what appears to be an entire day hunting for someone with whom to share 'his second favourite thing in the Universe'. Ultimately he coaxes a bemused Delenn into joining him – to eat popcorn and watch Daffy Duck in *Duck Dodgers in the 24th-and-a-half Century*, showing that popular culture has a degree of continuity and creating an important link between the audience and the characters.

Equally, *Farscape* relishes every possible opportunity to reference sf and other popular culture alike. When the Scorpius chip creates a duplicate Scorpius inside Crichton's mind, Crichton dubs him 'Harvey' after the 1950 James Stewart film; Spielberg and Captain Kirk are mentioned on a regular basis. In a tour de force, Aeryn practises her English in 'Kansas' by watching *Sesame Street*, featuring the Jim Henson Workshop Muppet Kermit the Frog on television, whilst the Jim Henson Workshop Muppet Dominar Rygel sits beside her in-diegesis. *Stargate SG-1* also frequently makes sly jokes at the expense of – or in communion with – other sf series and films. In the time-travel episode '1969', the show selects and points to famous sf films and television shows. O'Neill is captured by the American military and accused of being a Russian spy; asked his name on several occasions, he tells his interrogator that it is James T. Kirk, then Luke Skywalker. When the X303 experimental interstellar vessel is thrust into early mission to save the Asgard in the two-part 'Prometheus'/'Unnatural Selection', O'Neill confuses Major Carter by saying that the joint chiefs-of-staff won't 'go for it'. Carter believes he means the mission, but in fact he is referring to his proposed name for the ship, whereupon Carter reveals why: 'Sir, you *can't* call it "The Enterprise".'

LANGUAGE

If intertextuality, mannerist expression and self-reflection are not *Star Trek*'s favourite arenas for innovation, it does play with one of the key means by which sf can create a schism between the real world and the fictional: language. If Tom Paris' love of the 1950s in *Voyager* is manifested in the argot of fast cars and fake sf series, *The Next Generation* delights in a level of technobabble that would confuse most NASA scientists. *Deep Space Nine*'s 'Little Green Men' features a sly dig at technobabble from Quark and a parody of its worst examples from Rom. Their ship in danger of imminent destruction, Quark urges Rom to think of something:

> Rom   The Chemocite! If we vent plasma from the warp core into the cargo hold, we may be able to start a cascade reaction in the Chemocite. Then we can modulate the reaction to create an inversion wave in the warp field and force the ship back into normal space. If I time it just right I should be able to get us close enough to Earth to make an emergency landing.
>
> Quark   Rom! You're a genius!
>
> Rom   You think so?
>
> Quark   How should I know? I have no idea what you're talking about.

Babylon 5's 'Walkabout' parodies this *Star Trek* tendency: when Lennier begins to explain the advantages and operation of the organic Vorlon-based technology behind the White Star, his momentary leaning towards technobabble is dismissed by Sheridan with 'Well, as my great grandfather used to say – "Cool!".' In itself, this use of language emphasizes for us the importance of the technology, or the ship. Just as the stories of Jules Verne were often less focused on the adventure itself and more concerned with the technical ability to travel through the adventure – by submarine, or rocket, or flying machine – so the focal point of our modern equivalent is undoubtedly *Star Trek*'s various Enterprises. Renamed, but in an identical role, the ship is also the focal point for *Voyager*. Crews come and crews go but the starship remains an interstellar icon, a constant manifestation of the Federation and its values in uncharted space.

Although *Star Trek*'s 'universal translator' generally removes some of the linguistic functions previously identified by Rabkin by automatically translating between languages, the use of language in sf is frequently a means by which concepts of difference can be interrogated. Most other series avoid the problem by similar means: *Farscape* has 'translator microbes'; in *Stargate SG-1*, archaeologist Daniel Jackson serves as a sort of mobile Rosetta Stone. *Babylon 5* demands that the various races learn each other's languages, although of necessity for the audience English serves as the language of diplomacy. One of the more reflective stories from *The Next Generation* offers a simple but clear example of sf's linguistic challenges and potentials, as well as demonstrating the manner in which ancient tales become metaphors for human life. The Enterprise's crew seldom has problems with language and difference thanks to its universal translator – when this fails it is generally a plot device to create humour.[27] However, in 'Darmok', the Enterprise crew encounters an alien species, the Children of Tama, with whom successful contact has never been established. The Tamarians are called 'incomprehensible' and, for once, the inability to instantly translate meaningful sentences provides an opportunity for linguistic exploration. The computer can provide nouns and prepositions, but precious little else.

Picard is transported from the bridge of his ship, apparently kidnapped, and finds himself on the planet El-Adrel with the Tamarian Captain, Dathon. He is unsure of the latter's motives – until they are both attacked by an alien beast, and the Tamarian is wounded. Meanwhile, as tension increases between the first officers who have remained on their respective ships, Counsellor Troi and Lt. Commander Data can use the Enterprise's extensive computer database to locate words, but cannot translate the Tamarian syntax. Picard and Dathon's attempts at communication are more successful. United against the alien beast, when the action lulls in the twilight, they attempt to communicate by telling each other the stories of their ancestors in words and pictures drawn on the ground. Enthused and impressed by the Tamarian's determined attempt to make himself understood, Picard recognises a parallel between the alien's story and a memorable tale from human history. Dathon's tells how two warriors named Darmok and Jelahd joined forces in order to defeat a dangerous enemy and battled to victory at a place called Tenagra. Using drawings in the sand to enhance his explanations, Picard relates the legend of Gilgamesh and Enkidu battling the Bull of Heaven, realising that the incredible risk taken by the Tamarian captain was a selfless one, made with the intention of creating communication where there had been none. It was an act carried out, naturally, in the abstract manner of his people.

Asked to study the language and try to find some common ground, Data and Troi are at a loss, but at least note the repetition of certain proper nouns, notably 'Darmok' and 'Tenagra'. Searching the ship's database for the sector's records of these nouns, they discover a communality: on the planet Shantil III, there are records of a mytho-historical hunter called Darmok, and an island continent called Tenagra. They present their findings to Riker and Crusher:

Data   The Tamarian ego structure does not seem to allow what we would normally think of as self-identity. Their ability to abstract is highly unusual. They seem to communicate through narrative imagery, a reference to the individuals and places which appear in their mytho-historical accounts.

Troi   It's as if I were to say to you: 'Juliet on her balcony.'

Data   The situation is analogous to understanding the grammar of a language, but not the vocabulary.

As Dr Crusher then recognises, unless we are familiar with Shakespeare's tale of *Romeo and Juliet* (where the image of Juliet conjures up the idea of tragic romance) context is meaningless and therefore so is the image. Thus communication between the Starfleet crew and the Children of Tama is initially impossible because the metaphors and their temporal locations are contextually empty: the Tamarian language appears to be just random names and locations, rather than a sophisticated form of syntax. Hence the computer can make no sense of the language; it can translate individual words but not speculate as to the semantic context: 'Shakka, when the walls fell' and 'Darmok, at Tenagra, his arms wide' mean nothing in isolation. Just as our own language demands metaphor for expression, so the Tamarian language is based upon its own system of metaphors. In this case, situations are related to a template provided by their historical predecessors. The examples 'Darmok' offers are simple; it takes little invention to realise that 'In Winter' said sharply probably implies that someone is 'frozen out', but the problem of functional comprehension is nevertheless genuine. However, *The Next Generation* offers a successful resolution. Although the beast on the planet kills the Tamarian, Captain Picard survives. He returns to the Enterprise able to explain what has happened to the Tamarian Captain, and expresses his grief by saying 'Shakka, when the walls fell', thus avoiding violent recriminations. The Tamarian officer responds by elevating the story of Picard and his captain to a status similar to that of Darmok and Jelahd at Tenagra, saying 'Picard and Dathon at El-Adrel'. In essence, 'Darmok' has resonances both in- and ex-diegesis. The episode not only presents a simple story of Picard encountering an alien, it also enters human storytelling history as a direct parallel with Gilgamesh. The narrative parallels the internal (diegetic) narrative of Darmok and Jelahd at Tenagra in the experiences of Picard and Dathon; their experiences enter into Tamarian legend, becoming part of their history and thus their discourse.

Janeway has a unique and somewhat different linguistic function in *Voyager* – whereas culturally *Voyager* denies many connections with its era of production, Janeway's perceptions are entirely of its era. Like Spock in the original series, Data and Worf in *The Next Generation* and Seven of Nine and Tuvok in *Voyager*, she allows us to interrogate and reposition 'normal' human assumptions and actions. Janeway's role is to relate the future to the present for us by her literary knowledge and her use of current idioms. Her passion in the holodeck is a *Jane Eyre*-style story of a governess, first seen in 'Persistence of Vision', although she also spends time with Leonardo da Vinci when she is feeling more creative – and her ability to create imaginatively is part of her potency. When the Cardassian spy Seska leaves Voyager, she also leaves a virus in a holodeck program, which asserts itself in 'Worst Case Scenario'. With the ship in imminent danger of destruction, Janeway

105

has to continually rewrite the scenario in order to save Tom Paris and Tuvok, who are trapped within the holo-story. With considerable literary flair, she invents an alien attack, which buys her the time necessary to rescue her officers: the *deus ex machina* is, Janeway announces, far from 'an outdated literary device'. In the marvellously indulgent 'Bride of Chaotica', Tom Paris' 'Captain Proton' program is the focal point for an alien attack; Voyager's commander cheerfully assumes the role of the vampish Queen Arachnia, acts her heart out in a black and white parody and again saves the day. Janeway is the sole character allowed to make contemporary references (Tom Paris' are all retrospective), and this extra-narrative role is important, because with 'history' absent, it links our present with her future. As the Barretts argue, she makes jokes about a 'think tank' and a 'space race' and, most importantly, on more than one occasion she confesses to temporal physics giving her a headache when she tries to think about it – allowing an immediate identification with the viewer, who is enduring the baffling technobabble of her senior officers regarding innovations in multi-phasic shielding, tachyon particle dispersion and slip-stream technology.[28]

IMAGERY

It is not only language which can be used to create the necessary 'break' or cognitive estrangement so central to science fiction: imagery can also be used and, as argued in the first section, with the advent of more advanced televisual technical capabilities, the successful foregrounding of the background becomes a far more realistic ambition. The original *Star Trek* had little in the way of budget, and the miraculous 'transporter' effects were actually invented to avoid the costs of filming a shuttlecraft landing on a weekly basis.[29]

However, there were still some remarkable effects, including a journey beyond the galactic rim in 'Where No Man Has Gone Before', as well as some rather awful ones – the Enterprise's twin ship 'Constellation' at the mercy of a planet-munching ice-cream cone in 'The Doomsday Machine'. The emphasis was very much on the exploration of all things new and the very human response to that discovery. In *The Next Generation*, the entire quadrant is figured out, mapped and charted: there is little left to explore. Far from going boldly 'where no one has gone before', under Jean-Luc Picard the Enterprise mostly potters around a secure little galaxy delivering medical supplies, dropping off passengers and supplying Q with frivolity and amusement.[30] If it was daring in killing off one of its ensemble in 'Skin of Evil', that was its first and final act of rebellion. After the first few episodes, the universe plays a mere backdrop; it is ironic that *Star Trek*'s *mise-en-scène* resembles the repetitive black and white starfield we now use on our computers as a screensaver, because that is mostly all we see of space. The bridge's view-screen acts like a car's windscreen, framing the stars outside and creating the kind of artificial composite vista Bierstadt and Church created in their depictions of the western frontier. Standing on their bridges, Kirk, Picard or Janeway create latter-day examples of this uni-directional magisterial gaze Albert Boime associates with frontier landscape painting, although mostly they only glance briefly at a starfield, planet or, more commonly, an alien commander in close-up. As a result we are not drawn into contemplation of the view as would be a staffage figure, and any televisual flourishes are diminished in power.

A majority of episodes from *The Next Generation*, *Deep Space Nine*, *Voyager* and *Enterprise* limit images of the ship in planetary orbit (used as an establishing shot between commercial breaks) or the stars seen from warp speed, flickering through the portholes of the observation lounge or the Captain's 'ready-room'. Even 'The Best of Both Worlds', where the Enterprise locates remains of the Federation fleet destroyed by the Borg at Wolf 359, lacks any substantial visual-narrative dynamic. It is also linear, offering gentle, gradual sweeping turns, lacking use of different planes and more appropriate for vessels in gravity than in space. In the later series, such as *Voyager*, there is little use of sfx beyond the technologies and techniques Caldwell identifies. Physical action and descriptive dialogue dominate, while a static *mise-en-scène* offers a mere indication of the location. The sets are stark, functional and impersonal, while the ship interiors are predominantly beige, or grey. The camera moves little, offering mostly close-ups or middle-distance shots, classically edited or, occasionally, keeping abreast of the characters/ship, heading purposefully toward their destination. Likewise, *Enterprise* seems far more interested in the technology of the vessel than the wonders of space, although 'Cold Front' depicts a fabulous proto-star burst, the Great Plumes of

Agosoria, which occurs only every twelve years, and 'Breaking the Ice' is visually impressive, and depicts the crew's genuine astonishment at the beauty of a passing comet.

Eric Chauvin worked as a matte artist for both *Babylon 5* and *Voyager*, creating cgi backdrops – onto which analogue props and actors' performances are later mapped digitally. He suggests that the latter lacks visual flair and aesthetic innovation: 'Paramount knows it has a franchise with a known financial return, it doesn't want to fool around with the formula. Consequently, it doesn't do anything very daring or original because that wouldn't be part of the *Star Trek* style.'[31] The *Star Trek* image has been carefully forged over thirty years; to change it substantially risks the established audience dynamic. There is no reason why it should be, and genre television generally demands safety, not risk, in narrative style and format. If the various *Star Trek* series can guarantee good returns and a solid audience, they clearly fulfil their audiences' expectations to a greater or lesser degree. Whether they always function as science fiction, providing cognitive and linguistic estrangement, is more doubtful. They also tend to rely upon the anachronistic bland background of pre-1980s television, allowing their dialogue (especially technical discourse) to dominate, rather than paying attention to the potential of a dynamic *mise-en-scène*, something which can greatly enhance sf television.

The titles of *Voyager* contain some splendid examples of space imagery; sadly, this is not often extended into the episodes themselves. However, combined with the pioneering journey home, they are indicative of the ideology underpinning the series. The sequence contains what we might call the 'elemental' – as Voyager crosses the screen we see fire, water, earth (rocks) and air (gas). The ship first passes through a scarlet and yellow solar flare, then sends ripples through a multicoloured pastel gaseous cloud (which simultaneously resembles water and air). We look up to see Voyager crossing above an ice-bound planetoid, then the camera rises through the ring of tiny asteroids, which clatter on the 'camera' as we travel through them, ultimately coming level with, and then above, the ship as it passes the Saturn-like planet. Finally, as the warp engines come on line, the ship moves toward a glorious purple, blue and scarlet nebula backdrop, vanishing in a point of brilliant white light. Just as Voyager's journey home recalls the adventures of Sinbad and Odysseus in its sense of wonder, so the basic elements so precious to explorers are shown to us (water, air, earth, fire), making the connection between those ancient heroic voyages across Earth and Voyager's journey through space. The images echo the sense of destiny we observe in pictures of the frontier, except rather than heading west to new lands, the ship is heading home through new lands. Equally, the celebratory and triumphant brass-based theme music, just like that of *The Next Generation*, could be that of any Western. Indeed, the closing image of its journey is against a backdrop not dissimilar to the promise offered within pictures produced by the Rocky Mountain art school. The same light we find in Church's *Twilight in the Wilderness* infuses the imagery here.

And this is the key. *Voyager* is backward- not forward-looking. The Western articulated its demise as it articulated its existence: it was a self-fulfilling prophecy. The frontier hero, whether the eponymous Shane or *The Searchers'* Ethan Edwards, is condemned forever to ride further west, further into nature, further towards the sunset and the end, as the frontier is swallowed up by civilisation: it is the very place they protect yet can never truly inhabit. But the western states were settled long before the Midwest, and where east and west meet, the frontier, like the setting sun, is gone. Bierstadt's paintings of Yosemite were notably often of sunset, the end of light. They are therefore a retrospective of what *was*, as well as what they actually depict – ideologically and culturally. *Voyager* offers a similar kind of directional retrospective.

NAUTICAL FAMILIES

On several occasions, Janeway is asked why she refuses to let the crew settle in the Delta Quadrant, given that their journey home is estimated to take seventy years. But she steadfastly refuses; there is no settling here, the values and customs of Starfleet are honoured and obeyed, there is little deviation despite circumstances, as 'Equinox' confirms. In 'Resolutions', when she and Chakotay contract a virus and are unable to leave a planet, the ship carries on – only to return once the Doctor has located a cure. Seldom does the crew learn from others: it is far more interested in teaching everyone else Federation values, Federation ideology. One of the continuing threads is the

5. *STAR TREK: THE NEXT GENERATION* — WORF SEATED), PICARD AND DATA ON THE BRIDGE OF THE ENTERPRISE.

gradual humanisation of Kes, Neelix and Seven of Nine: they are taught the values that Janeway holds dear. Seven of Nine offers the most resistance, repeatedly noting how she is encouraged to be an individual and then condemned for her individuality, a charge to which Janeway is curiously reluctant to respond. Even the Maquis crew rapidly accepts the change – Chakotay, their commander, most of all. In the aforementioned 'Nemesis', he initially expresses his surprise at an alien race's desperation to destroy its 'enemy', saying that his people would try to 'talk' things out; yet he was a Maquis rebel, fighting desperately to save his adopted planet, ceded to the Cardassians, just a few brief years earlier. Even in 'Course: Oblivion' (a story following on from 'Demon', when the ship and its crew are copied by a newly sentient life form on a 'Demon' class planet), the copy of Janeway ignores the scientific evidence from Chakotay and Tuvok that she is in fact from the demon planet, saying 'I'm from Indiana', and demands that they stay on course for Earth. The copy of Voyager ultimately implodes as the real Voyager arrives in response to its distress call.

The nautical heritage of the first four *Star Trek* series has been explored by Michèle and Duncan Barrett – the opening credits from *Enterprise* could not reiterate their case more clearly. Not only do they draw upon the iconic image of the Earth from space, they also take us back to early voyages on Polynesian rafts and mighty galleons to the (HMS) Enterprise. We journey on through the history of earthly exploration via balloons, to Kittyhawk and the first manned flight, the jet plane, the Apollo programme and the space shuttle 'Enterprise', before making an elegant segue from historical fact to future fiction with a finished and extended International Space Station, a pre-warp commercial vessel to the arrival of Zefram Cochrane's 2061 warp engine and, finally, the first starship: the Enterprise itself. There is a seamless transition from document to documentary, from recorded space video to cgi imagery, in essence from documentary to drama, and this works to prevent us from losing pace with the narrative while we admire the sfx, a tendency which is positively encouraged in some sf series and in many sf films. Underlining these technical advances are *Enterprise*'s titles: although they begin by linking global human exploration, the higher levels of actual and projected technology are clearly entirely American.

At the narrative heart of *Star Trek* is the Captain's love for his/ her ship and the ship's family. The concept of family runs deep through *Voyager*, and all of *Star Trek*, yet, paradoxically, families are invariably absent or surrogate. Janeway's equality demands that she make the same sacrifice as every member of Starfleet's senior field officers, male or female, seems required to do – her personal life is far from fulfilled. In *Voyager*'s pilot episode, 'Caretaker', we see Janeway involved with Mark, but throughout her travels she is alone. This is underlined when communications are restored with Starfleet in 'Hunters', when Mark sends her a 'dear John' letter, confessing that after three years of her being 'lost' in the Delta Quadrant he has given up hope and married someone else. Kirk enjoys romance after romance with alien women of literally every colour and creed, but his love for the ship always wins. Picard is also single, although he too enjoys various romances, most notably with the mischievous archaeologist Vash in 'Captain's Holiday' and 'Qpid', but also with stellar cartographer and musician Nella Daren in 'Lessons' and with metamorph Kamala in 'The Perfect Mate'. Each time, however, his deep sense of duty prevents him from more than a brief and entirely honourable liaison. Beverley Crusher is widowed, likewise Benjamin Sisko has lost his wife – although, like Crusher, he has a son. Even his final season marriage plans with Cassidy Yates are denied in the final episode, 'What You Leave Behind', when his ancestry is revealed and he elects to return to his origins with the 'wormhole aliens'. Worf, whose character straddles both *The Next Generation* and *Deep Space Nine*, is put through tragedy twice. His first partner, K'Ehleyr, is murdered not long after they confess their continuing love for one another ('Reunion') and, years later, no sooner have he and Jadzia Dax tied the knot in the traditional, painful Klingon fashion, than Jadzia is killed ('Tears of the Prophets'). Tuvok is married, but his wife is on Vulcan. Perhaps the only successful long-term relationship we see in the *Star Trek* universe, apart from the brief glimpse of a happy future for Paris and Torres in *Voyager*'s 'Endgame',[32] is that of Miles and Keiko O'Brien. They marry in *The Next Generation* and by the end of *Deep Space Nine* not only have their lives and relationship intact, but also have two children.

Without a real family, Janeway demonstrates her willingness to go to extraordinary lengths to preserve her ship and surrogate family in the two-part 'Year of Hell', refusing to abandon her role as Captain and succumb to medical rest, because 'right now it [Voyager] needs one of us'. Her last actions are in fine nautical tradition, she goes down with her ship – finally crashing what remains of Voyager into the Krenim Imperium timeship (captained by the wonderfully named Annorax), thereby restoring the entire timeline, including Annorax's former life and love, and Voyager itself. In 'Scientific Method', Tuvok describes her actions as 'reckless' when she heads Voyager between a binary pulsar to shake off aliens who have been conducting medical experiments on the crew. Indeed, although Picard may be explicitly linked to Ahab in Melville's *Moby Dick* (1851) in the film *Star Trek: First Contact*, Janeway shares more of his obsessive nature concerning her goals and dedication.[33] In *Deep Space Nine*, Sisko is initially denied a vessel, given instead an aging Cardassian space station to command, although the pleasure of sailing the starry sea in a more 'ancient' fashion is depicted in 'Explorers' when Sisko and Jake build a vessel according to ancient Bajoran tradition. It is perhaps harder to convince an audience that a *Star Trek* captain can 'boldly sit', and the third season opens with the arrival of the experimental vessel the 'Defiant', from which time Sisko and his crew zip around the Alpha and Gamma quadrants in a tradition more associated with Kirk and co.

With the notable exception of *Deep Space Nine*, the various *Star Trek* missions clearly stem from the classical heroic/epic journey, and also clearly draw upon speculative fiction's fascination with technology epitomised by the works of Jules Verne, H.G. Wells and others of that ilk. The experiences of Voyager's crew echo a theme initiated in sf television by the 1960s series *Lost in Space* – where updated versions of the Swiss Family Robinson find themselves lost and alone. *Voyager*'s journey commences with powerful references to America's frontier. The chase takes them immediately into 'the Badlands', an uncharted and unpredictable region of space, and the crew's subsequent experiences are not unlike those of the pioneer. Thrown from the charted Alpha Quadrant to the uncharted Delta Quadrant, they are effectively plunged into the wilderness and must learn to cope with new and dangerous situations in order to emerge, at the end of their journey, new and better people. Their first encounter is with the 'Caretaker', a mysterious being who has swept them, along with the Maquis ship and crew, into a holographic farm-like area of blissful nineteenth-century Americana – a pastoral idyll located between the artificial social stratifications of civilisation and the dangers of the wilderness.[34] Of course, Janeway, her crew and the Maquis are far from happy to remain; they reject the illusion and confront the Caretaker. In order to make good Voyager's escape, Janeway swiftly incorporates the doubtful Maquis crew into her own, sacrificing their vessel in the process, before setting off through the wilderness of this unknown quadrant for 'home'. Voyager's subsequent journey is a reversal of the pioneer's journey, but similar in meaning – if anything, it is more reactionary, looking determinedly backwards rather than forwards. Just as Bierstadt and Church depicted a safe, god-given Edenic future in the far west of their pictures, but depicted a carefully delineated area of wilderness in between, and as the western frontier narrative demanded that pioneers and frontiersmen essentially travelled from civilisation to civilisation via a total immersion in the wilderness, so Janeway's journey starts with Federation civilisation in the Alpha Quadrant, passes through the unknown Delta Quadrant (allowing for numerous explorations en route) and ends with the established status quo of 'Federation' civilisation as Voyager reaches the Alpha Quadrant, earth and home in 'Endgame'.

Janeway's mission in this unmapped quadrant of the galaxy is essentially the same as that of Kirk in the original *Star Trek*, but it also harks back to classical Greek tales: it is the *Odyssey* and the *Aeneid* all rolled into one. It is a quest for the knowledge that will permit a triumphant return home and requires a loyalty and devotion to the ship itself above all else. The Maquis are rapidly absorbed into the crew: Chakotay as Janeway's trusted First Officer; B'Elanna Torres becomes Voyager's Chief Engineer. The rest of the Maquis crew knuckle down, and any ideological differences are dealt with briefly and subsumed within the general principles of Starfleet. The ship creates a community.[35] The only lasting and potentially dangerous rebellion comes from the unappealing Seska, who turns out to have been a physically altered Cardassian spy in the first place and who soon defects to join the equally unpleasant Kazon. Even in the Delta Quadrant, seventy years from home, the ideals of the Federation dominate. Voyager is quite literally and metaphorically the vessel containing them and Voyager's welfare is paramount; its technology and the advances enforced by the very situation in which the crew finds itself create further scientific innovation. This kind of gadget-oriented sf allows for an extension of the ancient and fantastic heroic voyages of Odysseus and Sinbad in a context often more plausible (via a kind of 'natural law' or 'common sense') than that of pure myth or fairy tale. Jason's Argonauts have become Janeway's Astronauts.

NARRATIVE IDEOLOGY

The heroic quest for knowledge (technical or otherwise) is a primary focus for such epic journeys. It is perhaps telling that the more stationary narrative of *Deep Space Nine* was rapidly complemented by a return to more traditional maverick adventurism in the shape of *Voyager* – and more so in the raw, pre-Kirk *Enterprise*. Alongside its five humans (Sisko, Jake, O'Brien, Keiko and Bashir), *Deep Space Nine* offers a multi-planetary ensemble: Odo the shapeshifter, Kira the Bajoran, Dax the Trill, Quark the Ferengi and Garak the Cardassian. It is a remarkable collective. *Voyager* may be notable as the first *Star Trek* series to have a female captain, but Janeway's gender offers the only difference: in every other sense, *Voyager* echoes the original series. In effect, after *The Next Generation*'s quiet and secure diplomacy, with the advent of *Deep Space Nine* and *Voyager*, the *Star Trek* universe fragmented.

The potential schism was beginning to announce itself even during *The Next Generation*'s television run. In the fifth season's two-part episode 'Unification' (1991), Captain Jean-Luc Picard takes a message to (now Ambassador) Spock from his dying father, Sarek. Undercover and in enemy territory on Romulus, Picard roundly criticises Spock for his dangerous 'cowboy diplomacy', an explicit reference to the clear-cut ideology of the original *Star Trek*. However, by the end of the narrative, that same cowboy diplomacy has resolved the problem, whilst Picard's more delicate diplomacy has faltered and failed. As *The Next Generation* finished, so *Deep Space Nine* began, offering a darker, politically astute and gradually more thread-based story based on a space station. Within a year, *Voyager* had arrived, providing a nostalgic return to the grand old days of Kirk's considerably less politically aware exploits. Forged in the heat of the cold war and the new frontier politics of Kennedy, the *Star Trek* universe had nowhere else to go. As Gareth Roberts observes, 'born of the old order ... [it] has responded to the multiplicity of influences and pressures from within and without its culture by fracturing.'[36] *Enterprise* neatly avoids any such difficulties; set prior to the original series, it can return to maverick heroics and wild adventures with a wry and knowing postmodern smile. The films as a whole tend towards a less subtle approach to the *Star Trek* universe in their narrative, and certainly play more to the gallery through android Data's 'emotion chip', alien incongruities and so forth. In *Star Trek: Generations* (1994), Data most clearly articulates the frontier values lurking close beneath the surface most clearly, saying: 'Saddle-up, lock and load.' *Star Trek* still possesses an underlining ideological anachronism, which betrays itself occasionally by its metaphors, but more often by its scenarios.

The dangers of ideological historical distortions are demonstrated in 'Living Witness' through the holographic Doctor's experiences in a museum 700 years in *Voyager*'s future and, in 'Remember', Torres experiences the memories of a woman who experienced the systematic extermination of an entire section of society – a hidden holocaust. In 'Memorial', the crew experience at first hand a massacre on the planet Tarakis via a faulty memorial projector. In 'Darmok', Picard's diplomacy and knowledge of storytelling avoid an unnecessary conflict and, in the lyrical 'Inner Light', he experiences the life of the musical family man Kamin, from the long-dead world of Kataan. The experience of an entire life as a father and husband, something absent from his own life, stays with him and helps foster the unexpected romance with Commander Daren in 'Lessons', something 'entirely consistent with *Star Trek*'s insistence that individual experience, in this case transmitted through memory, is the essence of human identity', according to Michèle and Duncan Barrett.[37]

In a sense, *Enterprise* is rewriting *Star Trek* history and along with it the identity of its humans. Jonathan Archer is a captain reminiscent of Kirk in his more maverick moments: a man who keeps a young Beagle called Porthos and wears his heart on his sleeve. His crew, uncertain of what the brand new Enterprise NX-01 can do and endure, go boldly where only aliens have gone before with the assistance of T'Pol, the Vulcan liaison officer, and the result is a storyline which maintains a degree of freshness despite covering old ground in this 'new' sf frontier. There is considerably less reliance upon advanced technology and its concomitant technobabble, but more upon the development of technology through inspiration and dedication. This Enterprise is not about the Federation of the future, it is about the NASA-like technological expertise that can take us to that future. The episode 'Silent Enemy' concentrates upon the deployment of sub-space amplifiers so as to speed up communications, others upon the use of the feared transporter – a piece of technology Kirk and his compatriots took for granted. Just as the technology of mass communication – trains and other transportation, the telegraph and oloctricity – facilitatod in tho taming of tho Wild Woet, eo tochnology again is helping humanity to 'tame' space. Enterprise shows space as the final frontier, but it relies upon anachronistic 'old frontier' ideologies in much of its approach, a sad comment upon Star Trek's overall ideological direction.

FOUR

THE SACRIFICE OF ANGELS

MILITARY HISTORY AND IDEOLOGY

The previous chapters have shown how narrative trends changed in the 1980s and 1990s. Predominantly episodic series became sequential, their characters and themes creating long-term narrative arcs. One particular series that developed a definite story arc and demanded careful audience attention was *Space: Above and Beyond*. Not only does it offer a long-term narrative strategy, one which was just reaching its potential when the series was cancelled at the end of its first season, but it also offers a challenge to ideology in an arena seldom open to such challenges – the world of the military.

This chapter explores representations of individuals and the military and also the involvement of armed forces in a variety of sf series. It concentrates upon the depiction of military men in *Space: Above and Beyond* and the break with post-Vietnam conservative military ideology suggested by the character of Colonel T.C. McQueen. Had the series been made and screened after the events of September 11th, with a resurgent American military involved in Afghanistan and Iraq, the military theme may have been more in keeping with its era, and the juxtaposition of McQueen's carefully considered values and the very real terrorism and warfare of the early twenty-first century would have afforded a remarkable contrast. As it is, perhaps the

Clinton era suggested different values and, although McQueen's ideology in particular is more liberal and more in keeping with the ideals of the Democrat party (and therefore very much of its time, in terms of production), there was maybe less of a contrast between the ideology of the futuristic story and perceptions of the real world. *Space: Above and Beyond* therefore may have found less of a desire and less of a need to explore its military scenario in its potential audience.

ALIEN INVASION

Whereas many of the sf series examined so far have been concerned with private individuals or ensembles, few borrow from military or pseudo-military organisations to facilitate their premise – other than depicting them as antagonists and forces for oppression. *Star Trek* works hard to deny its military basis, yet the naval language and traditions of the star 'ships' belie this claim and many sf stories work around the threat of invasion and war; this is at the heart of *Deep Space Nine*, for instance. *Stargate SG-1*'s long-term narrative deals with the threat of a Gou'ald invasion and a variety of other aliens who also have access to the Stargate system or interstellar capabilities. The horror of the Earth under threat from some hostile force has percolated through sf literature, film and television since its earliest days. *The Outer Limits* is particularly fond of this theme and, in episodes such as 'Birthright', 'Music of the Spheres' and 'Feasibility Study', humanity is tested with political deceit, addiction and slavery respectively. Mostly the threat comes from outside, and programmes such as the remarkable 1983 mini-series *V* and its 1984 sequel *V – The Final Battle* showed the way for sf in the televisual era.

V opened with massive alien ships appearing over the world's major capitals and the superficially humanoid aliens pronouncing friendship, peace and an end to famine and disease, in return for some minerals their home planet did not possess. As scientists began to disappear, people became suspicious of these benevolent humanoid visitors. TV cameraman Mike Donovan (Marc Singer) boarded one of the alien vessels, discovering in the process that the new human friends are in fact repulsive, cold-blooded reptiles in disguise, with a penchant for rodent hors d'oeuvres and a main course of roasted or boiled human.[1] Although the truth is broadcast, it is dismissed as terrorist propaganda by the invaders and the world continues to welcome its new friends. Fortunately, the humans are aided by a rebellious alien 'fifth column' that helps to defeat the invaders. During this collaboration, one of the aliens mates with his human girlfriend, and within a short space of time she gives birth to twins. One, an alien-human hybrid dies, but the surviving human-alien twin, Elizabeth, survives, and her rapid metamorphosis into a 'Starchild' offers hope for humanity and the pacifist aliens alike. The series suffered somewhat from poor and limited sfx and whereas its Neo-Nazi aliens (replete with cunning propaganda and swastikas) may have lacked subtlety, its message of anti-totalitarianism was entirely of its time.[?]

Set just a few years into the twenty-first century is Gene Roddenberry's *Earth: Final Conflict*, which works along much the same lines as *V*. Based upon a storyline written by the late Roddenberry and brought to fruition by his wife, Majel Barrett (also responsible for the posthumous *Andromeda*), the story opens some time after Taelon 'Companions' have arrived offering peace and goodwill to the people of Earth – when, in fact, amongst other dastardly plans, they intend to harvest the human race for genetic material. *Earth: Final Conflict* is essentially a political thriller set in the future, with double-dealing politicians and adamant ideologists pursuing their goals at the expense of human and Taelon races, whilst at its heart are those same humanist values we find in *Star Trek*. As the series evolves, we encounter yet more aliens, a race of dedicated and merciless hunters called the Atavus. They are eventually revealed to be not alien at all, but the original inhabitants of the earth – they went into a state of stasis to avoid the consequences of a catastrophic asteroid collision, and when they awoke millions of years later, the earth was 'infested' with homo sapiens. The issue of ownership was not much debated, given the intransigent and uncompromising attitudes of both parties.

Similar in its invasion theme is *War of the Worlds*, which picks up from where the 1953 film of the same name left off, reactivating the Martian invaders by means of a toxic spill and having them pursued by astrophysicist Dr Harrison Blackwood, whose parents were killed in the original invasion. The other main tale of alien invasion offers Cade Foster as a 'running man', almost alone in his knowledge of the imminent danger, and following in much the same mould as David Vincent in the similar and earlier series *The Invaders* (1967–1968). The Francis Ford Coppola production *First Wave* is based loosely around the 'Millennial Prophecies' of Nostradamus; these predict that an alien enemy (the Gua) will destroy the Earth in three 'waves'. During the first wave, aliens will disguise themselves as humans, making way for the second wave: invasion. The final wave will destroy the planet, unless humanity can find a twice-blessed man, who holds the key. Reformed thief Foster is framed for his wife's murder, discovers that he is subject 117 in a series of psychologist tests, the previous 116 having resulted in the subject's insanity or death. With the aid of Crazy Eddie, a conspiracy theorist and editor of the Paranoid Times, and more latterly, a renegade alien called Joshua, Foster tries to stop the invasion.

The paranoia associated with alien invasion or alien abduction has been explored as a secondary theme in programmes such as *Project UFO* and *Kolchak: The Night Stalker*, progenitors of the more darkly paranoid *X-Files*, and the short-lived *Dark Skies*, which provided a brief period of heaven for conspiracy theorists, with John Loengard and his wife Kim battling against invasion, government conspiracy and alien impregnation. *The Visitor* turns this around slightly, its pilot protagonist Adam was abducted in the 1940s by aliens in the Bermuda Triangle – an area off the eastern seaboard, which has entered into American folklore because of the various strange sightings and the lost ships/aircraft it has claimed. Adam has now escaped his captors, returning to steer the planet away from imminent destruction. Adam's experiences make him no longer comfortable with Earth, least of all with how it has changed in the fifty years since his abduction. As we will see with Crichton in *Farscape* and Sheridan in *Babylon 5*, Adam's experiences and his unique perspective now make him as much an alien as those who abducted him. *Roswell High* (1999–2002) – which subsequently ditched the '*High*' in a quest for reinvention – touches upon this theme but its aliens, descendants of the infamous Roswell incident aliens, are stranded and trying to not only understand themselves, but to find a way home. As a result, its scenario is often closer to a rite-of-passage teen-drama (and during puberty what parent and teen does not regard the other as totally alien?) with occasional use of slick sfx. Nevertheless, through the teenage scenario, sf's traditional concerns regarding aspects of humanity projected as 'otherness' or 'difference' are addressed in the strongest tradition. A different kind of invasion is depicted in *Alien Nation* (1989–1990). The Tenctonese are slaves who escape bondage when the ship commanded by their Overseers crashes in the Mojave Desert. The humanoid aliens seek sanctuary and become refugees on earth, welcomed in human society with slightly less than open arms. They are intellectually superior, and get drunk on sour milk, so naturally they become a new underclass, officially called 'Newcomers', but commonly called 'Slags'. The series is really an LA-based detective story, focusing on the relationship between rough and tough cop Matthew Sikes and his suave Newcomer partner George Francisco, but it makes clear points in its exploration of humanity through otherness.

SEDITION

Occasionally, the horrific plots to take over the earth (or the USA) in such series stem from purely human agenda. *Freedom* (2000) is marginally sf-based, although it is really concerned with political intrigues and extrapolations. It depicts a near-future America where a renegade section of the military has deposed the legitimate government and taken power, resulting in America being run by an oppressive military dictatorship. The only hope for society emerges from four dissidents, all of whom are accused of treason, who band together to return the elected civilian government to power. *The X-Files*, in particular, offers a combination of external and internal forces in its long-term narrative, which is concerned with both alien invasions and government cover-ups and alien-human collusion, as well as a more regular explanation or documentation of the paranormal.

In the more explicit *Prey* (1997), bio-anthropologist Dr Sloan Parker discovers a new strain of human DNA with a 6% differential from homo sapiens, 'homo superior' – a new species. The opening credits offer a context:

> Forty thousand years ago, the most advanced species on Earth was wiped out by a powerful new life form. Now another species has evolved – stronger, smarter, and dedicated to our

annihilation … Once again it's survival of the fittest … And this time we are the prey.

Prey is all about a desire to halt the next stage of human evolution, a reversal of the more common sf theme of advances, enhancement via cybernetic implants, medical breakthroughs, etc. This unexpected evolution is not one modern man wishes to contemplate, and Parker battles against the remarkably strong, intuitive new species confronted initially by Tom, who then defects to join the battle, and later against one of the leading 'homo-superior' beings, the clinical and sadistic Lewis. The only real weapon Sloan has is a call for humane behaviour, but these new life forms are absolute Darwinists and have no truck with emotions or ethics – rather like *Earth: Final Conflict*'s Atavus.

Dark Angel (2000–2002) takes the idea of advancement from the point of view of a genetically engineered woman, Max Guevera, on the run from her creators. In a careful juxtaposition of respective mental and physical ability, she teams up with a wheelchair-bound scientist to fight injustice. *Mutant X* (2001–2002) offers a team of enhanced beings bordering more on the superhero narrative area of *Batman* and *Superman*, and contrasts the potential benefits against the dangers of a genetically advanced group of humans let loose on an unwitting society, whilst *The Sentinel*'s James Ellison uses his jungle-honed hyper-senses for the purposes of detection. *Jeremiah* operates a slightly different tactic, showing a post-apocalyptic nightmare world of our own making, where a virus has wiped out the adult population, leaving mostly only the pre-pubescent alive. Set ten years after the devastating virus, *Jeremiah*'s eponymous protagonist sets off on a quest for a mysterious place, somewhere that his father called 'Valhalla'.

Often sf television's battles against internal or external enemies are fought by civilians, but they are also sometimes rooted in government-sanctioned, occasionally secret, military action. *Stargate SG-1* epitomises this secrecy, a problematic fact articulated in several episodes, such as the two-part 'Redemption'/'2001'. *The X-Files'* operatives Dana Scully and Fox Mulder (and later Doggett and Reyes) are FBI agents; *The War of the Worlds'* Dr Blackwood has his own military advisor, Colonel Ironhorse. Series like *Stargate SG-1* offer a team of trustworthy individuals who are more than happy to go against the grain and fight 'City Hall' – their project may be secret but they demonstrate repeatedly that they are working to protect the public. The government and other arms of the military we encounter are clearly doing no such thing. 'Politics' and 'Shades of Grey' are plain examples of this, as the political establishment in the form of Senator Kinsey, does everything it can either to destroy the Stargate project or to ignore the advice of its team. Of course, the irony of the secret stargate on earth is thrown into relief when they meet up with aliens who haven't shared the secret of their stargate with other races on their planet ('Homecoming').

The respective submarine commanders of the environmentally focused *Seaquest DSV* (subsequently renamed *Seaquest* for its second season, and *Seaquest 2032* for its final run) work almost in isolation, constantly saving the day whilst their military and political masters invent intriguing new ways of destroying the planet, starting wars, making obscene amounts of financial profit and enslaving the world's population in the process. Even within a military-based series like *Stargate SG-1*, both the military and political establishment en masse are generally cast in a negative light, whilst maverick ensembles and individuals like SG-1 and the Seaquest's Captain Oliver Hudson are held up as protectors and saviours.

THE LEGACY OF VIETNAM

Historically, there is good reason for this attitude in both film and television. Just as the frontier experience was a key moment and fundamental basis for the forging of a national identity, so the Vietnam War offered a second and vital moment in American history and mytho-history and explains to a great degree the level of ambivalence towards the military (and the politicians) in post-Vietnam narratives. Since the 1960s and the withdrawal of American troops from Vietnam, there has been considerable unease in the screen portrayal of its military officers.

From John Wayne's Colonel Kirby in *The Green Berets* (1968) through Kilgore and Kurtz in *Apocalypse Now* (1979) to Tom Cruise's gung-ho self-oriented Lt. Mitchell in *Top Gun* (1986), the soldier's integrity and honour, so constant and unquestioned in earlier

Hollywood films and television, has been ravaged by the horrors lurking in the collective psyche of post-Vietnam America. A state of impasse exists for these screen soldiers and rather than creating an arena for the re-examination and evolution of 'American' values, in a drive for self-protection, representations of the Vietnam War have created a 'large-scale renegotiation and regeneration of the interests, values, and projects of the patriarchy', leading to a revitalisation of the traditional frontier values of bourgeois individualism.[3] The problem percolates through all genres, confused as they have been since the collapse of the studio system and the fragmentation of a presumedly homogenous society in the 1960s.

America's very insistence upon its isolationism in combination with its occasionally intensive military and political involvement overseas is problematic and paradoxical. Hollywood's initial posture towards the Vietnam War is exemplified in the title of Julian Smith's book *Looking Away...* (1975). Only after the war ended did American cinema really attempt to deal directly with any issues connected to the war itself. Some films focused upon alienated, injured or violent returned veterans – *First Blood* (1982), *Coming Home* (1978), *Taxi Driver* (1976) – others suggest that they were confused and wounded victims – *Birdy* (1984), *Born on the Fourth of July* (1989) – and a handful tried to come to terms with the rationale for the war – in particular *Platoon* (1986) and *Full Metal Jacket* (1987).[4] Other films, especially *Rambo: First Blood Part Two* (1985) and *Rambo III* (1988) use the vet motif to justify 'the kind of violent and racist disposition that initiated the war in the first place'.[5] These kinds of films became a means of affirming the militaristic, patriarchal and entrepreneurial base of the 1980s, creating, as it were, a new, post-Vietnam era.

Ryan and Kellner suggest that after the period of self-doubt and isolationism following Vietnam, the conservative means of countering this national trauma emerged through:

> a triumph of the will, a purgation of doubt through action, and an interventionist military stance that brooked no restraint ... Both *The Deer Hunter* and *Apocalypse Now* contribute to that revival by incorporating Vietnam not as a defeat from which lessons can be learned, but as a springboard for male military heroism.[6]

So the fallout from the Vietnam War created a resurgence of militarism in the USA, and war films of the late 1970s and early 1980s are part of what is essentially a conservative backlash. They amplify this by rewriting history: if Vietnam is a source of national shame and the location of America's first military defeat, in film history it becomes a location for pride in individual victory. Hollywood representations of soldiers post-Vietnam suggests that the USA has been re-fighting Vietnam on a personal level, creating a potential hero in everyone, but simultaneously failing to address the real issues arising out of the war. *Saving Private Ryan* (1998), *We Were Soldiers* (2002), *Courage Under Fire* (1996), *Behind Enemy Lines* (2001), *Black Hawk Down* (2001) – regardless of their narrative's diegetic era (WWII, Vietnam, the first Gulf War, Bosnia, or Somalia), each story is about individual or small group victories, about individual honour and integrity.

Along with most producers of American popular dramatic arts,[7] Hollywood seemed far happier recreating wistful images of the USA's early settlement and colonisation, glorifying man against the wilderness, re-articulating its Manifest Destiny, explaining how its morality allowed it to win the Second World War for the rest of the world's own good, than it was in examining one of its founding ideologies: the concept of self-determination and free will, something as applicable to Vietnam as to the USA. As has already been established, central to the politics of American westward expansion lies the attitude towards the country itself – its civilised and its wilderness landscape. The manner in which historical and/or mythical events are transcribed, translated and retold within the arts offers frequent insights into what director Stanley Kubrick calls the 'shadow side of the nation's psyche'.[8] From the evocation of America's illusory and entirely masculine frontier spirit erupted John F. Kennedy's 1960s New Frontier, precipitating the world to the brink of a nuclear holocaust. Similarly, the reactionary 1980s propaganda of Ronald Reagan – significantly, an ex-cowboy actor – offered a final frontier in the shape of the Strategic Defence Initiative against the Soviet Union – 'Star Wars' versus the 'Evil Empire'. Repeatedly, the mythical historical scenario relied upon by Americans from William Bradford to Oliver Stone revolves around the dialectic of the frontier: a juxtaposition of an evil darkness in a wilderness inhabited by the 'Other', and the perceived shining light of American civilisation.

America's myth-making faculty – most notably the fantasy apparatus of Hollywood – has employed and embellished this individualistic, anachronistic and genocidal frontier dialectic as a paradigm for its portrayal of both domestic and foreign affairs. Metaphorically, the Vietnam War was simply yet another rite of passage through ungodly wilderness.

THE GREEN BERETS

Writing of representations of the war, J. Hoberman feels that Vietnam offered many Americans what initially appeared to be the 'fulfilment of something', observing how astonishing it was that GIs so frequently:

> referred approvingly to John Wayne, not as a movie star but as a model and standard. Nineteen year old Americans, brought up on World War II movies and westerns, walking through the jungle, armed to the teeth, searching for an invisible enemy who knew the wilderness better than they did, could hardly miss these connections. One after another said, at some point, something like 'Hey, this is just like a movie'. You probably remember the famous scene in *Dispatches* when a wounded marine turns to Herr and says 'I hate this movie!'[9]

If the link was obvious to the nineteen-year-olds serving in Vietnam, it was equally blatant to the ever-hungry film industry. Appropriately enough, it was *The Green Berets,* a retro exercise in polemical cinema-history co-directed by John Wayne alongside Ray Kellogg, which emerged from Hollywood as the first Vietnam War film. Wayne's screen persona and his publicly proclaimed ideology combine a military model with the most cherished ideals of patriarchal capitalism and the American frontier ethos. Although Wayne was named by the Green Berets as the model American, his selection of the Berets as his film's focal point is ironic, and historically inappropriate – by the time of the film's release (after the Tet offensive of January 1968), few Green Berets were still operating in Vietnam. However, at a stroke, his focus connects the mythological world of Ford's cavalry trilogy, *Fort Apache, She Wore a Yellow Ribbon* and *Rio Grande* (1948, 1949, 1950), with Wayne's public devotion to the late President Kennedy's concept of a new 'Camelot'. The film's obsession with hi-tech gadgetry carries echoes of James Bond and espionage, and of the missile age, benchmarks for Kennedy's New Frontier ethos. Perhaps, to those involved with *The Green Berets* in 1968, the only way to make a Vietnam War film that could win the hearts of any wavering American was to have it starring the all-American hero, Wayne. Likewise, the collective jokey camaraderie of the stalwart Berets echoes the collective in Howard Hawks' films, many of which were notably Westerns, several starring Wayne – *Red River* (1948), *Rio Bravo* (1959), *El Dorado* (1967). The soldiers exude honour and decency, and all those values which mainstream American cinema delights in representing as unique to itself, whilst they continue fighting an unappreciated and seldom comprehended battle again the evil empire of Communism.[10]

Wayne's character, Colonel Kirby, has no doubt that this war is for professionals. Far worse, he tells us that the type of war waged by the Communists is a perversion of the vital and natural frontier rite of passage for American manhood. Kirby also makes clear that there is no frontier in Vietnam, and this actually seems to be the specific problem that he has with the place. The battle is one of insurgency and counter-insurgency, there are no demarcation lines; even 'Dodge City', the hill that they defend, so frighteningly similar to the heroic failure of the Alamo in concept, fails to delineate a safe area. The only safety is the bastion of God-fearing frontier morality, the camaraderie of the Green Beret unit itself, a symbolic tower of American strength in the midst of unholy chaos.[11] Amidst gut-wrenching emotional blackmail, war-hungry patriarch Kirby stands impervious. Kirby's final words to the Vietnamese orphan Hamchunk confirm the importance of the undisturbed rite of passage: 'You're what this war's all about.' The Green Berets fight so that Hamchunk can grow up in a world deemed safe by mythical, anachronistic and faked frontier values. It isn't man against man in Vietnam, it is white American manhood against anything else: 'us' versus 'other', a re-enactment of victorious mythical campaigns against the wilderness and the Native American. As Frances Fitzgerald observes:

> in Vietnam, American officers liked to call the areas outside GVN control 'Indian country'. It was a joke of course ... but it put the Vietnam war into a more definite historical and mythological perspective: the Americans were once again

embarked upon an heroic and (for themselves) almost painless conquest of an inferior race.[12]

Except, of course, it was becoming far from painless, and every effort was made by Wayne to get his desperate propaganda message across. In *A Year in the Dark* (1969), the *New York Times* critic Renata Adler takes up the point made by Fitzgerald, describing Wayne's polemic as:

> a film so unspeakable, so stupid, so rotten and false that it passes through being funny, through being camp, through everything and becomes an invitation to grieve not so much for our soldiers or Vietnam (the film could not be more false or do greater disservice to them) but for what has happened to the fantasy making apparatus of this country.[13]

Adler touches upon a crucial issue in her vitriolic dismissal of *The Green Berets*. It broke no new ground in either metaphor or verisimilitude and makes no pretence of being anything other than a temporally and spatially displaced Western, a genre itself torn asunder by the 1960s re-evaluation of civil rights. Whether audiences went to see it because it starred Wayne or because they were in collective communion with the broader sentiments is a moot point.

Around the time of *The Green Berets*' release, the fortunes of war took a bad turn for the American forces in Vietnam; shortly afterwards, it was perceived by others than those in the peace movement as an unwinnable operation. With Nixon's withdrawal of troops underway, Hollywood seemed to want the war out of the way, 'thus operating within the regime of wish fulfilment'.[14] Production of the war film ceased abruptly between 1970 and 1975 – images of a near-defeated American army in retreat from a lost cause would fill few cinema seats. Small surprise that if few film directors were unwilling to touch the issue, even fewer distributors were willing to associate themselves with such films. For a long time, American cinema and television merely dipped its toe in the quagmire or edged nervously away, retreating into nostalgia with films like *American Graffiti* (1973) and television shows like *Happy Days* (1974–1983), which were set in an idyllic version of the 1950s and essentially used the war as a structuring absence.

FILM AND TELEVISION

Between 1979 and 1985, there was a concerted effort made by Hollywood to at least consider the issues: *Apocalypse Now* and *The Deer Hunter* were just two of a sudden rash of films. In *Apocalypse Now*, an adaptation of Conrad's seminal novella of colonialism *Heart of Darkness* (1902), Captain Willard sets off into the furthest reaches of Vietnam/Cambodia in search of a renegade, Colonel Kurtz. Heir to the protagonist of the Western and film noir, and his voiceover commentary constantly reminding us of his own confused state of mind and his gradual loss of direction, Willard begins an investigation that leads him to reject the only basis upon which he may function in US society. He is defeated by the impossible ideology of his nation, an ideology which Kurtz pursues to an extreme and finds lacking. Alongside Willard's rejection comes the harsh realisation that with the myth destroyed inside its holiest temple (the Green Beret Corps), no one remains either willing or able to avert anarchy and chaos: Armageddon ensues.[15]

But if *Apocalypse Now*'s journey beyond Vietnam and into Cambodia showed the flaws of the American Dream, it failed to exorcise Kurtz's heart of darkness; there is no future for the unfortunate Willard, who inherits Kurtz's dismal hollow-man role. The Western hero and his city equivalent, the noir protagonist, are stranded in a new and alien mindscape; their ideologies are shown to be bankrupt, their values destroyed. They have stared long and hard at the American mythical landscape and found no redemption. Kurtz has tried to recreate American civilisation in the wilderness of Southeast Asia and, having failed, turns instead to embrace the wilderness. The vision of his action provides Willard with no alternative to the impossible contradictions, only knowledge of the degeneration and fall into savagery resulting from blind adherence to either extreme. Therefore, Coppola's film offers no hope, no way forward.

The Deer Hunter is more to do with ethnicity than the war in Vietnam.[16] Set initially in a Pennsylvanian steel-town, it sends its three protagonists headlong into the Vietnam conflict, where they are captured by the Viet Cong, tortured and forced to play Russian roulette, before finally escaping and making it to friendly territory. The film's sole unscathed survivor is Michael, a misplaced frontiersman archetype who believes in the one-shot mythology; he is a paranoid man, who merely adapts to new environments better than his colleagues. Stevie is left crippled, bitter and lonely, while poor Nicky, Mike's protégé, and the youngest, most subversive and fascinating character in the film, dies, gambling away his future in his addiction to the game of Russian roulette. Both the challenge and hope he offers are repudiated until too late by the physical and vocal discourse of Michael's frontiersman. Michael's words to one of his hunting companions in an early scene provide a clear example of the problem. Gripping his rifle and shaking it, he insists, 'This is this, Stanley – this ain't something else' – but 'this' is enigmatic to the point of meaninglessness within the context of Vietnam.

Much of the paranoia located within these two films descends directly from 1950s film noir, which pitted its protagonist against a corrupt and corrosive system, but left him to discover only personal extrication from that world. As Larry Gross observes, film noir 'postulates the existence of a "bad" society, but the stress is laid on the efforts of the hero to extricate himself from that society, rather than the social structure itself. Society and the individual are at odds without even coming into view of one another.'[17] More to the point, the actions described are for self-preservation; they do not take into account the experiences and fortunes of those around – they are individualist and ego-driven. Basically, they concentrate upon winning the individual battle at the expense of the collective war. This is a major difference between Occidental and Oriental philosophies, the latter of which essentially requires a concentration upon the welfare of humanity above the welfare of the individual self, and, via Vietnam, illuminates the USA's confusion of community values with communist doctrine.

Other Hollywood films of the past thirty years have touched upon the subject of Vietnam, but few address either its greater impact upon society or the changing attitude of society towards it. They offer J. Hoberman's 'remaking' of the war except, in the remake, individual American soldiers can win against the odds – thus Oliver Stone's *Born on the Fourth of July* provides the disabled vet Ron Kovacs with the happier ending reality denied him. And so we return to the Western rite of passage, with nineteen-year-old soldiers reliving the Martin Pawley 'questing' role in John Ford's *The Searchers* (1956). Except it doesn't work – Mike's quest for Nicky in *The Deer Hunter* is the filmic proof of this, and cinema's repeated attempts to depict the war within the Western paradigm is proof of America's difficulty in coming to terms with the lessons of history.

But what of television? As we have established, the domestic medium is arguably the least daring of any country's media, and American television was reticent in entering the debate: few series about Vietnam have either graced or debased the small screen. Those that did distanced themselves from the issues and morality of the war either spatially or temporally or both: *M*A*S*H* (1972–1983) and *China Beach* (1988–1991) were basically about the ancillary workers, doctors and nurses who remain beyond the theatre of war, and thus their agenda is vastly different; like the film which spawned it, *M*A*S*H* further removed itself by being set nominally in Korea. Likewise, *Tour of Duty* (1987–1990) avoids any larger, metaphysical questions by concentrating purely upon the soldier's physical experience (much like the 1987 film *Hamburger Hill*, itself an effort to deal simply with the experience of the average soldier, or 'grunt'). The larger issues are not really addressed, although group loyalty and camaraderie are demonstrated, and the limited specificity of the subject matter denies extension of the arguments. These programmes also follow Vietnam War films in many ways, celebrating small personal victories, ignoring the greater problems. And yet serial television allows repeated visits to issues, and thus has the potential to deal with the traumas and complexity of an experience like Vietnam in far more depth than a film ever could. Representations of the war singularly fail to address the more pertinent points arising from it, and demonstrate only how America's myth-making faculty has refused to respond to its challenge.

SPACE: ABOVE AND BEYOND

American mythology was fundamentally trapped by the problem of Vietnam: it could neither comprehend it nor be educated by it.[18] Manifestations of the future would seem to be a perfect place to analyse and explore the subject, but the subject remains mostly closed. Small, personal victories are safe representations, national tragedy and self-examination has little place in any genre in any medium. Only one television series has offered a decidedly military-focused vision of the future, one that is very carefully linked with our own time and our own history and yet takes advantage of the cognitive challenges offered by science fiction – *Space: Above and Beyond* (henceforth '*Space*'). Created by Glen Morgan and James Wong, who served as both writers and as executive producers, *Space* is a complex programme with an equally complex historical narrative, which is gradually revealed as the season progresses. The story arc is clearly a long-term project and, although there are episodic elements, the gradual tales of possible government and big business deception were incorporated from the beginning. Although the primary focus of the series shifted from the original group of three young marine officers to a seven-strong ensemble, this did not affect the fundamental direction of the narrative. Its scenario is perhaps best described by the introductory voiceover accompanying the titles for the later episodes:

> We thought we were alone, we believed the universe was ours – until one night in 2063, on an Earth colony sixteen light years away, they struck, and now we are at war. My name is Lieutenant-Colonel T.C. McQueen. I am an In-Vitro, a race of artificially gestated humans. I command a Marine Corps squadron, the 58th: they call us 'The Wildcards'. We fight when we are called, in space, on land and at sea. To lose this war means more than defeat, to surrender is to never go home. All of us must rise to the call – above and beyond.

Essentially, the narrative covers the experiences of young Marine Corps cadets in 2063 as they endure training, become members of the 58th Squadron, the Wildcards, and head to war with mysterious aliens known only as 'The Chigs'. Two significant historical events have shaped the world they know, the A.I. Wars and the development of a race of In-Vitro humans, created to help naturally born humans after the world population is decimated by plague and warfare. The A.I.s, or 'Silicates', were originally created as robot soldiers and servants for humans, and are identified by their uncanny eyes – white, with cross-hairs for pupils. When an unhappy computer programmer infected them with a virus, instructing them to 'Take a chance', they responded by becoming addicted to risk and rebelled against their human masters in the A.I. Wars, eventually taking off to find freedom and a new life in space. The second race humanity has 'created' to help get back on its feet are the In-Vitros, disparagingly known as 'Tanks', because they are grown in artificial gestation chambers and held there until they are fully developed eighteen-year-olds. Identified only by a navel at the back of their necks, they are initially used as slaves and then as indentured (bonded) labourers. Their emotions are poorly developed, and they are people who essentially open their eyes as adults: they have no family, no culture, and no history.

COLONIALISM

Space opens with the alien attack on two new Earth colonies – Vesta and Tellus. It is worth noting here that the explicit idea of a new human colony is itself an unusual scenario in American sf television; whereas journeys to other worlds with a view to human habitation occur occasionally in episodic series like *The Outer Limits*, they are otherwise rare. *The Next Generation* touches upon it, occasionally mentioning Federation colonies – emphasising that they are not just *human* colonies – and otherwise dealing with it mostly through ideas of terraforming dead and unoccupied worlds, with the suggestion therefore that no sentient life is being disturbed, or that to do so would be morally unacceptable, as 'Home Soil' demonstrates. Only two series really take it further as a part of their diegesis rather than as an 'a priori' fact. *Earth 2* (1994–1995) is set in the twenty-second century; after humanity's destruction of the earth's eco-structure, humans are forced to live in massive space stations. Devon Adair and her fellow Eden Project pioneers are trying to establish human life on a distant planet; arriving in orbit of the new planet amid political intrigue and the unmistakable stench of corruption, the main ship is blown up, and they are forced to land on their new home with only vestiges of the equipment and supplies intended for their expedition. They also discover that the new earth has its own life form, the Terrians, whose existence is interlinked with that of the planet; any changes to the eco-structure, even the very presence of the humans, have immense ramifications.

Also illuminating ideas of colonisation is the brief light that was *Firefly*. In a galaxy devoid of aliens, humanity has stretched out across the stars, terraforming and colonising dozens of worlds. The series establishes a sharp divide between the rich and the poor: the wealthy upper class rule with a rod of iron and the poor struggle to survive in hostile environments short of water, food and medical supplies. The title sequence takes us to the stars via the Firefly-class vessel 'Serenity', but it also depicts wagons, gun-toting cowboys and whorehouses, and closes on a freeze-framed image of magnificent stampeding mustangs. *Firefly* makes no effort to be metaphorical: this is the frontier, America's Wild West made manifest.

In *Space*, the significance of the human colonies on Vesta and Tellus changes as the series progresses, our perception of it shifting from an apparently ghastly attack on innocent pioneers to questioning whether humans were in fact committing a wanton act of imperialism by colonising planets that were already the home of another highly developed species. Initially, however, the alien attack seems utterly ruthless and totally unjustified. Removed from the Tellus mission at the last moment so that an In-Vitro can take his place, Nathan West watches in horror as news of the settlement's destruction comes in: his girlfriend, Kylen, was one of the colonists. The Earth forces strike back at the alien vessels, sending up the 127th squadron, the legendary Angry Angels, but they are all but destroyed and the Earth forces start losing badly. Enlisting in the Marine Corps, West meets up with Shane Vansen, the In-Vitro Cooper Hawkes, who has been sentenced to service, Paul Wang and Vanessa Damphousse, who ultimately become the Wildcards, along with their new commanding officer, an In-Vitro and one of the few surviving 'Angry Angels': Lt.-Col. Tyrus Cassius McQueen. It is McQueen whose very existence epitomises most strongly the daring and ideological debate intrinsic to the series. Much like the character of Commodore Ross (played by Tucker Smallwood), McQueen was not initially conceived of as a focal figure, and the precise nature of his development ultimately seems to have evolved largely from how Morgan and Wong's sketchy ideas combined with the philosophical sensibilities of James Morrison, the actor who portrayed him throughout season. Morrison explains that whereas the other characters were clearly delineated from the start, McQueen was less well defined. However, he also recognised the potential for both the character and the series and suggests that, although the producers 'weren't clear what they really wanted when they started with the entire concept of the show', they were open to collaboration.[19] The series moved away from its early lost-love basis and soon became a dark, sophisticated war drama, owing as much to novels such as *The Red Badge of Courage* (1895), *The Naked and the Dead* (1948) and *Guadalcanal Diary* (1942)[20] as it does to the tale of alien attacks and, ultimately, the origins of humanity.

GENRE: SCIENCE FICTION OR WAR?

Space demonstrates very clearly the difficulty of generic labelling, reminding us of how very useful we may find Steve Neale's arguments for an ideological rather than thematic basis. In shifting genre we notice the ideology behind it in a different light, maybe even allowing us to confront its ambiguities – which suggests that genre's thematics are indeed more complexly intertwined than we tend to assume. *Space* is a futuristic drama, its impressive cgi imagery includes space flight and spacecraft but, just as *The Next Generation*'s language illuminates its central technological preoccupations, so *Space*'s fundamental verbal discourse articulates its military basis. Although wormholes are mentioned, for example, they are mentioned purely in passing as a means of transportation. The pilots live aboard the carrier 'Saratoga', they fly Hammerhead fighters, they eat in the mess, the marine war cry of 'semper fi' echoes around as they enter battle, and more time is spent discussing missions and enemy advances than in admiring the spectacular galactic backdrops. The heart of the show is 'about the nature of war ... what it was like to be at war' and, set against a background of political turmoil and deception, the links to previous wars and the politics of post-Vietnam America are stunning.[21] This is clearly articulated in the season's cliffhanger finale, '... Tell Our Moms We Done Our Best', where three of the five pilots are missing in action and McQueen is gravely injured. As Morrison says:

> the way we ended it, the possibilities for the next season were really exciting, because he would have been a disabled Vet, and of a war that nobody really wanted ... so that the parallels that we could have drawn [to Vietnam] could have been wonderful, especially in the recovery.

REPRESENTATION AND CHARACTER

But there are other precious observations and dialectics in the series that rise above the promise offered even by direct parallels with Vietnam. McQueen is discriminated against because of his genetically engineered ancestry, a point raised especially clearly in 'Ray Butts'. Here, the eponymous natural-born Lieutenant-Colonel responds to McQueen during interrogation with a sneer: 'We may wear the same ribbons from our nipples when we put on the dress blues, but don't you think for one second that we are equal, *Tank.*' McQueen comments on his lack of equality on several occasions, perhaps most eloquently in 'Mutiny'. Hawkes, the only other In-Vitro on the Saratoga, objects to the Colonel's glacial façade, saying, 'Even pain's part of being human.' McQueen's response is curt: 'Who said you're human?' But in many ways McQueen represents the egalitarian future of America, of humanity – he is a being of the twenty-first century, a mixture of the gene pool, not born of some 'pure' aristocratic concept of bloodline. He is not some space-age Western hero, a Luke Skywalker fantasy, the lost son of an elite Jedi knight born with a romantic destiny to fulfil. McQueen will have none of that: 'I don't give a damn for destiny', he says.[22] His origins are those of broad humanity, and thus he offers both a distillation and repudiation of all those horrors of miscegenation which have haunted America, particularly the South, since its founding.[23]

Although he is developed and given a higher profile later in the series, McQueen's character does not change awkwardly or markedly: his fundamental traits are merely gradually illuminated and accentuated. Morrison says, 'You can't describe McQueen with words, he's a man of action, and a true enigma can't be [defined],' but points out that you can 'define him by the things that he puts around himself, the comforts that he finds in his world'. So the Colonel is described primarily through his actions, by what he does every day,[24] and secondly, in context, through the aesthetic and philosophical influences in his quarters, shown to us in 'The Angriest Angel'. As the camera roves around the room, we see his many books, ranging from US and world military history to Greek Classics and Oriental Philosophy. Ueshiba's *Art of Peace* counterpoints Sun Tzu's *Art of War*, and while McQueen reads Homer's *Iliad*, he also consults the *Tao Teh Ching*.[25] There are pictures of W.C. Fields and George Washington; Shoichi's poem 'The Circle' hangs from the wall; calligraphy brushes sit atop his desk next to an ink-stone and pressed ink; and he nurtures a Bonsai. This is a man of tradition, aesthetics and patient discipline.[26]

McQueen adheres to the Way of the warrior, bushido (the Japanese warrior's code), which generally demands 'a resolute acceptance of death'.[27] Science fiction television generally allocates this trait to 'noble' alien warriors, such as Worf in *The Next Generation* and *Deep Space Nine* and Master Bra'tac in *Stargate SG-1* – so again McQueen's 'difference' is highlighted. The most well-known work defining bushido is probably Miyamoto Musashi's *Book of Five Rings* (1045), which offers not only a guide to Kendo swordsmanship, but also a combination of philosophical beliefs stemming from Zen, Shinto and Confucianism. It is this that Morrison draws on in his explanation of McQueen's philosophy:

> In a warrior, which is what McQueen is, if you go into battle and think about anything but the greater good, if you think about your own well being, you'll die. If you think about everything *but* yourself, if you go in as a dead man, if you think, well, nothing can happen to me, I'm dead already, then you can win. You can actually win the battle for the greater good.[28]

And this point demonstrates that we have new, yet very old, sensibilities emerging from McQueen. He can be defined by actions epitomising the Way: the code to which he adheres simply to deal with life. This soldier-poet radiates dignity and honour, and his strength comes from his internal ability to validate his selfless actions by his code, not from a desire to seek external sycophancy. This is no Kurtz, Kirby or Kilgore, no shallow 'Top Gun' pilot or Marine corps cipher. McQueen transcends such definitions. He was created to be a slave and a soldier, and as Morrison observes:

> his reaction was a peaceful one; get the job done well, without regard for self, so it will end well for the greater good. He is not a gung-ho reactionary or jingoist patriot. He is a munificent humanitarian forced to kill for a society that

harmed and enslaved him. And he made the best of it. What greater conflict could there be in a warrior?[29]

McQueen's disenfranchisement and enforced eclecticism allow him to draw on the finest human philosophies and create out of them an enduring set of inter-cultural principles that transcend the gulfs created by political ideologies. McQueen's In-Vitro character also explores in detail a problem that haunts all our lives: the issue of self-determination. A quick trip through some of the episodes shows us his calibre. McQueen's tireless devotion to the 58th squadron – but not at the expense of others – is demonstrated repeatedly. In 'River of Stars', the Wildcards are missing, presumed lost, but he keeps up the search until every possibility is exhausted, and in doing so locates them – demonstrating that he is always there for them. However, this has a price, one he pays with resolute acceptance. As their commander he can seldom afford to allow them any expression of gratitude, nor can he express any towards them, other than in the most formal manner. Taken away for loyalty questioning in 'Eyes', simply because he is an In-Vitro, he dismisses Vansen's outraged refusal to go on the mission without him with a brisk 'I expect you all to do your duty.' Only to his senior officer, Commodore Ross, can he ever allow himself to admit to any emotional involvement, as he does prior to the near-suicidal mission of 'Hostile Visit': 'Most In-Vitros have a hard time with love. We don't get many opportunities to feel it, or give it. But I know that I love those kids.'

When Lt.-Col. Butts temporarily wrangles command of the Wildcards away from McQueen, in 'Ray Butts', in an attempt to atone for a tragic error, the 58th are distrustful of their abrasive new commander's motives and ask McQueen if he would follow Butts into a fire-fight. He confirms immediately, 'He's an officer of the Corps, trained to care about his Marines, and yes, if so ordered, I would follow him.' Yet he adds more gently: 'But I'd watch my six, and I'd watch each other's sixes real close' – a quiet and permissible expression of his concern. If the Wildcards dislike Butts, out of hearing of his juniors, McQueen has even less time for him, denouncing his maverick behaviour:

> I want you gone. I don't know how or why you're here, or what you think you're doing – abusing subordinates, disrupting morale and unity. Whatever you're doing I take one look at

you and know that it's *only* about you, and anyone pulled in is going to die, while you just drive on.

Butts responds by showing McQueen orders which virtually give him carte blanche. Recognising a battle he cannot win, McQueen acquiesces, whilst maintaining his stand against individual glory by issuing a dire warning to Butts as he departs with the 58th:

> Butts. I know they're not my children, they're Marines, life-takers and heart breakers, and I know we're at war, and pooplo dio, but if any of *my* pooplo dio booauoo of *you*, all your recon skills and black ops training won't be worth a damn. I'll find you.

McQueen demonstrates here that he has no time for loud heroics, for individuals out for glory: 'We're in the middle of a war. If we stop following orders there will be no order', he says. However, he doesn't adhere blindly to his instructions, but contextualises them with a humanitarian consideration of the necessary principles upon which order is founded. In 'The Furthest Man from Home', West goes AWOL to search for his lost lover, Kylen. McQueen, still a new commander and thus an unknown quantity to the 58th, condemns West's actions, yet simultaneously intimates that someone should look for him, thus demonstrating not only the spirit of the Marine Corps, which looks after its own, but also his principles, his code, which transcend orders and the chain of command, saying:

> He's beyond insubordination, he's out there operating with no regard for good order or proper conduct. He thinks he's putting only himself in danger, but by bailing out of the mission he puts all of your lives on the line. He threatens every grunt that hits the beach and relies on our recon. This war wasn't made for Nathan West – *every* life in this war is tied together.

Vansen tries to argue that it was a selfless act, but West was thinking of himself, of Kylen – he finds other survivors only by happy accident. In the later episode 'Mutiny', he acknowledges this, and his selfish heroics and the similarly selfish, yet initially incredibly sympathetic, desires of the In-Vitro crew to save their cargo family of unborn are juxtaposed with McQueen's universe of cold equations, his pained but immediate and logical decision to switch off power to the unit containing the In-Vitro cargo (thus condemning them to death) in order to save hundreds more human lives.

LEARNING FROM MILITARY HISTORY

In 'Sugardirt', the invasion of the alien planets is underway and along with many other of the Earth forces, the Wildcards are trapped on the planet Demios. An unexpected opportunity emerges to engage the enemy at the planet Ixion, potentially cutting the war by two years; the decision is made for the fleet to move on. McQueen draws on his historical knowledge, paralleling the situation with the Second World War battle for Guadalcanal, and advises that the push should indeed be made, regardless of the circumstances of his men and women on Demios, the lives of the 25,000 soldiers being a lesser cost, though no lesser loss, than the lives of one million. He absolves Commodore Ross of guilt in accepting their senior officers' decision, saying that the 'right thing to do is rarely the easiest'. But the two men also make their pain clear, Ross saying how hard it is for him to leave, and McQueen admitting he too wants to join them. Ross denies him permission to join the 58th on-planet and quietly, soberly, McQueen continues his duties. The traditional US screen soldier would have rushed off on some desperate mission to save his squad, or save face, as did West and Butts, regardless of the danger it created for others and the lack of order created in its wake. McQueen does not succumb to such egotistical compulsions: his heroism is honesty and a sacrifice of his own desires, it is greater than he, greater than his people, more genuine and selflessly principled.

In 'Hostile Visit', the Saratoga encounters a drifting enemy bomber and, rather than have it destroyed, McQueen suggests using it as a latter-day Trojan Horse. The night before their departure, a gloomy Commodore Ross muses on the potential suicide mission while McQueen begs to be allowed along, despite his grounded status. Ross asks him why, after 'all we did to your people, why would you give your life?' McQueen replies, 'I would consider it my gift to you, Sir, to have you wonder why I did.' It is an exceptional moment, and the common discrimination perpetrated by whites against blacks is reversed in the juxtaposition of the disenfranchised and white McQueen alongside the enfranchised and black Ross, illuminating racial discrimination in an uncommon and striking manner. In his actions, McQueen demonstrates not just his qualities of leadership and his devotion to the men and women who serve with him, but also, given his background, his extraordinary capacity for munificent behaviour towards greater humanity. 'Choice or Chance' is the conclusion to the story: the bomber is shot down, with the Wildcards escaping in a life-pod. Four of the squad are captured, but McQueen and Hawkes are conscious after the crash, evade the enemy and set about finding and releasing their companions. Now it is the naïve Hawkes's turn to question McQueen's rationale and, speaking to his fellow In-Vitro, McQueen opens up slightly, explaining that 'I did it, I'd do it, for every In-Vitro who's ever been called a "Tank" or a "Nipple Neck", I'd do it so that no-one, human or In-Vitro will ever be able to say that all In-Vitros are lazy, or cowards, or don't stand for anything.'

DEFINING MOMENTS

Morrison believes McQueen to be a strong metaphysical source in the series, saying:

> he's the only poet there. The others reach a level of poetics but they're not aware of it happening to them and I think when McQueen does it, he knows it's happening, so what do we call that – aside from an acute awareness of life, a sense of irony?

McQueen's opening monologue to his single intentionally expositional episode, 'The Angriest Angel', epitomises this awareness, asking questions fundamental to humanity – 'Who am I?' and 'What's the point?' – before continuing to comment on his impending battle with the alien 'Red Baron':

> My name is Colonel Tyrus Cassius McQueen, but I know nothing of who I am. The answer, I feel, is near. The defining, perhaps final, moment is close. Everyone, *everyone* in this life knows when the moment is before them. To turn away is simple, to ignore it assures survival, but it is an insult to

life because there can be no redemption, no second chance. Beyond death there's nothing, just darkness and cold. The instant his existence was confirmed, every action, every breath of my life became horrifyingly clear. He's out there tonight, sending our women, our men to that cold, dark place, and nothing, *nothing* will stop him until I face the moment.

Later in the same episode, his child soldiers push him beyond the edge. They have become overly familiar with him, temporarily forgetting his keen sense of duty and his responsibilities to them as their commander. One of the key characters here is Flight-Lieutenant Winslow, who appears in a few prior episodes. Here she serves essentially as a narrative device and is perhaps representative of the audience, since she is arguably the most well-adjusted member of the Wildcards. Winslow flirts with McQueen in the bar, contributing along with Wang to his uncharacteristic emotional outburst. Rounding on Wang, who summons the Colonel over to be 'another guy on my team' in a table game of 'foosball', McQueen loses his exceptional control, blasting him and his other juniors with an acutely self-aware description, one which defines not only him, of course, but his audience, both in- and ex-diegesis:

> *Guy?* What do you think, we're back on the block, smoking and joking? Hear this loud and clear Marine: I am not your guy. I'm not your Joe, I'm not your damn drinking buddy, and I sure as hell am not a mark in a singles bar. You hear this CFB. I am not here to make friends. When this war ends and – you go back to raising money for charity – and you're eating dogs at Wrigley – and you go back to Mayberry, I'm still going to be out here waiting for the next one. That's why I'm here. That's what I'm good for.

The tragedy that emerges here is that having found his calling as a warrior, having found what he is 'good for', McQueen is then denied his purpose, grounded through injuries received in the decimation of the Angry Angels. Now convinced that he must face the newest and most deadly enemy fighter, one which has already destroyed the 19th, 31st and 42nd squadrons, McQueen indulges in desperate masochism to get himself un-grounded, certain that this new enemy brings with it the defining moment of his existence. It is now that we see his quarters for the first time, immediately after the bar scene, and hear him read in voiceover Achilles' reproach to Hector – clearly foreshadowing the narrative to come:

> Looking darkly upon Hector, swift-footed Achilles answered 'I cannot forgive you; as there are no trustworthy oaths between men and lions there can be no love between you and me. One or the other must fall before then to glut with blood, Ares, the god who fights under the shield's guard. Remember every valour of yours for now the need comes hardest upon you to be a spearman and a bold warrior. There shall be no escape for you, you will pay in a lump for all of those sorrows of my companions you killed in your spear's fury.[30]

During this episode, an Elroy-L silicate model is captured. McQueen interrogates it, seeking the location of the alien Red Baron. Responding to McQueen's threat of violence, Elroy remarks that 'A silicate doesn't feel pain' and taunts McQueen about his allegiance: 'You're gonna get your asses kicked. And then, *Tank*, you lose. And because we're allies with them, we win.' Dismissing Lt. Paul Wang[31] and thereby absolving him of any guilt in what follows, McQueen warns it that 'I've got no problem in going all the way with this,' before indulging in some ad-hoc re-wiring until finally, its voice reduced to a mechanical stutter, the unit responds with the information. McQueen immediately recalls Wang, telling him: 'Take this thing down to the shop, and inform the flight surgeon that I wish to see him.' The symmetrical irony is immaculate here, for Elroy and McQueen, both artificially created by humans, one a broken computer with a virus and an attitude problem, the other an In-Vitro pilot grounded through injury and greatly troubled by the concept of his own humanity, will be 'repaired' at the same time.[32] McQueen's actions toward Elroy-L could be construed as revenge – for the lost squadrons, for Wang's suffering, or for his own torture as a POW in the AI Wars, or for honour and pride – in his own code and that of the Corps. But torture clearly runs against every principle he holds dear. And his action is about neither revenge nor honour. It emerges from stark necessity and the choice to remove Wang from the room says more about the man than any other action, as Morrison says:

McQueen absolved him of any association with what might
be construed as a crime – out of respect for Wang's conscience
and because he didn't want a witness – by making him leave
the room. What it really comes down to is this: do you want
Gary Cooper to ride off with Grace Kelly and live happily
ever after or do you want him to go back to town and do what
needs to be done?[33]

Thematically this is perhaps the strongest demonstration we have
that the Colonel's sense of duty, loyalty and honour extends beyond
his rigid personal code: his behaviour is focused upon the greater
good once more and he needs to locate the alien vessel. McQueen
is prepared to sacrifice even his own values, willingly bearing the
consequences of his actions, regardless of how they must affect him
psychologically and whether they manifest themselves physically in
death or injury through battle, or in punishment for his unwarranted
behaviour.[34]

When Winslow visits McQueen to apologise for flirting with
him in the bar, the maturity of her contrite action (which is partly
of course what McQueen's outburst is all about) is combined with
her humanitarian and compassionate recognition of his isolation.
She apologises, then comments: 'Sir, the Lieutenant has observed
recently inordinate behaviour by Colonel McQueen and realises that
due to circumstances or by design the Colonel has no one with which
to communicate his feelings.' Picking up the wedding photograph
sitting on his desk, McQueen replies: 'It's by design, Lieutenant,
but not mine.' He talks briefly about his human ex-wife and the
bigotry they encountered. As Winslow leaves, he thanks her for both
her apology and her concern. She thus provides this very private
individual with a reason to reflect more personally and less angrily
on his existence. When she is later killed by the mysterious alien
pilot, her cockpit destroyed after she has ejected from her damaged
Hammerhead fighter, she serves as the final catalyst for McQueen's
defining moment: the edit cuts directly from her death to McQueen,
looking at the stars from the Saratoga.[35]

PREDESTINATION AND FREE WILL

McQueen was initially denied the mission because of his grounded status. Now, after Winslow's death, he pulls out the trunk containing his 127th 'Angry Angels' flight gear, and immediately goes out alone to face the alien vessel. Morrison says of McQueen in this episode that: 'to be able to take control of a situation, to step so far beyond the boundaries of circumstance and actually take action to change the outcome – it was almost god-like.' In a short but telling scene with Ross, the Colonel explains why he must undertake the task himself. His words are superficially reminiscent of the American Western hero; the episode notably carries echoes of the seminal Western *Shane* (1953), to which Morrison alluded earlier, and its eponymous, definitive hero, yet the signification differs because McQueen's actions emerge from such a contrasting ideological and philosophical stance. Asked why he would carry out the mission by Ross, he replies simply, 'I have no choice.'

Free will is very much an issue with McQueen; there has been little choice for him in his existence. His questions in the opening of 'The Angriest Angel' frame this: 'Who am I?' and 'What's the point?' But if he believes that life is a series of causes and effects, in 'Dark Side of the Sun', when an edgy Vansen asks if he's ever felt that something is 'out there waiting', McQueen dismisses any notions of fate. He tells her: 'There's no such thing as predetermination, and there's no such thing as luck. You make things happen. Keep your head together, and don't make mistakes, and you'll come back. It's that simple.' Again, we hear echoes of the Way:

> If you keep your spirit correct from morning to night, accustomed to the idea of death, and resolved on death, and consider yourself as a dead body, thus becoming one with the Way of the warrior, you can pass through life with no possibility of failure and perform your office properly.[36]

McQueen certainly leans towards determinism at times, with a resigned acceptance that everything follows on logically and inexorably, each thought and action determined by the previous thought and action. This is in direct contrast to Hawkes, a mere six years out of the 'tank', who constantly questions his commander about life much as a child questions a parent, longing to make things different. For a former slave, a man denied free will from the moment of his 'design', McQueen's tendency to determinism is both understandable and appropriate. He is the only character in *Space* aware that he is not free to create himself – he has already been created.[37] As he departs for battle, the chaplain calls after him, suggesting that he should make peace with his maker. McQueen is scathing: 'My "maker" was some geek in a lab coat with an eye-dropper and petri-dish. What do I need to make peace with him for?'

The climactic dogfight takes place to the strains of the funeral march from Beethoven's Third Symphony, *Eroica* (Heroic); the self-aware McQueen is playing it as he sets off. In line with the Homer he quotes, the fight occurs in the nearby Achilles star system. As McQueen despatches the alien with appropriate élan, in careful keeping with the tenets of his philosophy, there's a complete absence of any personal celebration. However, there is a grim dedication, uttered before he closes for the kill: 'This one's for you, Winslow.' Appropriately, and with perfect symmetry, just as McQueen's opening speech of destiny is inter-cut with aerial combat and the death of Brandt, so the dogfight leading to the alien's destruction is inter-cut with Winslow's funeral. The physical manifestation of McQueen's 'moment' is the combat with the alien pilot and, when it occurs, it is a poetic act of catharsis and thus one of redemption – and he knows it. The episode may well remind us of the Western gun-fighting ritual, except that in the vacuum of space, stripped of its frontier context, its binary ideology is clearly out of place and out of time. Its logic eludes even the philosophical McQueen, who returns safely to the Saratoga. As he later drinks a bottle of Scotch in salute to the dead, McQueen gazes out at the stars and ponders the anachronistic scenario: 'I now know with certainty who I am. But I'll be damned if I'll ever know the point. And now all I can ask is who was he, and who was she? And what *was* the point?'

McQueen's unprecedented act initialises an epiphanic moment; it not only frees his character from its narrative bond, but also combines with his other actions to provide catharsis and thus potential salvation for the future US screen soldier. His solid integrity, his surety in his remarkable professional competence and his ability to validate any action internally according to his code sustain his difficult decision-making. His rejection of ego, the personal indignity he willingly suffers and the knowledge that he will be self-serving if he argues that his men and women are his primary concern are all remarkable in their selflessness and greater awareness. But more importantly, with his self-awareness and his concurrent denial of self-worth within the context of other lives, McQueen distances himself from all those previous screen protagonists who have undertaken a frontier-style rite of passage and thereby gained individual fulfilment from an ideology that relies upon the concept of free will and individual choice. He challenges the fundamental American belief which asserts that you have the right and the ability to make of yourself what you wish. He demands that you make the best of yourself despite the dictate of circumstance.

Of course, McQueen has his flaws. The *Tao Teh Ching* asks that we are natural in our behaviour. McQueen can never truly behave naturally, since he regards himself as unnatural, outcast, inhuman. His pain is intense, his anger deep and, when his self-control fractures, he lashes out in fury. Self-denial and self-control may well be his prize assets but they are also his prize problems. The ascetic Colonel clings desperately to regulations, to routine and to his code, because they allow him to deny that he does not live, but merely exists. In 'Mutiny', Hawkes is devastated by the loss of his unborn 'sister' and McQueen confides that he never had the courage to look for his In-Vitro family, not because he was frightened of what he might find, 'but of what I might feel'. The structure and discipline of the Marine Corps creates a surrogate family for McQueen, himself a surrogate child. Hiding behind protocol, and with the benefit of that infinite capacity for selflessness, he assures Hawkes that when he dies his military family will know what to say. 'You got that right,' says Hawkes, but one wonders whether or not McQueen really believes it – or if he has a choice.

Likewise, McQueen has all too human needs but constantly sublimates them, substituting those of others. This is clear in the final episode, '... Tell Our Moms We Done Our Best'. An explosion devastates the newly commenced peace talks. Ross is absent with a cold, McQueen has taken his place; in the carnage, he loses his right leg. Later, as the Colonel lies on a gurney waiting to be taken to hospital, an emotional and grief-stricken Ross clasps his hand. But it is McQueen who speaks first, selfless as ever, dealing vicariously with his own emotions by absolving his commander of guilt. 'It should not have been you,' he says, before his fine sense of irony prompts him to remark wryly that it should not have been him, either.

CREATING AN IDEOLOGICAL BREAK

In 1996, *Space* was cancelled after only one season. The apparent confusion over its genre and marketing niche didn't help; even Fox seemed unaware of what they had, pitching it alongside Paramount's *Star Trek: Deep Space Nine* and Warner's ground-breaking *Babylon 5* and then making frequent changes to its time-slots.[38] Perhaps the low audience figures identified by the Neilsen ratings explain its demise and doubtless the demanding narrative threads did not help, but perhaps its focal issues – the uncomfortable backdrop of political intrigue; the complicated, bravely articulated metaphysical debate and McQueen's challenge to the most fundamental American ideology – are more pertinent to its cancellation. Yet McQueen's character articulates the potential for a redefinition and reaffirmation of the best of humanity, to allow America's popular but manufactured mytho-historical basis to evolve, to move on.

Every nation needs its mythology and, while America's myth-making faculty in Hollywood film and television recognises this, it simultaneously refuses to accept a great deal of responsibility for adjusting the depressing cycle of superficial heroics and small-scale victories, thus making the audience unsure of how to handle those rare and challenging efforts which transcend the norm. In McQueen, we find a man who combines the philosophy of Musashi with the poetics of Homer, an awareness of classical strategy with the context of modern warfare, a man who gives redemption to the tragic post-Vietnam soldier-type by offering us a warrior for beyond the millennium. He has faced the harshest judge, himself, and is resigned to his disenfranchised existence. He has very human failings, which trouble him, but he responds by working tirelessly to be the best he can be at all times, never for himself, but for the benefit of everyone else.[39] His every action and utterance challenges the concept of free will and self-determination so manifestly demanded by American ideology. He offers a solution requiring no individual cowboy heroics, instead demanding a denial of self in the greater cause of the community. He fights to win the public war, not the private battle. He motivates collective community values, pitching them against the personal values and ideology dominant in American cinema and television.

McQueen's potential solution, which demands a resolute acceptance of determinism, works heavily against the American grain. Yet it is that same depth of character integrity as we find in the writings of John Dos Passos, Ralph Ellison and John Steinbeck, who, with *USA* (1930–1936), *The Invisible Man* (1952) and *The Grapes of Wrath* (1939), are responsible for some of the most innovative but also the most fundamental American texts concerning political ideology, discrimination and class. McQueen moves us beyond the young, naïve and egocentric hero soldier, rejecting the hypocritical values of an anachronistic and mythical frontier, drawing not from the culturally specific human traits and aspirations of pride, self-aggrandisement and entrepreneurial skills as demanded by late twentieth-century western society, but rather from the enduring metaphysical concepts of life, humanity and universal truth. His suturing of western and eastern philosophies, the constant and total denial of his own self-worth within the context of other lives, creates a new soldier protagonist whose redemptive power is perhaps in danger of being recognised only long after he is gone. McQueen's gift to us is that same gift he offers Ross, that same gift we are offered by science fiction – he has us wonder why.

6. *STARGATE: SG-1* — THOR OF THE ASGARD.

FIVE

WORMHOLE X-TREME!

IMAGES OF TIME AND SPACE

The two previous chapters considered issues of representation, language narrative structure and ideology in specific sf television series. The other dominant feature of series produced from the mid 1980s onwards concerns imagery and the ever-increasing ability of television to offer plausible alternative realities enhanced by sfx and cgi spectacle as never before. However, the creation of alternative realities is not limited to sf; it is a feature of the televisual era also found in sustained alternative realities in shows like *Moonlighting* and *Twin Peaks*. The invigorating *CSI: Crime Scene Investigation* (2000–) currently employs the technique in an innovative fashion, depicting the experiences of the Las Vegas forensic experts. As Gil Grissom's team investigates aspects of the murder case, the viewers are treated to the experience of several brief 'alternative' worlds. Visually, we experience a grainy and oddly angled temporary mindscape created by the investigator as he or she speculates as to a possible scenario of, for instance, a bullet entering the body at a particular angle or repeated scenes depicting various angles. Throughout the investigation the images are simply conjecture, until all the evidence is finally drawn together as proof and the final mental scenario becomes a record of the act of murder. Each vision is accompanied by non-diegetic rock music, which is absent from the external diegetic-world, thereby enhancing the sense of both speculation and artifice in the characters' cognitive processes.

This chapter explores how advances in visuals have aided narrative and allowed television to create spectacular narratives which might not quite rival cinema for size, but which certainly add to the creation of plausible sf worlds. Considering two of the most consistent themes in modern sf – space travel and wormholes, and how they are visualised in contemporary science fiction – it also explores parallel universes, alternative realities that occur within the already 'alternative' reality of science fiction. This is a feature akin to that within *CSI: Crime Scene Investigation* and demonstrates great confidence in sf's ability to sustain its speculative worlds.

SPACE TRAVEL

Star Trek introduced and familiarised us with the concept of high-speed interstellar travel: it gave us 'warp drive'. Sadly, with our current ability in space travel, it would actually take 40,000 years for NASA's exploratory craft 'Voyager' to reach even the nearest star, Proxima Centauri;[1] clearly, without warp drive, the Enterprise would have serious trouble getting beyond its galactic driveway on its mere five-year mission, let alone harbour ambitions of reaching beyond the galactic rim. So science fiction, drawing on modern astrophysics and imagination, yet still far away from the vanguard of scientific research, offers intriguing ways of avoiding this problem. Carl Sagan suggests that the Earth:

> is now thoroughly explored. It no longer promises new continents of lost lands. But the *technology* that allowed us to explore and inhabit the most remote regions of the Earth now permits us to leave our planet, to venture into space, to explore other worlds. [My emphasis][2]

Just as technology informed the stories of Verne and Wells and imagination took them beyond our capabilities, so science fiction today can use scientific theory as a platform for its futuristic technical imaginings. This in turn provides us with yet more advances in technology through more discovery and development, or from alien sources. If classical physics' theory of relativity was rigid and unforgiving towards science fiction, the road to quantum physics has itself said 'what if?' and offered delightful potentials in its probability scenarios. More importantly, modern sf television can present immaculate and highly realistic images of these scenarios.

The future offers an ideal realm for the technology of advanced space travel (Suvin's novum) to be presented. In many cases, just as *Star Trek*'s contented Federation exists previously to our introduction to it, so does high-speed space travel. We understand that the Enterprise can travel at sub-light speed or at warp speed, but although a great deal of time is spent discussing topics such as 'warp manifolds', 'the warp field' and fear of a 'containment breach in the matter/anti-matter chambers', the theoretical physics of the technology are seldom discussed, because, quite often, the technology is in itself implausible, as Laurence Krauss, amongst others, has demonstrated at length.[3] Within the diegesis, we are merely treated to the descriptive technical discourse – which has an alienating effect, part of sf's process of cognitive estrangement (neologisms) – and we can watch the associated imagery. This raises the issue of 'user interfaces', a question central to the *Star Trek* spoof *Galaxy Quest* (2000). Believing the television episodes of the film's diegetic sf series 'Galaxy Quest' to be historical documentaries, aliens seek an alliance with these potentially powerful allies (the actors' characters), in order to defeat a terrible enemy. They design a ship with technologies based solely upon how they saw the 'crew' operate the props. The actors can manipulate the ship's technology merely by copying how they pretended to operate it in the television series.[4] Skill is required to invent the systems but not to operate them – and here most of us can find a simple parallel in our actual understanding of how a computer functions set against our regular use of computer software.

There are various preferred methods of achieving high-speed space travel in current sf television, and all of them are related to our concept of space and time as a single conceptual sphere. We can use warp drive to warp space, we can find a passageway in hyperspace or some special 'corridor', and we can use wormholes, which may take us through space or through space and time. Since well before the original *Star Trek*, a popular approach has been to use some high-speed means of travel, and nearly all series demonstrating distant space travel draw on the idea of warping space or via some sort of hyperspace. *Babylon 5*'s hellish swirls of hyperspace are a less friendly version of the 'slipstream' through which the 'Andromeda Ascendant' travels in *Gene Roddenberry's Andromeda*; whilst *Farscape*'s living Leviathan, Moya, can 'starburst' to avoid capture. The basis for wormhole travel can be easily demonstrated – if you lay a book open on a table, the tops of the right-hand and left-hand pages are far apart, but begin to close the book and they draw closer and closer until the distance between them is reduced. Wormholes are a manifestation of this process, they effectively bend space-time – except that the book pages remain open: the wormhole simply connects them as if they were at their minimum distance. Another approach related to the idea of utilising wormholes is to assume that if you can enter some sort of fixed corridor, often represented as 'gated' at either end, it creates a kind of short cut from one location to another. *Stargate SG-1* and *Sliders* depict the most obvious example of this, and *Babylon 5* depicts the entrance to hyperspace as similarly 'gated', but larger ships can create their own jump-points, as can the Andromeda Ascendant, Gou'ald vessels and Moya in their respective series. The effect for the traveller is the same as the folding of space: two distant points are suddenly a few seconds apart.

Science fiction's other area of interest concerning wormholes or conduits is not to journey to distant parts of the universe, but to parallel universes. Stepping through a portal or gate, another dimension/universe is reached, offering another possibility for life. In these scenarios, the quantum theory of every moment (past, present and future) co-existing at the sub-atomic level coincides with the philosophical concept of each and every decision made creating different possible futures. Just one small decision or action can have a tremendous impact upon everything in the universe, as *Babylon 5*'s Japanese stone garden suggests – each stone causing a series of ripples across the sand, each ripple impacting upon other stones and ripples. Each variation is a new universe or reality, closely or distantly related to the last. This brings us to the final area of interest – time travel. Whilst physicists study space from the 'big bang' to the curvature of time, it is also natural for sf to speculate upon the concept of going forward or backward in time in order to explore, change things or, in the case of history, most commonly to ensure that events remain as they originally took place. As Nicholas Packwood suggests, although

> science and the tourism industry have yet to conspire a round
> trip ticket to classical Greece or the twenty-third century, our
> conceptions of time travel and its paradoxes owe as much
> to *The Time Machine* and *Dr Who* as they do relativistic
> physics. Indeed, the speculative technologies upon which
> these conceptions are based have themselves advanced
> independent of science proper. What was once HG Wells'
> Victorian time travelling wing-chair has been transformed
> into the TARDIS and beyond.[5]

Wormholes, jump-gates/event horizons, time travel and the
exploration of parallel universes have provided tremendous
inspiration for sf television series for many years. *The Time Tunnel*,
a progenitor of *Quantum Leap* (1989–1993), is perhaps the most
famous of the older series, trapping its two protagonists in the past
or the future, casting them from century to century – but never back
home. *Sliders*, for example, offers a series of parallel Earths rather
than travel off the planet, whilst *Sir Arthur Conan Doyle's 'The Lost
World'* (1999–) offers a dinosaur-occupied plateau *itself* caught in a
time warp which facilitates a variety of zone-like arenas for adventure.
Crichton's entire existence in *Farscape*'s 'uncharted territories'
is premised upon wormholes and wormhole navigation, while
Quantum Leap, *Odyssey 5* (2002) and *Seven Days* (1998–2001) are
all concerned with time travel, particularly with changing the past.
A central storyline in the continuous narrative of *Babylon 5* concerns
the impact of just one instance of time travel, but an instance whose
impact permeates the entire diegesis. *Stargate SG-1* combines all
three versions of the novum: its ancient stargate serves as a means of
high-speed interstellar travel between a variety of 'addresses', whilst
we are also invited to consider life in parallel universes from time to
time, and possible futures and past experiences occur in a handful of
time-related episodes.

PARALLEL WORLDS

Many series have occupied themselves with ideas of parallel worlds,
and one series touching upon them in the 1980s is the short-lived

Otherworld (1985). Its theme echoes an earlier series, *The Fantastic Journey* (1977), whose characters were scooped up from the past (pirates), present (a shipwrecked crew) and future (the musical healer) and deposited on a bizarre island. The island comprises a series of 'zones', located within (or parallel to) the mysterious Bermuda Triangle. *Otherworld*'s ubiquitous 1980s American family, the Sterlings, accidentally fall through a portal in an Egyptian pyramid only to find themselves in an alternative universe of unfriendly 'Zones', pursued by the relentless Kommander Kroll and his Zone troopers. The various zones hold up different ideas for consideration – reverse gender roles, robots with feelings, a quest for immortality, rock star fame, Mad Max-style biker communities, who deny the concept of 'family', and a lyrical version of *Beauty and the Beast*. In its eight episodes, *Otherworld* offered some fairly wretched material, its 'special effects' consisted primarily of obtuse camera angles and chiffon or grease on the camera lenses, but in its anodyne and prosaic way it still articulates one of the basic premises of sf: it turns the tables on us and asks 'What if?'

Sir Arthur Conan Doyle's 'The Lost World' has no entry 'portal' as such, it is merely set on a remote and almost inaccessible South American plateau, and the protagonists' problem of returning to the known world is the same as for the Sterlings. Having reached the plateau by hot-air balloon, the explorers find that it cannot make the return journey, so they must search for another way out. Although *The Lost World*'s early twentieth-century protagonists not do travel through time to reach their lost world, they begin exploring a land which time has forgotten. The idea of living dinosaurs echoes a theme popular throughout sf history, but was given a new lease of life on the big screen following the tremendous success of *Jurassic Park* (1993). The basis for the 1920s expedition is scientific, and Professor Challenger, the renowned hunter Lord Roxton, the journalist Ned Malone and Marguerite Krux, the adventurous heiress, are (as the voiceover introduction worryingly explains) 'befriended by an untamed beauty', a sort of female Tarzan called Veronica, the only daughter of missing explorers and the plateau's sacred female Amazon warrior protector. They create an entertaining enough group, but the series' science fiction premise would appear to be limited. Once the narrative reaches the plateau, it really takes on its original role as an adventure story with thoughtful/action men and headstrong/ duplicitous women, while a worrying preponderance of naïve and/ or dangerous dark-skinned 'primitives' are set against a singularly white ensemble. Yet there are gateways and portals scattered across the plateau, areas where time shifts from past to future, where single events are repeated time and time again, and in its historical format it reiterates many of the questions arising out of other sf series. *The Lost World* initially concerns itself mostly with the travellers' desire to get home, but much like *Voyager*, which positively dawdles around the Delta Quadrant and explores every possible nook and cranny, the group are fairly comfortable in Veronica's elegant tree house. They spend time collecting gems, fighting off savages and dinosaurs and having the occasional romantic fling. However, the role of myths and legends in communities is explored in detail, as are their origins and, importantly, the scientific/technological ability of the squabbling travellers, as well as their logical approach to incidents, is demonstrated more than once to be the reason for their survival. They build a windmill for running water and electrical power, create an electrical fence around the tree house to keep out Raptors and design a new gas balloon to explore the plateau, all technological inventions which serve to keep them alive.

Sliders takes an alternative attitude to portals and dimensions. Rather than them being the mysterious creation of some ancient or unknown race – as in *Otherworld* and *The Lost World* – they are very much of the present, rooted in more recent theoretical physics and, as a result, neither perfectly nor entirely predictable. Quinn Mallory is a brilliant young student who creates the technology in the basement of his San Francisco home. His device is a means of opening up wormholes between a series of parallel universes: the 'sliding' of the title. Mallory explores these universes with his overbearing but caring physics professor, Maximillian Arturo, a computer-literate girl-Friday/girlfriend, Wade Wells, and a washed-up soul singer, Rembrandt 'Crying Man' Brown. Mallory's opening narration from the first series describes its premise, asking:

> What if you could travel to parallel worlds – the same year, the same Earth, only different dimensions? A world where the Russians rule America, or where your dreams of being a

superstar come true, or where San Francisco was a maximum security prison. My friends and I found the gateway. Now the problem is finding a way back home.

Aside from the premises mentioned above, the series offers a line of fascinating scenarios, such as a world where America lost the War of Independence ('Prince of Wails'), a disease-ridden land where antibiotics are unknown ('Fever') and a place where Einstein withheld the secret of nuclear energy and the world has no defence against a meteor hurtling towards it ('Last Days'). There is even an Earth about to be destroyed by a pulsar ('Exodus') – the sliders escaping along with various others to a new dimension, fortunately just before the planet explodes. America's heritage is considered carefully in most episodes, and two actually take the form of Wild-West excursions: 'The Good, the Bad and the Wealthy', where corporate takeovers are settled by gunfights, and 'Way out West', where the travellers find themselves on a frontier-style planet Earth. The benefit of this approach for viewers is that, stripped of its everyday context, the origins of the one-shot frontier/gunfighter ideology and the validity of its premise and other ideological positions can be interrogated more freely whilst under the episodic microscope. It is a similar approach to that taken in *Space: Above and Beyond*, when McQueen questions the purpose and result of his confrontation with the Chig super-fighter. The problem in *Sliders* is that the three men mostly hold sway over 'Miss Wells' with a 'common sense' balance of opinion, and gender stereotypes are perpetuated even as the episodic narrative presents its critique. Quinn's apparent shock at a woman 'sizing me up like a piece of meat' in a job interview in 'The Weaker Sex' is a somewhat jaded idea for 1995, regardless of how advanced or not we find our society's degree of equality. The series does rebalance this later with the arrival of soldier Maggie Beckett, who joins the travellers from a parallel Earth after the death of Professor Arturo.

What *Sliders* does well is to comment upon how small incidents can change the course of history. Much like *Quantum Leap*, it ponders the effect of introducing new elements from other realities into the current reality. Since its earlier episodes are mostly set in the same San Francisco location each episode, it enjoys introducing characters who remain almost the same in each reality, including the Dominion Hotel manager, Gomez Calhoun, and taxi driver Pavel Kurlienko. *Sliders* demonstrates an episodic narrative to begin with, concerned only with independent episodes in which the sliders attempt to reach home. But in the later series it demonstrates the slow-burn longer narrative threads discussed earlier, and characters, issues and ideologies touched upon in previous episodes are brought back to create at least some sense of a coherent overall narrative. The series has little need to play around much with linguistics, nor does it rely heavily upon sfx. It is more a question of a challenging narrative scenario, but the ability of its characters to walk not just around but to interact with cgi avatars thanks to new post production techniques is of tremendous benefit in creating a narrational *mise-en-scène* and sense of sublime spectacle. Like the loosely connected narrative strategy, these flourishes of technology are another aspect of sf television and film in the post-1980s era and are explored in more detail later in this chapter.

FARSCAPE

Perhaps the series most fascinated with wormholes is the marvellous and whacky 'lost in space' story of *Farscape*.[6] Not only does it utilise state-of-the-art cgi and sfx, it also incorporates a remarkably mixed collection of main characters, two of which are actually Muppet-like animatronics, created and operated by the Jim Henson Creature Shop. Testing the Farscape module on its maiden flight, astronaut John Crichton (the son of a moon-landing veteran astronaut) hopes to confirm a new means of interstellar travel by means of a planetary slingshot manoeuvre. Both times he attempts it when there is a solar flare from the sun, and wormholes appear. On the final attempt his craft is hit by a massive electro-magnetic wave and sent hurtling down the wormhole, ending up on the far side of the universe. Taken aboard the living vessel Moya, with a Pilot who exists in symbiotic harmony with the ship itself, Crichton and his companions set out to find their way to their respective homes. The presence of animatronics/ Muppets in a central role suggests a youngish audience for the series, but the frequent and blatant sexuality of its crew, its often-complex physics and grim narrative and a tendency to bondage/torture scenes suggests otherwise. However, it does not quite reach the heights

7. *FARSCAPE*: CHIANA AND SIKOZU.

of that bizarre but entertaining romp through the Forbidden Zone: *Lexx* (1997–2002), with its phallic living vessel, where the quest for unending sex is the most permanent narrative feature.

Crichton's quest for home provides the main narrative thread to *Farscape* after his encounter with 'the Ancients' who have wormhole knowledge and are anxious to protect it from rash younger species. He develops an absolute obsession with wormholes, describing them thus:

If D'Argo wants to get from one end of Moya to the other, he
has to walk the whole distance. But if I could fold Moya in
half – so that her front and back ends are close enough to
be connected by a short tunnel – then I could slip through
that tunnel and have my feet up and a drink in my hand
by the time D'Argo arrives ... You don't go faster than light;
you bend space-time itself, and take a serious short cut while
light slogs through space the long way.[7]

Farscape links the various types of theoretical wormholes: not only
do they bridge space-time, allowing a unique ability to navigate
across vast distances (and thus through time) they also traverse
dimensions (or universes) other than our own. Quantum theory
suggests that all possible outcomes from each variable event actually
occur simultaneously (therefore concepts of past, present and future
become meaningless), but each leads off into its own quantum reality.
In effect, we are offered a potentially infinite number of what *Farscape*
dubs 'unrealised realities' within our own universe, none of which
actually exists until we encounter it.[8]

One of *Farscape*'s most complex wormhole episodes is 'Unrealised
Realities', an episode directly linked to the subsequent 'Kansas' and
'Terra Firma'. In 'Unrealised Realities', Crichton is floating in space
near Moya, waiting for a wormhole: the knowledge of the Ancients
in his head gives him the uncanny ability to predict when the next
opening will be. He is drawn into the wormhole by a being from
another dimension, who demands to know what Crichton knows
about wormhole travel. The alien acts as a sort of guardian between
dimensions which cannot interact because such an action would
'result in a cataclysmic unravelling of the precise mathematical
harmony'. His mission is to kill Crichton, but as they sit on an iceberg
in a temporary reality, he changes his mind and agrees to let Crichton
return to Moya, first showing him the dangers of backwards time-
space travel in a variety of unrealised realities, since each wormhole
has infinite exit points. The *Farscape* pages of the Sci-Fi channel's
website contain Crichton's 'notes', echoing his dialogue in the
programme and explaining the problem. They demonstrate again
the laws that sf texts create for their own single or multiple realities:
travel through a wormhole:

> [F]rom point A to point B; now, attempt to travel back. You could arrive at point A immediately after you left. Or a cycle later. Or a cycle earlier. Or ten. Or ten thousand. There are millions of permutations – millions of chances to unravel the past and completely erase everything you ever cared about. In other words, going *forward* in time is no great shakes; it's going backward that screws the pooch. A traveller who appears earlier in the timeline of his own existence is like a rock dropped on still waters; the ripples radiate from the point of disruption and cause bigger and bigger circles of change as they move outwards. But if you fix the first thing that goes ape before the other temporal dominoes fall, time is elastic enough to recover its initial shape. If events are matched closely enough to their original course, they have a way of restructuring themselves to familiar outcomes.[9]

Released by the alien, Crichton now understands that the wormhole knowledge is instinctive, that he can 'command the stars' (he acknowledges this sometime later in 'Hot to Katratzi'), and 'thinks' himself out of the wormhole as he is instructed, 'feeling' his way back to Moya and a way home. He finds himself gazing at the moon and, in the closing scenes of the episode, turns to face the Earth. In the following episode, 'Kansas', he makes it back to Earth, but finds that it is the wrong year. It is 1986, his very presence means that history has changed, and his father is about to captain the doomed Challenger shuttle mission. Following the advice of the alien about fixing the first thing which deviates from history, he and Moya's crew, who have joined him on D'Argo's cloaked vessel, fix the mistake and prevent Crichton senior from making the flight. Reasonably sure they have fixed history, they return to Earth orbit and reunite with Moya, who has travelled through the wormhole from the uncharted territories and appeared in the solar system in 2003, four years after Crichton was lost on his Farscape mission. Waiting on board is Crichton's father, and an assortment of officials from Earth.

The subsequent episode, 'Terra Firma', is a strikingly brave and sensitive effort to present the bigger picture, both within and beyond the story. Filmed in the aftermath of September 11th, the episode seeks to cast the events of that day and the policies they provoked into a more considered light. Returning to Earth from Moya with his father, Crichton discovers that he has indeed corrected history. However, he is also unaware of the past four years of human history, particularly of events in the USA since his departure. He returns to find an isolationist USA, his homeland embittered and shattered by the tragedy of the Twin Towers and the attacks on Washington. Aware of the dangers lurking beyond the wormhole, Crichton wants to share the alien technology he has to hand with the world; his father and the space agency want him to supply only the USA, repeatedly telling him that since he has been away he has lost sight of the 'bigger picture'. In the context of *Farscape's* dark and dangerous diegesis, this is a ludicrous and arrogant statement: aside from Crichton and his companions, no one on Earth has any concept of the 'bigger picture'.

As Crichton and his Moya associates stay in their Florida compound, we are treated to a fragmented sense of culture both in- and ex-diegesis. 'Terra Firma' is able to articulate the anger and paranoia felt in post-2001 America, but it also depicts the despair of Crichton. Returned to his beloved home after such a long absence, he cannot locate the innate democracy and the decency of his fellow Americans (of which he has spoken so proudly to his squabbling alien companions) in any of the people around him, even his father. The astronaut and his alien companions now represent all of the best aspects of open-minded humanity, but the people surrounding them depict only fear and loathing: humans stripped of their humanity. Eventually, Crichton reminds his father that he always taught him to do what he believed in, refuses to hand over any technology unless it is shared, and points out the 'bigger picture' – that just on the other side of the wormhole is an invasion force of aliens who will devastate not just the USA, but the entire planet. Finally, Crichton's father accepts his decision and persuades the space agency to invite all nations to take part in the 'continuing Farscape project', admitting that although he is 'afraid of what will happen if we do', more significantly he is also 'afraid of what will happen if we don't'. The long-term bigger picture is thus not only contrasted sharply with short-term shattered pride, but more positively, those values treasured by Americans prior to September 11th are still seen to be equally important after consideration and reflection. This is how the alternative realities of sf television can offer an arena for ideological debate, stripping individual moments and events of narrow and short-term considerations, and replacing them with broader, more contextualised concerns.

LOOKING BACKWARDS

Farscape links various ideas of travel in space-time with its use of wormholes, but time travel itself is often the central novum for sf stories. The British series *Doctor Who* may provide the best-known time traveller in the world, but America also introduced a variety of thought-provoking programmes concerning time travel in *Babylon 5* and *Quantum Leap*. *Babylon 5*'s attitude to backwards time travel is reminiscent of that in *Farscape*. There is only one actual instance of time travel in *Babylon 5*, focused around the disappearance and reappearance of the previous station, Babylon 4, although it is a significant occurrence for the overall story arc and occurs for different people at different times, a thousand years prior to the story's era, and in 2054, 2058 and 2060: it is thus explored from a variety of perspectives. For the next station commander, John Sheridan, and Minbari ambassador Delenn, the time travel means glimpses of the distant and near future respectively; for security officer Garibaldi, it is a potential future; for Commander Sinclair, it is his future, his present and his past. In 'Babylon Squared' and 'War Without End' Parts 1 and 2, the characters are confused not only as to *where*, but also *when* they are.

The impact of these episodes reverberates throughout the series. Even the opening voiceover narration is subverted by the events of 'Babylon Squared'; Sinclair's first-season introduction proudly declares: 'The year is 2258. The name of the place is Babylon 5.' Yet on Babylon 4, no one knows what the date is. Zathras adds to the confusion; quizzed by Krantz and Sinclair, he responds in brief sentences, confusing 'chronologies of tense and time from the offset'.[10] Zathras is an alien, he has spent his life in the Great Machine on Epsilon 3, and when Garibaldi asks him what year it is, he says '4993'. The information is useless because, like *Babylon 5*'s visions and predictions, it has no context. Questioned further by Krantz, Zathras genuinely can't help: 'Much apologising. Mathematics not Zathras's skill.' In 'War Without End', Delenn may be more articulate than poor Zathras, but she is a source of precisely the same kind of confusion. Firstly, she shows Ivanova, Sheridan, Marcus, and Sinclair a recording of the White Star, gathered by Draal and the Great Machine on Epsilon 3 (in 'Voices of Authority', we learn that it sees the future and the past). It is of the near future and in it the White Star destroys Shadow vessels carrying a fusion bomb to destroy Babylon 4. They are attempting to prevent it from being taken back in time a thousand years to provide a base of operations for the Minbari and Vorlons; they are trying to change the course of history. Delenn then tells her colleagues, who have not yet shot at the Shadow vessels, but who have heard Ivanova's message from eight days in the future, that 'it's history. It's already been done. All we have to do *now* is to make sure that we do it *then*.'

This is a more complex rendering of the format of the detective story identified in the previous section by Todorov's *Poetics of Prose*. The plotting of the story and the connection between story and plot (more complex than in mundane narratives), create a convoluted experience and, because it stretches across time and space, the significance of 'Babylon 4' cannot be explained within a single narrative episode. Instead, it is part of the greater myth of Babylon 5 and, whereas the threat of destruction to Babylon 5 is only explained after the two-part 'War Without End', the actual destruction of the station does not come to fruition (nor to absolute clarification) until 'Sleeping in Light'. As Sinclair says when he tells Marcus and Ivanova that he will take Babylon 4 back in time: 'I'll take it back because I have always taken it back, and I always will. It's already happened,' *Babylon 5* is myth, it is ongoing and never ending, existing both diachronically and synchronically, and as such is impossible to pin down exactly. Its very function is to avoid such a fate, it must remain mutable and flexible – yet recognisable. Like *Doctor Who*, perhaps the closest to it in format and purpose, its characters are finite, but its story is infinite.

A recurring feature of time-travel stories (until very recently) is that the antagonists are the ones who travel through time to change things. The forces of good invariably time travel only to stop history from being changed. *TimeTrax* (1993–1994), much like *TimeCop* (1997), is concerned with this concept, sending agents from the future back to the past to stop others from disrupting what has already happened. Lingering on the edges of sf, their protagonists are essentially detectives, sent from the future to collect villains who have stolen technology or money and taken refuge in the past. *Odyssey 5* has shades of this, but here the protagonists, the surviving members of 'Odyssey' space shuttle's crew, are going back in time to prevent the destruction of the planet – something that has already happened. In *Babylon 5*, history is done, it is set, it has happened: it should not be changed, and thus the action of the antagonists, the Shadows, is illegitimate. History must also be protected, which is perhaps why *Babylon 5* is so insistent that we are true to it, and do not create false memories of it. In the Shadows, we encounter a force determined to win at whatever cost. If they succeed in destroying Babylon 4, Delenn warns that the Shadows 'will emerge from the last war stronger, their forces intact'. History will change, and the Alliance will not be able to defeat them. As a follower of prophecy, and of the knights of order, the Vorlons, Delenn must have order, time must work the way it is intended, the way it has always worked. The sacrifice required of her is the temporary loss of Sheridan ('this was not part of the plan'), and the permanent loss of Sinclair ('He's my friend, Lennier'). From this point on, prophecy (history) has little place in Delenn's life (or Sheridan's), although for others, like G'Kar and Londo, it begins to take priority: Londo has repeatedly seen his destiny and death, with G'Kar's hands around his throat. It is first seen in 'Midnight on the Firing Line', and then in 'Dust to Dust', where G'Kar finally shares the Centauri's vision of their demise – later confirmed by the timeline that Delenn insists is set in 'War Without End' Part 2, which we see during Sheridan's future-flash.

What complicates the time travel in *Babylon 5* is that it takes us not just to the future or to the past, but to both. When Sinclair and Garibaldi travel to Babylon 4 in 'Babylon Squared', they have no idea where the station was moved in time. As a result of their experiences in 2258, Ivanova remarks in 'War Without End' that when Babylon 4 vanished, they 'assumed it was into the future'. It does, of course, move both ways. On the White Star, Delenn tells Sinclair, Sheridan, Marcus and Ivanova that they must enter the time rift and travel back six years in time, thus moving from 2260 to 2254, the year Babylon 4 was to have come on-line, and the year it vanished. The faulty acceleration of the machinery Zathras fixes to the station's reactor core pushes the near-completed Babylon 4 four years into the future, to 2258, where the Sinclair and Garibaldi of *that* year find it, staffed by a skeleton crew and Krantz, its temporary commander. Krantz introduces them to Zathras, whom they find on board as they become 'unstuck in time'. Zathras recognises Sinclair, then denies it, saying 'No, not the One', having already been warned by the Sinclair of 2260 that the Sinclair of 2258 will not recognise him. The Sinclair and Garibaldi of 2258 evacuate the station, leaving Zathras, who begs them to go, telling Sinclair he has 'a destiny'. The Sinclair of 2260 watches the evacuation transports leave for the Babylon 5 of 2258, and then takes Babylon 4 (and Zathras) back a thousand years as a gift to the Minbari in the last Shadow war. Meanwhile, Sheridan, Delenn, Marcus and Ivanova return to their own Babylon 5 and their own time, 2260, secure in the knowledge that they have ensured history has occurred as it should have done.

In a sense, Valen is also a forward time traveller. As the former Sinclair, he knows of the future and can pass it on in the form of prophecy – but only until Sinclair takes Babylon 4 back in time. Sinclair remains unaware until he and Delenn receive their messages from Valen, in Sinclair's handwriting. He must make happen with Babylon 4 what prophecy (his confirmed history) dictates has already happened in that future. Likewise Sheridan, having experienced the future of Centauri Prime in 'War Without End', recalls it in the present of 'Z'ha'dum'. Thrown some 17 years into the future he is accused by an incandescent Emperor Mollari of:

> the crime of neglect, the crime of convenience. During your little war you drove away the Shadows, yes. But you did not think to clean up your mess. If a few of their minions, their dark servants, came to Centauri Prime – well, where is the harm in that? You want to see the harm? *Do you*?

Londo shows him the once beautiful city. Palls of black smoke tower above crumbling edifices, fires flare from the windows of greying, collapsing homes, a Centauri version of the fall of Rome. A possible history of the future is thus laid out for Sheridan, raising yet more questions for the audience. Gifted with the 2277 consequences of what he and the others are doing in 2260, when he returns to his own time, in 'Z'ha'dum', he wants to try and save Centauri Prime. Fearing that he has heeded Delenn's repeated plea ('Do not go to Z'ha'dum') in the past of the future timeline he glimpsed, which might have led to Centauri Prime's destruction, he demonstrates responsibility across time for his actions, and in his farewell message to Delenn, explains his reasoning:

> I began to wonder, what if that future happened because I listened to your warning, and didn't go to Z'ha'dum? What if I could prevent the fall of Centauri Prime *and* end the Shadow war by going there? What I want is to stay alive, to be with you. But you were right before, this is about more than what I want.

The timeline Sheridan sees in the future actually remains the same; he realises that trying to logically calculate, or even second guess, an infinite number of possibilities in a finite life is futile. Faced with not only the temporal mystery of Babylon 4, but also the physical role of Babylon 5, Sheridan and the others cannot interpret the situation; they can only act according to their fashion. Krantz repeatedly mumbles that they are 'unstuck in time', whilst Sinclair, Sheridan and Delenn do what is required of them. Marcus' flippant aside to Ivanova that Zathras is 'quite mad, you know', provokes the ever-practical Commander into commenting: 'Marcus, we're stealing a space station to fight in a war that was over a thousand years ago – we're *all* mad.'

These episodes fit perfectly with the cause-and-effect philosophy underpinning the series, and its insistence upon the knowing use of free will, but they also partly explain how the judicious employment of Suvin's novum and other narrative devices (such as flash-forwards) help maintain *Babylon 5*'s audience. Of course, with a predetermined arc rather than a variety of smaller threads, there are limitations to the audience's loyalty. Nevertheless, with this approach it is very clear that subtle (or not so subtle) hints can be dropped into the early narrative, even from the pilot episode, and can later be drawn into the story – or not. There is a marvellous symmetry – one only obtainable through such a preordained narrative structure, which allows its own kind of flexibility – and a full use of the most modern television technologies. In series like *The X-Files* or *Deep Space Nine*, both of which draw upon major storylines, this cannot happen easily because, even though a regular team of writers and producers work on them, in comparison with *Babylon 5* the stories are developed on a relatively short-term basis. Thus, although convenient flashbacks from past episodes may be available to stress certain elements of continuity, they can never offer flash-forwards, images that form part of a future narrative thread. This demonstrates a remarkably innovative feature of *Babylon 5*'s narrative strategy. The majority of the episodes articulate something (however minor), concerned with the arc, 'War Without End' and 'Babylon Squared' are excellent examples of this continuity, respectively representing tales Barthes' identifies as a *texte de plaisir* and a *texte de jouissance*,[11] that is, texts which afford pleasure from explaining events, or texts that afford pleasure by denying us the information we desire.

REWRITING HISTORY

An alternative approach to time travel comes from *Quantum Leap*. Scientist Dr Sam Beckett (Scott Bakula) is experimenting with time travel, but finds himself cut adrift and 'leaping' between a variety of people at vital points in their lives, trying to improve history and hoping that each leap will be his last as he returns into his own body in his own time. His only guide is Al Calavicci, a fellow worker on the project, who appears as a hologram, invisible to everyone except Sam and dispenses somewhat world-weary advice about the current and approaching leaps, which he gleans from the project computer, Ziggy. Rather than follow the usual conventions of maintaining the past, *Quantum Leap* positively relishes in changing events, and this is the key fascination of the programme, allowing for a great many sly jokes – for example, in one of the early episodes ('Camikazi Kid'), Sam teaches a little Michael Jackson how to moonwalk.

The desire to rewrite history with the 20/20 vision endowed by hindsight is understandable but deeply troubling. To go forward in time is merely to explore possible futures, since they are not set and thus act simply as timeline indications of what *may* happen. But the main narrative threads of the sf series discussed here argue long and hard that what has happened is done and cannot or should not be changed. Nevertheless, the idea of going back in time and changing things, as did *Quantum Leap*, is again fast becoming a popular strand of sf on television. Like Hollywood's reworking of Vietnam, history is being restructured. The *Star Trek* series are not averse to the odd time-space trip and, although temporarily journeying home by conventional means, Voyager seeks a wormhole in order to return more quickly to the Alpha Quadrant. The strength of the crew's desire is such that, with the exception of Seven of Nine and young Naomi Wildman (who was born on the ship), the crew are easily deluded by an alien entity in 'Bliss' who shows them the image of Earth, apparently at the end of a nearby wormhole. Only Seven's attitude towards this 'unremarkable planet' and her ability to think beyond the 'home' desires of the crew allow them to escape. In 'Timeless', Voyager's crew develop a trans-warp drive, which should cut their journey drastically; Chakotay and Ensign Kim go ahead of the vessel in the smaller 'Delta flyer', guiding Voyager through the trans-warp conduit. However, there is an error in their calculations, and the ship crashes on an ice-bound planetoid on the edge of the Alpha Quadrant, killing everyone aboard. Years later, having successfully found a ship and the means to send a message back through time, Chakotay and Ensign Kim save their 'family', therefore changing history. In the two-part finale, 'Endgame', the crew makes it home, twice. They originally achieve their goal via twenty years of effort in crossing the Delta Quadrant and reaching Federation territory. Looking back on events some ten years after Voyager's return to Earth, Janeway wants to shorten the journey home and save, amongst others, Tuvok and Seven of Nine. As a result, the ship returns home after only seven years away (the real-time duration of the series), via a Borg 'trans-warp' conduit and Janeway's reworking of history. Both 'Timeless' and 'Endgame' are superficially about individual matters of conscience or desire, but both actions wipe out decades of history for billions of other beings. Other episodes are concerned with time travel – such as 'Future's End' and 'Relativity', but in both of these the time travel occurs by accident and is a question of ensuring that the past is not disturbed – with the Temporal Prime Directive (itself from the future) as a guide.

Like *Odyssey 5*, *Seven Days* is also concerned with amending the past and rewriting history. It concerns a top-secret military project, 'Back Step', which permits time travel – backwards, for the seven days of its title. When a devastating event occurs, such as a plane crashing close to the White House (the pilot episode) or a deadly virus running riot ('The Gettysburg Virus'), Frank Parker is sent back in time with knowledge of the event. Arriving seven days before he departed, he calls his companions – who of course know nothing of the situation because for them it has yet to happen – with the codeword 'Conundrum' and engages their aid to stop a potentially fatal situation within the allotted time. 'There's Something About Olga' depicts Parker making repeated trips back to get the past exactly as he thinks it should be. The series provides a quick solution to plane crashes, plagues, military/terrorist action and so forth, but the complex rationale for why the American government and its forces should take responsibility for changing history for the rest of the world is never addressed. However, it is a clear example of rewriting history, just as the *Voyager* episodes discussed show, and, in a sense, it demonstrates an unwillingness to either take things as they come or to take full responsibility for actions.

EVENT HORIZONS

Based on the film *Stargate* (1994), *Stargate SG-1* uses wormholes on a regular basis for its intergalactic travels. The SG-1 team can 'dial' an address using a particular string of hieroglyphs written on the ancient gate-system's numerous entry points. Each hieroglyph represents a location in space-time: together, they create a wormhole that leads from the point of origin to the point of destination. Air Force Colonel Jack O'Neill, Captain, later Major, and astrophysicist Samantha Carter, archaeologist Daniel Jackson (Jonas Quinn in season six) and Teal'c, the former servant of the Gou'ald Apophis, travel to a variety of alien planets within the Stargate system. Mostly the action takes place in the present, and in the universe of our own reality, but several episodes are concerned with parallel worlds and time travel and offer some of the most interesting scenarios in the entire series. The benefit of an essentially episodic show with strong main threads is clear, although there is an underlying theme of the ongoing battle against the Gou'ald, which regular viewers can appreciate, so that they are not required to have watched every episode. A simple 'Previously on *Stargate...*' over the titles can offer the context.

A group of episodes linked by the theme of time travel, and most obviously through their titles ('2001' and '2010'), straddle the fourth and fifth seasons. They also make reference to a second-season episode;

in '1969', in which the team is accidentally sent back in time because there is a solar flare which affects the time-space co-ordinates of the planet they are 'dialling' via the Stargate – a world which lies on the opposite side of the Sun to the Earth. They walk through the gate to – the gate-room, which promptly vanishes, and they find themselves in the 1969 version of the US military's Cheyenne Mountain base. They are suspected of being Soviet spies, and a junior officer called George Hammond is in charge of their transfer to a more secure location. But the older General Hammond from the team's own time has sent a note to his younger self, requesting that he help them, and giving two dates and times as a key. The SG-1 team returns safely (via a brief trip into the future) to the 'present'.

'2010' and '2001' offer a careful time-theme sequence, and the order in which they are screened creates an extra-diegetic narrative function for the loyal audience. '2010' shows a now-defunct Stargate command ten years after a treaty has been negotiated with apparently peaceful and forward thinking humanoid aliens known as the Aschen. General Hammond is dead, Carter is married to Joe Faxon, the ambassador who negotiated the treaty, and is working on an astrophysics project with these alien friends. O'Neill has retired to his beloved log cabin to fish and the unpleasant anti-Stargate senator, Kinsey (who tried to close down the Stargate programme in 'Politics'), is now President. The war against the Gou'ald is over, and Teal'c has returned to his home world of Chulak. At the anniversary reunion, attended by Dr Frasier and the rest of the Stargate team (except O'Neill), Carter confesses that she and Joe have been trying for a child for three years. Her Aschen doctors have assured her that she is healthy, but Dr Frasier's tests show precisely the opposite: Samantha Carter cannot have children. Further research on the Aschen computer, to which Carter has some access, shows a 91% drop in the human birth rate. Instead of the short-term Gou'ald plans for the destruction of Earth, it transpires that the Aschen, who repeatedly refer to themselves as a 'patient people', are prepared to wait a couple of hundred years for dominance by reducing the birth rate through their medical 'assistance' programme.

The former SG-1 team makes plans to change history, although Dr Frasier has doubts. Contacting O'Neill, Carter finds much the same reaction as Dr Frasier's – do they have the right to try and change

8. *STARGATE SG-1*: GENERAL GEORGE HAMMOND.

history? 'You want to erase your mistakes... not happy with the way things turned out?' O'Neill says, because he alone had warned that the Aschen were too good to be true. As if the Aschen deceit were not enough, Carter finds her husband (and the President) knew that the human birth rate would be cut because 'it was unsustainable', but had expected a reduction of just 30%, not the 90% discovered. Nevertheless, as SG-1's members make their plans, they find O'Neill is with them, and once Carter predicts the next solar flare (which should create a possibility for time-travel) they set out to dial Earth's own gate, activate their old recognition signal and send a message. The Stargate is the only heavily defended point on the planet, and the team die one by one – Carter's final action is to throw the message through the Stargate's event horizon. The scene cuts to the familiar gate-room in the year 2000, and SG-1's signature code is received, much to the confusion of the SG-1 team and General Hammond. The message reads 'Under no circumstance go to P4C-970'; it is covered with blood and signed by Colonel Jack O'Neill. The address is removed from the computers but not before Carter ponders to O'Neill: 'I wonder why you sent it. I wonder *when*.'

Later in the same season, '2001' completes the chain of events for us. Whilst on the agrarian Volian homeworld, SG-1 discovers that the few thousand Volian farmers have a beneficial trade agreement and membership of something called the Aschen Federation. The SG-1 team has no knowledge of forewarning of the Aschen, but since the events occur after the regular audience seen what transpired in '2010', that audience is fully aware of the trap into which the team is walking. The Volian homeworld also has another gate code, P3A-194, so no immediate connection is made with the world deemed off-limits by O'Neill's note in '2010' warning of P4C-970. Immediately, the negotiations begin between Ambassador Faxon and the humourless Aschen Federation, and we discover their main concerns. They regard the possession of Stargate addresses as most desirable, remark upon (and remind the audience of) their patient nature and offer defensive weapons systems to Earth for protection against the Gou'ald and bio-weapons which can be coded to destroy a specific DNA base. During the negotiations, Teal'c and Daniel Jackson are digging around, quite literally; one of the local farmers has discovered 'iron-root' in his field and wants some help removing it. Beneath the grassy fields, Daniel discovers the remains of a city – but there are no bodies – and from a library he obtains a tattered newspaper. The headlines (in the alien language) say that there has been an epidemic, the Aschen arrive in spaceships offering a vaccine, but it causes something – and the 'something' is a word that Daniel cannot translate. The location of the Volian homeworld is beginning to cause concern; if the Aschen have no Stargate and limited stellar transport, within a 300 light-year radius there are only four other known planets, three of which are unexplored, and one of which is P4C-970.

At the negotiations, Carter brings various wormhole addresses for the Aschen, whilst she also enquires politely if they can translate Daniel's missing word. 'Sterility' replies the Aschen assistant. Carter manages to escape through the gate to warn Earth, just before the

Aschen release one of their biochemical weapons, but the Senator sacrifices his life to ensure she does so. As an injured Carter is taken for medical treatment, Daniel Jackson worries about the Aschen now having access to the Stargate system, but O'Neill is not concerned. Drawing upon another previous episode ('A Matter of Time'), he explains the first gate address should stop the Aschen, it 'being a black hole and all' and finishing rather grimly with the comment that the addresses 'get progressively darker after that'. The chain of events in space and time is complete.

The other type of wormhole travel is that between parallel worlds, another novum utilised by *Stargate SG-1*. If '2020' and '2001' demonstrate potential futures, and allow those futures to be changed by a warning from the possible past, the parallel world scenario also allows 'unrealised realities' to be manifested and to intertwine, albeit briefly. Whilst on an apparently deserted world in 'There But for the Grace of God', Daniel Jackson discovers a series of relics in a warehouse, including a strange kind of mirror. It is a portal and, upon touching it, Daniel is transported to a parallel universe. In this universe, the SG-1 team has not been to Abidos; Teal'c is still First Prime of Apophis; the Gou'ald are in the process of systematically destroying the Earth; Carter is a civilian astrophysicist in love with General Jack O'Neill; and Dr Catherine Langford, a woman involved with the original Stargate project, is the archaeologist assigned to the programme in what should be Daniel's place. As the Gou'ald destroy this parallel Earth, one of their motherships lands over the Cheyenne Mountain base. O'Neill is killed by loyal Jaffa Teal'c; Carter and Langford are also killed, but not before they help Jackson escape through the Stargate, and return through the portal to his own universe, to warn SG-1 of the imminent Gou'ald invasion – a story followed up in the next three episodes ('Politics', 'Within the Serpent's Grasp' and 'Serpent's Lair'). Some time later, in 'Point of View', another Samantha Carter arrives at Stargate command from Area 51, where the inter-universe portal that Daniel found is stored. She has come from another parallel universe with Kawalsky, a soldier killed in SG-1's own reality in an early episode, 'The Enemy Within'. With the team's assistance, she manages to stop the invasion of her parallel Earth.

SFX AND CGI

If series like *Stargate SG-1* and *Farscape* rely upon wormholes for their means of transport and narrative drive, they must also manifest those wormholes in a convincing fashion. Both series excel in their creative use of cgi spectacle. In its 'purest state, spectacle exists for itself, with images that dazzle and stimulate the eye (and by extension the other senses)'. Andrew Darley suggests that 'spectacle begins and ends with its own artifice, it is simultaneously both display and on display.'[12] Intentionally or not, spectacle also disrupts the flow of the action narrative: the combinations and display of exotic and strange staged events produce astonishing viewing and also exhibit their own fundamentally fabricated nature. In the past, the cost and number of sfx limited the sense of spectacle in both film and particularly in television, but now sfx are no longer 'intermittent of isolated digressions and flashes of virtuosity', but are the predominant aesthetic character of a great many sf films and television programmes.[13] *Stargate SG-1* and *Farscape* both use a great many sfx as regular ammunition in their episodes, but most exciting of all is their blending of the digital and analogue realms. This integration creates a battery of effects based upon illusionist spectacle, demonstrating the shift from storytelling to 'formal preoccupations and excitations'.[14]

The problem for the cgi effect is that ultimately it must establish a powerful illusion, the visual resemblance of reality – an analogical effect – even in scenes of the utterly fantastic. James Cameron's 1989 film *The Abyss* was one of the major breakthroughs in this seamless blending of real and unreal, and television sfx have moved on so fast that *Stargate SG-1* uses the technique on a weekly basis when its characters enter the gate. For effective cgi, the computer has 'to produce the effect of a photo-realistic representation in a scene which is conceptually fantastic in character – a scene that could have no direct correlate in real life'. This digital effect must be convincing in the film's diegesis and diegetic action, an analogue setting of high definition and high fidelity which contains real actors.[15] It does this in three ways associated with cinematic (or televisual) transparency. Discussing the pseudopod sequence in *The Abyss* (the Stargate event horizon is a direct corollary), Andrew Darley notes that three particular cinematic and diegetic aspects must be satisfied – and these are equally applicable to television. Firstly, regardless of its fantastic nature, the pseudopod has to look and behave in a credible manner. 'This involves surface or descriptive accuracy: naturalism.' Simultaneously, it must be 'alien' in relation to the characters around it to enforce the sense of difference. Secondly, it has 'to appear to occupy – to be ontologically coextensive with – the same profilmic space as the human actors. This involved the seamless combining to two differently realised sets of realistic imagery', one of which exists in real life and time, analogue and cinematic, and another that is apparently cinematic: a digital simulation. Finally, it has to integrate seamlessly into 'the diegetic dimension: the story space'.[16]

In *The Abyss*, Mary Elizabeth Mastrantonio's character appears to physically interact with the pseudopod: she touches its watery 'head' with her finger, and announces that the creature is made of salt water. This creates the seamlessness and plausible event of which Darley writes. In addition to having the SG-1 team walk through the gateway itself (an analogue 3-dimensional prop) interacting with the shimmering cgi event horizon at the moment of 'embarkation', *Stargate SG-1* frequently mobilises the camera, intensifying the belief of an actual, physical presence, tracking from behind the actors as they walk up the ramp, into a position where the gate is sideways on, so we can see the shimmering light from the event horizon to the right of our picture, along with the ramp, but only the dark gate-room to the left of the screen. As the actors reached the gate, the event horizon ripples in response to their touch, and they vanish from sight within the narrow side aspect of the gate rim *as if* they had walked through it and stepped into the wormhole. The Stargate is used in nearly every episode, and the experience of travelling through it not always commented upon, but when a new character or someone who has not travelled through the gate before encounters it, such as Ambassador Faxon in '2001', then cgi imagery of the journey itself is called upon to 'describe' his experience. This combination of innovative camera mobilisation and the constructive use of cgi ensures that the 'impossible' cinematic images are foregrounded and remarked upon by the audience.

Essentially what this technique creates is an unusual form of reception. Series such as *Stargate SG-1* dispense with a reliance solely upon the willing suspension of disbelief and acknowledge instead that 'pleasure and gratification can emerge from a different positioning' and a simultaneous pleasure in sensational image and action. The series both points to and denies its artifice, creating in its wake a new kind of formal engagement for the audience. The manner in which audiences respond to such sfx is certainly fascinating, and many journals and books are dedicated to explaining how effects are created – suggesting that there are diverse whole groups of viewers who wish to determine how the unreal is filmed – yet whilst watching the programme the same audience is paradoxically willingly to suspend its disbelief. This is a dual focus and a dual action: we gain pleasure from 'enjoying an awareness of the *process* of the illusion in which we partake'.[17] The strong humour in *Stargate SG-1* works to aid this process, drawing attention to it, whilst also balancing its spectacle. O'Neill, in particular, acts as a conduit for this on many occasions. A hologram of Anubis appears in the gate-room in 'Redemption Part 1' and threatens the Earth with destruction in the traditional manner of arch-villians: 'There is nothing that can stop the destruction I bring upon you. Prepare to meet your doom.' O'Neill looks disgusted, saying, 'Oh please, who talks like that?' He counterpoints Carter on a frequent basis as well, denying her the opportunity for her astrophysics jargon. Carter is not only an experienced combat pilot, but also a doctor of astrophysics, capable of interpreting the remarkable phenomena we see – black holes, wormholes, temporal anomalies. Her constant desire to explain everything in terms which, for the rest of the team, and probably most of the audience, equate to *The Next Generation*'s technobabble, and are frequently ridiculed by O'Neill, who repeatedly begs her to 'stop, stop it now!'

SHIFTING MODES

The sfx and technical images in sf films and television are often the central point of sf film; spaceships and battle cruisers are part of a reification of technology, but they actually disguise the technological elements for which we have true admiration – the cinematic apparatus, the technology behind the sfx. Adam Roberts takes up Jean Baudrillard's argument when he points out that the media's 'imitation of "reality" which [Baudrillard] calls the "simulacrum" has so replaced the real that it is all we have left. "Reality" has been replaced by the *hyperreality* of our simulated world.'[18] The simulated sciences of sf are much more exciting than real science because the 'technologies of reproduction, particularly in the realm of sfx, are at a far more advanced stage of development than the actual technologies of space exploration'. This is why '*Star Wars* is more fun to watch than a real shuttle launch; why the adventures of the real-life space shuttle Enterprise were so much less enthralling than the adventures of the fictional USS Enterprise'.[19]

Writing before the events of 11 September 2001, Geoff King and Tanya Krzywinska suggest that as we watch a film like *Independence Day* we can:

> experience the spectacle of New York and the White House being blown to smithereens in a convincing way, while knowing quite clearly that this is a sophisticated piece of artifice. We can enjoy the spectacular destruction of such hallowed landmarks, taking pleasure in what appears to be a highly detailed realism of images that we are unlikely to ever see in the real world. At the same time, we can enjoy the knowledge that this is not real, and that we are not so naïve as to be fooled; and, in case it matters to us, that such icons of Western democracy and power remain safely intact.[20]

However, a problem arises when this realistic unreality touches upon our own reality too firmly – when we do see a parallel act in our real world. Following September 11th, several action films showing acts of terrorism or sabotage were pulled or delayed – *Collateral Damage* (2002), for example. Images of a devastated New York in films like *Armageddon* and *Deep Impact* (both 1998) are less comfortable viewing given the grim reality of the World Trade Center's destruction and the thousands of lives lost. As a result, there are a great many contradictions inherent in such images, and our readings of the images are impacted upon to a high degree by our own life-experiences.[21] Using the *Challenger* disaster as his focus, Adam Roberts points out that as the appalling images unfolded before our eyes on television, what *Challenger* did:

> was to shift modes: from the 'real' mode of an actual launch to the SFX mode of a film. In SF films spaceships explode

all the time, and it is exciting. When *Challenger* exploded, the moment collapsed together our perceptions; that was one reason why, apart from being so terrible, it was so unsettling.[22]

Live television facilitates the kind of voyeuristic wish-fulfilment in viewers that is ordinarily legitimised by film and television drama. When this voyeurism accidentally intrudes into actual life, it becomes a tragedy of immense proportions, and as voyeurs we are riddled with guilt.

The awareness of the use of sfx brings one final point to mind. In a 1980 article about Samuel R. Delany's writings, Theresa Ebert suggests that the icons and conventions of sf are dispersing. Ebert is concerned with sf literature, but her point is applicable to all literature, not just science fiction, and also applies to television and film as well. She argues that, although mainstream sf still exists, a kind of meta-science fiction has emerged, radically reconfiguring the genre, displacing the old dominant internally, because:

> in terms of the writing conventions of science fiction, it is no longer effective – it has become 'automatized – and externally, in the context of the culture at large, it does not generate the imaginative energies it used to – the development of space technology has made it an almost routine *real* thing! The 'dominant' of postmodern science fiction consequently, has shifted, and a new aesthetic and thematic hierarchy has been established within the genre according to which the very 'fictivity' of science fiction is its primary element. It is perhaps important to emphasize that during the course of such a change none of the (older) components of science fiction is completely lost.[23]

Ebert's claim is that meta-science fiction backgrounds the traditional storytelling function and foregrounds the literary and aesthetic functions. As she says, fictivity – the fiction-ness of the story itself – has become the prime concern of the more adventurous sf author. It therefore revitalises the genre at a time when it has begun to take its own 'created reality' for granted, a tendency epitomised by the hardware-obsessed writings of Asimov, and the technobabble of *Star*

Trek: The Next Generation.[24] More importantly, it does so in an era when actual space exploration has itself become mundane, part of everyday life – the 1999 Mars Polar Lander, Beagle 2, the European Space Agency's Arianne commercial rockets, the gradual building of an international space station, the first space tourist – and when it is academically acceptable to study 'the future'. Ebert suggests that meta-science fiction: 'acquires its narrative force from laying bare the conventions of science fiction and subverting its transparent language of mimesis and believability ... it employs a self-reflexive discourse acutely aware of its own aesthetic status and artificiality.' So although examples of the old-style exploration of outer space still exist in sf, their relative position as hierarchical narrative elements within the scenario has altered.[25]

Science fiction television is now doing this, happy to draw attention to the brilliance of the cgi and other sfx it can now create and mobilising the gaze of the viewer in a process parallel to that identified by Ebert. Aside from general use of these sfx, episodes like *Deep Space Nine*'s 'Trials and Tribble-ations', *Voyager*'s 'Bride of Chaotica' and *Farscape*'s *Road Runner* cartoon parody 'Eat Me' become an absolute tribute to the technical ability of television. *Stargate SG-1*'s light-hearted 100th episode, 'Wormhole X-Treme' (2001–2002, fifth season), is a celebration of the real and unreal, and of science fiction in general, working on precisely the premise discussed by Ebert – and perhaps appropriately timed, given that sf television undoubtedly lags a little behind sf literature. Played unusually straight by Richard Dean Anderson as O'Neill and the regular SG-1 team actors, but hammed up by the fake film crew and fake Stargate team (most actually work on the real *Stargate SG-1*), it concerns 'Wormhole X-Treme', an sf series being made about intergalactic wormhole travel. Its writer and creator is Martin Lloyd, an alien with amnesia – who has previously encountered the real Stargate team in 'Point of No Return'. Unaware that his story is premised upon the truth, he is placing O'Neill's team and the real Stargate programme in danger of discovery and, under assault from a team of people from his own world, Martin has written an sf narrative, a military extravaganza reminiscent of SG-1's off-world experiences. O'Neill is assigned as the new military advisor, partly to stop Martin from endangering the real Stargate programme, but also to protect him. At the end of the episode, as Martin's own race arrive in a massive spaceship to collect him and/or his fellow alien pursuers, the 'Wormhole X-Treme' special effects staff are not impressed as they gaze up at the massive ship – they've seen much better sfx, but at least 'they can fix it in post' (production). The closing titles of the episode play with the hermeneutics and diegesis of *Stargate SG-1*: they contain 'interviews' with the '*Wormhole X-Treme*' actors, the producer is called Steve Austin (presumably in a nod to the *Six Million Dollar Man*) and the elements combine to create an exhilarating postmodern blend of 'fact' and 'fiction'.

SIX

BABYLON 5

BETWEEN THE DARKNESS
AND THE LIGHT

The previous chapters have demonstrated trends in narrative, ideology and imagery in a variety of sf series and have explored the use of language and theme. Yet none has come close to touching the ambitious complexity of *Babylon 5*, which forms the final, major case study for this book (indeed, it deserves much more). On a superficial level, *Babylon 5* offers a deceptively simple tale: after the Earth-Minbari War, a space station is established in neutral territory in the Epsilon system as a sort of United Nations in space. The five-season story is that of the station, and its inhabitants' efforts to create a new Inter-Stellar Alliance, thus ushering in a new era of peace. However, the greater arc concerns millions of years of past and future history. The voiceover to the pilot episode, spoken by Centauri Ambassador Londo Mollari, sets the scene and immediately establishes the nature of the series:

> I was there, at the dawn of the Third Age of Mankind. It began in the Earth year 2257 with the founding of the last of the Babylon stations, located deep in neutral space. It was a port of call for refugees, smugglers, businessmen, diplomats and travellers from a hundred worlds. It could be a dangerous place, but we accepted the risk because Babylon 5 was our last, best hope for peace.
>
> Under the leadership of its final Commander, Babylon 5 was a dream given form ... a dream of a galaxy without war, where species from different worlds could live side by side

9. *BABYLON 5*: RAIDER SHIP (TOP RIGHT)
ATTACKS STARFURY AND REFUGEE TRANSPORT
(SEASON 1, OPENING TITLES).

in mutual respect ... a dream that was endangered as never before by the arrival of one man on a mission of destruction.

Babylon 5 was the last of the Babylon stations. This is its story.

Five main races have a presence on the station, which is run by Earth Force military. The Centauri Empire is represented by Mollari and his aide, Vir Cotto; the Minbari Federation by Ambassador Delenn and her aide, Lennier; the Narn by G'Kar and Na'Toth; and the Vorlons by Ambassador Kosh. Although the other races, as well as representatives from the League of Non-Aligned Worlds, have ambassadors, the humans do not – first Commander Sinclair, then Captain Sheridan (or Lt. Commander Ivanova) and finally Captain Elizabeth Lochley, occupy roles as human, 'EarthGov' representatives at the Council. They also perform the administrative duties concerned with running the station, such as convening the Council, take care of security (Michael Garibaldi and Zack Allen) and medical needs (Dr Stephen Franklin) and oversee business arrangements if requested to do so (commercial telepaths Talia Winters and Lyta Alexander).

As the story of *Babylon 5* evolves, we discover that there are other major groupings and races, people who are far from committed to the peace-building ambitions of the station. First and foremost, danger comes from the Shadows, who are initially only identified by the occasional presence of the mysterious human Mr Morden. After the death of the Earth President Santiago at the end of season one, Vice-President Clark takes over; he turns out to be a Machiavellian character under the influence of the Shadows, responsible for the assassination of Santiago. His forces include the telepathic community of the Psi-Corps, represented by the Psi-Cop Alfred Bester, and a variety of organisations such as Night Watch, a Nazi-style organisation which needs no excuse to don its jackboots and dispatch terror in the name of purity and humanity. Finally, there are the ancient races known only as the First Ones, and the Drakh who are former servants of the Shadows. Following the Shadows' departure beyond the Rim and the destruction of Z'ha'dum, the Drakh seek to become masters themselves – and bring about the downfall of the Centauri Empire.

The greater narrative concerns the structuring and development of future intergalactic relations, and from the pilot episode an epic story arc is clearly and temptingly established.[1] To find out what happens, the viewer is committed to watching week after week, because resolutions may occur seasons apart. As the series progresses, so the questions mount; possible answers are given without context, leading only to more questions. This narrative structure distinguishes *Babylon 5* from the weekly resolution and gratification of other sf television and from short-term serials of mundane drama. As we have established, sf on American television is generally either episodic and discrete, episodic with some character or location linkages, or it incorporates some short- or long-term narrative threads which, although important, do not permeate the entire narrative nor place a specific demand upon the viewer that they be watched sequentially from start to finish. *Babylon 5*'s finite and unique narrative strategy lies in direct contrast to these general patterns of development.

Babylon 5's narrative follows the appropriate Greco-Roman structure for an epic tragedy, with five acts – in this case, five seasons. This structure (see Table 1) makes clear *Babylon 5*'s story arc, its poetic balance and overall epic nature.

TABLE 1: BABYLON 5 TIMESCALE

Earth years

Pre-series

1200s   *The last Shadow Conflict, Babylon 4 given to Minbari by Valen.*

2246–8   *Earth-Minbari War, Babylons 1-3 built and destroyed.*

2254   *Babylon 4 vanishes.*

2257   **Pilot – 'The Gathering'**

Introduction to main characters/station. Sinclair framed for assassination attempt on Kosh.

2258   **Season One – Equilibrium: 'Signs and Portents'**

Establishment of main characters, purpose of Babylon 5. Omens and predictions of the emerging threat of the Shadows. Babylon 4 reappears. Death of Earth President Santiago.

2259   **Season Two – Disruption : 'The Coming of Shadows'**

Sinclair assigned to Minbar as Ambassador. Sheridan assigned to Babylon 5. Increasing threat of Shadows. War between Centauri and Narn. Sheridan introduced to Rangers. Sheridan and Delenn tested by Vorlon inquisitor. Centauri assassin attempts to kill Sheridan.

2260   **Season Three – Conflict: 'Point of No Return'**

Shadow War, Civil War on Earth and Colonies. Babylon 5 declares independence. White Star Fleet deployed. Sinclair and Babylon 4 sent back 1,000 years. New Alliance formed between Narn, Minbar, Non-Aligned Worlds and Babylon 5 to fight the Shadows. Sheridan goes to Z'ha'dum.

2061	**Season Four – Repelling of Disruptive Force: 'No Surrender, No Retreat'**

Sheridan returns from Z'ha'dum with Lorien. Garibaldi used by Bester. The Shadows, Vorlons, First Ones and Lorien leave for beyond the Rim. War against Clark's Earth Forces. Civil war on Minbar. Sheridan captured, tortured, finally rescued. Marcus dies to save Ivanova. Earth saved from Clark's 'Scorched Earth' attempt. Sheridan and Delenn marry. New Inter-Stellar Alliance created. Earth invited to join. Ivanova accepts deep space assignment.

2062	**Season Five – Restoration of Equilibrium: 'No Compromises'**

Sheridan becomes President of Alliance. Captain Elizabeth Lochley appointed to run Babylon 5. Byron's martyrdom/Telepath crisis. Fall of Centauri Prime. Londo becomes Emperor under Drakh control. Inter-Stellar Alliance Headquarters established on Minbar. Lyta and G'Kar leave Babylon 5 to explore. Franklin becomes head of Xenobiology Division on Earth. Garibaldi and Lise Hampton take over Edgars' Industries on Mars.

Post-series

2278	*Delenn and Sheridan go to Centauri Prime to save their son, David, from the Drakh. Death of Londo and G'Kar. Vir becomes Emperor.*

2281	*Babylon 5 decommissioned and destroyed. Sheridan passes beyond the Rim. Ivanova becomes Leader of Rangers, Delenn takes over as Leader of Alliance.*

1,000,000	*The collapse of the Sun and destruction of the solar system.*

Despite some unevenness enforced by the lack of commitment (from Warner Bros.) and uncertainty about renewal for the final season (eventually through the Turner Network), the overall story remains clear. In some ways, that very uncertainty demanded a tying-up of most major/cosmic threads before the end of season four, and brought about a more sustained examination of the post-Shadow War situation, and the cost of independence on a more local scale, relatively speaking, in season five. This means that the episodes appear more as groupings of narrative threads, although collectively they still contribute to the overall arc of the series – almost a mirror of the early episodes in season one, which appear discrete but actually create a foundation for the overall arc.

The grim penchant for relentless paranoia in modern sf series makes a post-war space station located in neutral territory a curious choice as the setting for a new ideological dynamic. *Deep Space Nine*'s post-war scenario relies almost exclusively upon its nearby wormhole for adventure, whilst *Mercy Point* (1998) is a medical drama: *M*A*S*H* meets *ER* in space. However, the timing and location of *Babylon 5* are just the beginning of the series' subversion. Rather than stating that the future only lies somewhere 'out there', in exploration, conquest and/or empire,[2] in *Babylon 5* the future is all around. The meaning and existence of the station itself has as much bearing upon its past, present and future as do the beings associated with it, finding resonance in all that is said and thought and done, and emerges triumphant in that which the station comes to symbolise. Because Babylon 5 was, it also is and will be; because it will be, it also was and is. Time and space are confused with time and place in *Babylon 5*; the station exists literally and symbolically across and through time, simultaneously diachronic and synchronic.

PHILOSOPHICAL AND NARRATIVE STRATEGIES

A striking aspect of *Babylon 5* is that it does not shy away from discussing belief systems. One of its central themes articulates a dissection of the western world's dominant belief system – binarism, the fundamental reliance upon binary oppositions such as good and evil, black and white or day and night. It also quickly dispenses with the idea of some divine Manifest Destiny and refutes the basis of most dominant institutionalised religions – the concept of a creator controlling and rewarding or punishing his/her inventions, or merely standing by to watch their struggles. Most sf series avoid theological exploration, maintaining a strictly secular approach unless the theology concerned can be defined mythically – Norse, Greek or Roman – or as an exotic alien element, such as the wormhole aliens in *Deep Space Nine*. *Stargate SG-1* touches upon this theme with the transcendence of Daniel Jackson in 'Meridian' at the end of the fifth season and his rebirth in season seven's first episode, 'Fallen'.

However, although *Babylon 5* quarrels with institutional religion, it has no intention of debunking the concept of faith itself. The sharing of religious ceremonies in 'Parliament of Dreams' and 'Ceremonies of Light and Dark' is treated with dignity, whilst 'Convictions' shows Brother Theo and his fellow monks as useful members of society, not secluded holy-men on mysterious errands. Many episodes have religious titles – 'Believers', 'A Voice in the Wilderness', 'Revelations' and 'Passing Through Gethsemane' – whilst others involve personal spiritual quests which we are urged to respect, such as 'Grail'.[3] The first in a long line of people representing Earth's belief systems in 'Parliament of Dreams' is an atheist; in *Babylon 5* no ideology is still an ideology and thus, regardless of its source, 'faith manages'.[4] Nevertheless, *Babylon 5* carefully avoids any commitment to a particular deity, demonstrating instead a universal interconnectedness. This is most strongly iterated in the time-travelling episodes. Zathras' comments to Ivanova in the time rift in 'War Without End' Part 2 underline this.[5] When Ivanova suggests they are taking too long, Zathras reminds her that whereas they are both finite, they 'cannot run out of time. There is infinite time.' The episode constitutes a calculus-worthy example of 'infinity within the finite'.

The series carefully maintains that life forms have a soul – or spirit – and is perhaps the first sf programme to seriously suggest an existence beyond death. 'Soul Hunter' is the most detailed example, and 'The Paragon of Animals', courtesy of Lyta's telepathic scan, offers glimpses of a corridor of brilliant light along which a dying Ranger travels – one remarkably similar to the light announcing Lorien's return in 'Sleeping in Light'. The deceased who appear in 'The Day of the Dead' are far from the Gothic's ghoulish undead.

To 'pass beyond the Rim' or 'to go beyond the Veil' is physical as well as metaphorical: it does not represent the end of existence, merely the end of a stage of existence. Those who return are aware that they are dead, but reticent about the idea that they bring with them with some sort of astounding cosmic awareness. They seemed unchanged, yet they actually do bring knowledge. With characteristic relish, Morden reveals to a stunned Lennier that he will betray that which he holds sacred, the *Anla'shok* (the Rangers), and thus Delenn. Zoe, a substance-abusing friend from Lochley's wild youth, brings forgiveness for the Captain, and a message for Sheridan from the first Kosh. In turn, Sheridan's parting words in 'Sleeping in Light' are a gentle, awed, 'Well, look at that, sun's coming up', suggestive not of death but of metamorphosis. *Babylon 5* thus suggests that life in all its diversity – whether the universe itself, magnificent and timeless, or the finite beings inhabiting it, or the smallest sub-molecular particles – is sentient, integral, and thus eternally connected. The Minbari articulate this most clearly, rejecting the idea of a god and instead choosing a more secular, yet still spiritual, philosophy.[6] In 'Passing Through Gethsemane', we learn that they believe 'that the universe itself is conscious in a way we can never truly understand. It is engaged in a search for meaning, so it breaks itself apart, investing its own consciousness in every form of life. We are the universe, trying to understand itself.'[7]

The idea of conscious philosophical action reverberates throughout the series. Delenn suggests in 'The Gathering' that Sinclair does not spend enough time thinking about the significance of the ripples and intersections made by the rocks dropped into the fine sand in the Japanese stone garden. In 'A Distant Star', she tells Sheridan that 'We are the universe made manifest.' In the diegesis of *Babylon 5*, any word or action has an impact upon surrounding events: as we will see, however minor, casual, or flippant, nothing is unimportant and everything is connected. This is just one of the strategies that maintain audience interest in the series without too many revelations at too early a stage. Intrinsic to the narrative is a tendency for the odd early phrase or image to resonate throughout the series, usually in unexpected ways. Although the immediate mystery of Kosh's attempted assassination in 'The Gathering' is solved we are left with nothing but contextual questions. Why Babylon 5, for example? In

'Grail', Jinxo is frightened of leaving the station because he left the previous stations (Babylons 1, 2 and 3) only to see them destroyed. By whom, we wonder? Babylon 4, meanwhile, mysteriously vanished. Where? We thus remain none the wiser but the suspense and tension are considerably increased. These and other questions are partly answered in the later episode 'Signs and Portents', and questions established in that episode are partly answered in 'Babylon Squared' and 'War Without End'. However, 'Signs and Portents' also dangles an irresistible narrative carrot when the Centauri seer Lady Ladira offers Commander Sinclair a glimpse of the station's fiery future destruction, an image which remains distressingly unexplained and uncontextualised for over four years until the series' finale, 'Sleeping in Light'.

In the first season, episodes mostly reach a satisfactory conclusion with the immediate narrative concerns addressed or at least left at an appropriate moment. However, the careful combination of the overall story arc with additional narrative threads, replete with uncontextualised visual and verbal hints, ensures that, although sufficient small questions are answered, new and more significant ones are constantly posed. In line with Noel Carroll's theories of the macro- and micro-questions involved in the creation of a suspense narrative, this makes present viewing gratifying but future viewing a significant requirement.[8] It is just one of the ways in which *Babylon 5* plays with the concept of episodic and serial television. *Babylon 5* requires much the same degree of thought and attention externally, from its viewers, as it requires internally, from its characters, a risky, innovative strategy. Strong narrative continuity is a strength, but also one of the programme's weaknesses. Given the lack of verbal redundancy (so common to soap opera) in the series, there is little opportunity to 'catch up': in order to remain comprehensible to its viewers, the series demands complete commitment over a five year period, expecting to quickly catch its audience's attention, and assuming that it can maintain interest for the duration.

STORY ARCS

A useful example of how *Babylon 5*'s story arc emerges is revealed in 'Signs and Portents'/'Sleeping in Light' and 'In the Shadow of

Z'ha'dum'/'Into the Fire'. Lady Ladira's terrifying vision of the station's destruction is only 'a possible future', and she tells Sinclair that 'it is my hope that you may yet avoid it.' Of course, the characters *do* avoid the fire. The images of an assault on Babylon 4 hinted at in 'Babylon Squared' and Ivanova's desperate emergency broadcast in 'War Without End' Part 1, do not herald the destruction of the station. They are merely future-flashes, and as the story carefully establishes, the future is uncertain. Ultimately, Babylon 5 *is* encircled by Shadow vessels in 'Z'ha'dum', its inhabitants *are* forced to walk either metaphorically or physically 'through fire and darkness'[9] during the Shadow War, the liberation of Earth and the Minbari Civil War, and the fiery obliteration of the station *still* takes place. It simply does not occur in any expected or anticipated manner: in 'Sleeping in Light' the station is indeed blown up in a fiery spectacle – but only so as not to become a shipping hazard.[10]

Thus, although we receive tantalising information about its fate almost from the outset, the station's demise is brought about not by military action or grandiose expansionist politics, as we may have speculated, but by sheer practicality. It certainly occurs because of Sheridan and Delenn's new Alliance, but through its success, not failure. Babylon 5's ignoble demolition is a far cry from the five seasons of desperate courage in adversity demonstrated by its crew against determined invaders. A mundane everyday decision decrees its fate. In *Babylon 5*, everything is interconnected; we simply do not appreciate the context because it is seldom immediately revealed. Ivanova's characteristically gloomy prediction in 'Signs and Portents' echoes through the series – 'No boom today. Boom tomorrow. There's *always* a boom tomorrow' – and Ivanova is notably the one whose last moments we see in 'War Without End', and who is critically wounded during the assault on Clark's forces in 'Between the Darkness and the Light'.[11] *Babylon 5* has systematically denied its audience's expectations from the outset; although the station is not destroyed by the anticipated 'boom', it *is* still destroyed and the imagery of its destruction is that of Ladira's prophetic vision. There is indeed '*always* a boom tomorrow'. As ever, until the last, we are consistently denied any reliable framework or context and thus must struggle to create meaning as we go – an important facet of sf narration, as noted previously.

A second strong example of the overall arc structure occurs in the fourth season's 'Into the Fire', an episode containing most disturbing signs of universal connection and a clear example of narrative preplanning. On Centauri Prime, with the Vorlons approaching and the Shadow-touched planet under threat of destruction, Londo executes the Shadow's operative, Morden. Summoning Vir, he tells him to go out in the garden, where he has a surprise for him: Morden's head is on a pike. During season two's 'In the Shadow of Z'ha'dum', Vir is forced to meet Morden on Londo's behalf. Morden seizes the opportunity to ask Vir the Shadows' question: 'What do *you* want?' The inoffensive Centauri aide replies sweetly:

> I'd like to live long enough to be there when they cut off your head and stick it on a pike as a warning to the next ten generations that some favours come with too high a price. I want to look up into your lifeless eyes and wave – like this. Can you and your associates arrange that for me, Mr Morden?

Two seasons, two *years* later, 'Into the Fire' offers Vir an opportunity to recall the conversation, and to give Morden's 'lifeless eyes' that little wave. If the universe has a sense of humour, like its poetry, it is based in irony. Even at a table in a quiet bar in the Zocalo, with no one else apparently privy to their conversation, Vir's words create ripples.[12] Lady Ladira says as much: 'we create the future, with our words, our deeds and our beliefs.' The story unfolding before us demonstrates precisely this point.

HISTORY

The Babylon 5 station was built by humans, the youngest of the space-faring races and a natural choice as caretakers for its diplomatic mission. For the audience, the Earth Force command staff afford an acceptable connection between our present and the imaginary future history from the Earth year 2258. As the series commences, repeated references to the Minbari surrender at the Battle of the Line suggest that humans hold considerable sway as they enter the 'Third Age of Mankind'. This is underlined by the consistent war-like bickering of the other races, although as the narrative progresses it is clear that the humans share a propensity for splitting into warring factions. 'The Gathering' tells briefly of the Minbari surrender, but gives no reasons for it; at least superficially, they represent a defeated race. The first episode's pre-credits sequence sees the Narn, bitter from years of Centauri occupation, launch a devastating attack on a Centauri colony/listening post at Ragesh 7 ('Midnight on the Firing Line'). These Centauri/Narn skirmishes spark increasingly violent retaliations until war breaks out in 'The Coming of Shadows'.

Despite being run by humans, Babylon 5 contains marvellous diversity within its spinning shell. It would be daring sf television indeed that established a minor human contingent living on a station run predominantly by aliens, of course. *Farscape*'s John Crichton may be the only human in the uncharted territories but significantly he is not the only *humanoid*: of the regular Moya crew only Rygel and Pilot (and, to a lesser extent, D'Argo) differ extensively from that in appearance. The innovative concept over humans as a minority is given a disturbing bias in 'The Illusion of Truth' by an Inter-Stellar News (ISN) report. There are repeated rumblings from human isolationist movements such as 'Earth First' and the 'Home Guard', and constant anti-alien prejudice, articulated mostly through Clark's 'MiniPax' forces,[13] and 'Nightwatch'. Whilst the diegetic critique of intolerance is strong, the representation of the lesser alien species, particularly in the first season, is occasionally disturbing. Whilst we become increasingly familiar with the ways of the Narn, Centauri and Minbari as time is spent explaining their characteristics, the remainder of the aliens, who chiefly inhabit the alien zone where breathing apparatus must be donned, represent little more than a freak show. Glass walls separate species, whilst the predominantly human bipeds walk past, able to watch at will. This tendency rapidly evaporates: by season two, the unattractive exoticism of the alien 'zoo' is replaced by other, larger concerns as the major story arc comes into play, and the threat of the Shadows is developed.

Nevertheless, within the diegesis of *Babylon 5*, although individuals of each race act according to their individual nature, the qualities ascribed to humans and the capabilities of collective humanity are repeatedly shown to be both positive and important. Summoned to the Minbari Grey Council to be appointed leader, Delenn asks to remain on Babylon 5, commenting upon the remarkable ability she sees in humans. Guided by Valen/Sinclair's prophecy, she sacrifices the short-term honour of Minbari leadership for the potential greater good of the galaxy. In 'And Now for a Word', she again marks out humans as having an extraordinary talent. Asked by ISN reporter Cynthia Torqueman, whose 'special report' is as twisted as her name, if the Babylon station is worth the money and effort involved, Delenn says that it is, for a simple reason:

> Humans share one unique quality: they build communities. If the Narns or the Centauri or any other race built a station like this it would be used only by their own people. But overywhere that humano go, thoy oroato communitios out of diverse and sometimes hostile populations. It is a great gift and a terrible responsibility, one that cannot be abandoned.

From an historical approach, the sense of building communities and alliances from these 'diverse and sometimes hostile populations' relates more readily to a vast array of predominantly American but also worldwide historical moments. Colonialism offers an unpleasant memory here, but more positively the replacement of the League with the new Alliance parallels the League of Nations with the United Nations. *Babylon 5* also refers eponymously to the original Babylon, and to the epic of Gilgamesh, the Great Builder.[14] In political construction, the series clearly draws upon this but, more fundamentally, it utilises the creation myths of ancient Babylon, which tell how the universe was formed through the eternal conflict of two forces, chaos and order – the Shadows and Vorlons. *Babylon 5* is not about ancient Babylon,[15] but the choice of name is no coincidence. The mytho-history of that ancient land offers a foundation for the future scenario. History itself is fundamental to *Babylon 5*'s cause. The three-race alliance of human, Minbari and Narn (with support from the non-aligned worlds – and intermittent, indirect Centauri involvement) begins a war against the Shadows, but ultimately ends up fighting Shadows and Vorlons (and again, indirectly, the Centauri). The new Alliance's victory against the Shadows and Vorlons in 'Into the Fire' is more ideological than military and, unlike the ancient Babylonian alliances, what is then forged between the other races is no mere marriage of convenience.

IDEOLOGY

The destruction of the Narn regime, the collapse of the Centauri Empire, Clark's suicide, the pseudo-Earth Shadow forces and the Civil War on Minbar are tragic confirmations of the chaos caused by adherence to ancient binary oppositions. In seeking to create a new beginning, Sheridan and Delenn do not intend to merely build a new empire for themselves in the pattern of the old. They clearly have no such intention: they merely seek reasoned justice – although the 'special report' from ISN in 'The Illusion of Truth' suggests otherwise. The new Inter-Stellar Alliance rejects dictated binary choices, working instead around more fluid ethical and secular constructs for the benefit of all. There is no right way or wrong way, no absolutes, there are only various paths – some of which are more egalitarian, more positive in the long term and thus preferable to others. The Rangers will act as an interplanetary police force, drawing its members from all Alliance worlds – each neighbour will look after the other. The long-term viability of this new way is not really put to the test within *Babylon 5*'s story world; however, Delenn's voiceover at the end of 'Rising Star' offers an historical glimpse of the future and demonstrates realistic despair as well as fervent hope:

> It was the end of the Earth year 2261, and it was the dawn of a new age for all of us. It was the end of one chapter and the beginning of another. The next twenty years would see great changes: great joy and great sorrow, the Telepath War, and the Drakh War. The new Alliance would waver and crack, but in the end it would hold, because what is built endures, and what is loved endures, and Babylon 5 – Babylon 5 endures.

Babylon 5 openly identifies explicit ideological aspirations throughout its run, asserting a docu-historical strategy from the beginning. Intermittently, it highlights this perspective, and with the effective narrative closure of its final episode reminds us jarringly that we have been watching 'historical records'.[16] In this, and in a variety of other methods we shall explore, it achieves what sf does at its best: it creates a degree of cognitive estrangement. It rejects what we can readily recognise and offers instead new scenarios and perspectives for exploration and consideration, even as we demonstrate our reluctance to accept them. According to Straczynski, *Babylon 5*'s core meaning centres upon choice and responsibility; it is 'about our obligation to society, to each other, and to the future. It reminds us that actions have consequences, and that we must choose wisely if we wish to avoid extermination. Will we decide to lead, or to be led by others?'[17]

In Brechtian terms, James Brown finds that *Babylon 5*'s approach 'encourages one to think only "within the confines of the subject", rather than about it, in the stream rather than above it'.[18] This is a substantial problem for serial sf television: the longer the immersion in the alien world, the less alien it becomes. In series like *The Outer Limits* or *Welcome to Paradox*, the audience linkage is provided by the introductory voiceover or the location, whilst the story itself is discrete, lasting a mere 40 minutes or so. Series with longer story threads, like *Deep Space Nine* or even the occasionally revisited stories in *Stargate SG-1*, risk the audience's total submersion in the story: familiarity sets in rapidly and the familiar is science fiction's nemesis. The story world becomes predictable, we are put at ease by its recognisable theme music and credit sequences, location and establishing shots, readily understandable language, unchanging characters, etc. Unless poetic techniques similar to those identified by the Formalists are used to combat this effacement of signification – neologisms, transformed language, arcane or roughened language, juxtapositional and challenging visuals, significant character evolution etc. – we do indeed retreat within the cosy 'confines of the subject' *Babylon 5* takes pains to ensure this does not occur. Its characters, its imagery and its articulation of reality are in constant flux. Just as its characters are forced daily to renegotiate the political and personal situations in which they become embroiled, the institutions which they have previously taken for granted – even the station itself – so too are its viewers, denied the omniscience or semi-omniscience common to other television programmes. Sometimes this is subtle, sometimes it is more overt, as we shall see.

Brown's criticism of the series stems from his primary concern: industrial technology. Whereas *Babylon 5*'s mostly unacknowledged presence of technology (and capitalism), linked with a strong individualism 'and religion of some kind,' resoundingly echoes of 'the American way,' Brown's suggestion largely ignores the series' ambitions for balance. He walks perilously close to the trap of ideological polarity, of which *Star Trek* and its peers have historically fallen foul. If not 'their way', there is only the 'wrong way'. Yet I would argue that this is precisely what *Babylon 5* transcends. Its reality does not conveniently dispense with the ugly trappings of the world we recognise (iniquitous capitalism, social unrest, disaffection, etc.) in order to do so. Faced with the type of conflict born of class, duty or honour brought about by extreme political or military ideology, *Babylon 5* suggests fresh solutions. These are frequently condemned as politically naïve, as are Vir's ambassadorial reports from Minbar which Londo rewrites because they are too positive and enlightened, and the Minbari must be seen in a negative light ('Point of No Return' and 'Dust to Dust'), but this only serves to narrate the shift between the old and new orders we see jostling for position in *Babylon 5*. Vir's reports are honest and open, not couched in political jargon, prejudice or conceit. Sinclair and Sheridan create equally honest and open solutions to their problems and have no truck with political and military posturing or sabre-rattling. Whilst the new Alliance is being forged, Sheridan and Delenn certainly resort on occasion to manipulation – but always in the interests of the greater good, and they invariably demonstrate discomfort with the process.

Babylon 5 articulates a more plausible international vision of the future than sf television in the USA has ever previously attempted. Its primary goal is balance, a middle way – not some new and dogmatic ideological hegemony. In 'The Long Night', G'Kar remarks to the newly freed Narns that he 'did not fight to remove one dictator just to become another myself'. The very strength of this future vision is that it does not have all the answers: it is thus flexible. Commencing with a philosophical stance, Stephen R. Clark believes that most of us are:

> rational realists ... [who] believe that people may have different, and diverse, opinions, but that there are universal truths without self-contradictions ... To find scientific truths as firm as moral truths we have to embark on scientific theory: quarks are the same wherever we may be, though living creatures, crystals, rock formations differ unpredictably.[19]

He suggests that 'the moral if not the dramatic conclusion' of *Babylon 5* demands we take responsibility for our own destiny, and in doing so it merely rearticulates a desire for that same neutral path between demons and angels sought by artists and philosophers in perpetuity.[20]

Babylon 5 is entirely of its time, offering a kind of liberal New Age spirituality that locates 'God within the individual and evolved consciousness', although Kevin McCarron criticises its 'robust, even aggressive, faith in the endurance of capitalism, individualism, and humanism.'[21] If sf's preoccupations are essentially of its time, *Babylon 5* demonstrates only what *we* recognise from the era of its making. Along with the worst facets of individualism, western capitalism is enduring all too well, and this is a problem for those seeking to create a plausible, more egalitarian vision of the future. *Babylon 5* comments wryly on the horrors of capitalism in 'Acts of Sacrifice' through the visiting Lumati, who are favourably impressed by the effects of human capitalism when they see the poverty of the Lurkers. However, it is not so much the philosophy itself that is of primary interest, but more the timing of the desire to articulate it. *Babylon 5* is a definitive product of its cultural era – one of turmoil, desperate for diverse and troubled humanity to find a means of peaceful coexistence. Ultimately, *Babylon 5*'s epic approach, combined with its novelistic romances, only enhances its labyrinthine tendencies; its story may be complete, but even in that it denies us an absolute historical truth: it only offers unsettling and oftentimes unfamiliar choices.

These choices are echoed in *Babylon 5*'s articulation of its desire for peace and in G'Kar's 'Declaration of Principles' for the new Alliance, which celebrates unity and difference. Despite the establishment of a new Alliance, it has no ambitions for enforced homogeneity. The history of Earth – notably American history – is frequently referred to as a bloody example of why this would fail. Not only do we have the recent Earth-Minbar War, which erupted through a terrible First Contact misunderstanding, but also resentful colonies on Mars and Proxima. We find a yet more tangible connection in San Diego, which has been laid waste by atomic weapons which fell into the hands of terrorists following the collapse of the old Soviet Union. Like a soap opera, *Babylon 5* draws on present public fears and concerns to articulate its future. Unlike a soap opera, it cannot provide the continuous 'working through' of contemporary issues identified by Ellis, although it functions in a recognisable annual cycle, celebrating

Hanukkah, Christmas and New Year (as well as various alien festivals) and so retains a necessary degree of co-presence. The contrast of the familiar with the unfamiliar thus heightens both the degree of estrangement and (re)cognition.

Nor does *Babylon 5* blanche from reminding us that short-term worries are merely minor variants of long-term fears. The plague that wipes out the Markab in 'Confessions and Lamentations' has clear associations with AIDS and AIDS denial, and the growing cynicism and discontent about politics and politicians is appropriately extrapolated. In 'Voices of Authority', we learn that Clark arranged for the assassination of President Santiago in an action parallel to that of Shadow-influenced Emperor Cartagia (who is prepared to see Centauri Prime burn as a funeral pyre lighting his way to godhood). In a parallel move, and rather than facing the consequences of his own actions, Clark turns Earth's satellite defences on itself in 'Endgame'. *Babylon 5*'s protagonists must endure disease and fear, conflict and war before they can begin to build a future.

That future is by no means entirely peaceful, nor at any stage does it appear to desire conformity. In a sense it is earned, and there are only two minor characters who emerge relatively unscathed after five years – Vir Cotto and Zack Allen. Everyone else must pay a high price, whether through choice or manipulation, action or inaction. Characters change, Delenn, Sheridan, Sinclair and Lyta change outwardly or physically as well as psychologically. Others, like G'Kar and Londo evolve in more philosophical ways. Although it echoes the nobler desires for an idyllic new community and the brave foresight of the pioneer movement across the American West, *Babylon 5* avoids both the pitfalls of the false homogeneity of a White Anglo-Saxon Protestant predestination and the potential destruction of anything 'other' in its path. Science fiction's ability to create what Suvin identifies as cognitive estrangement is a subversion of our patterns of reference. This allows us to at least confront that which we consider abject, rather than merely reverting to binary notions of 'good' or 'bad', 'us' or 'non-us'. Delenn's claim for humanity stresses the importance of meeting-places like Babylon 5.[22] Her change from Minbari to human-Minbari hybrid, and Sinclair's later transformation into Valen, confirms this. On a smaller level, the alterations the Vorlons make to Lyta and Sheridan's connection with Kosh also stress this. Through their actions, a genuine sense of community is created gradually within the universe of Babylon 5, yet another subversion of television sf tradition.

The concept of an idyllic, fully co-operative interplanetary community is a theme common in sf. However, unlike the pre-designed communal manifestations of *Star Trek*'s Federation, which present their aspirations as a fait accompli, we join *Babylon 5*'s characters in their struggle to make a better future. When *Babylon 5* commences, its community-based ambitions are far from realised. The station has been operational for a little over a year in the 2257 pilot; by 2258, the planetary forces are still constantly feuding, the peace is under construction. It is not already created through a structuring absence that conveniently requires no explanation of the effort and sacrifices involved.[23] In a sense, series like *Star Trek* avoid the moral struggles, sacrifices, histories and, more importantly, the objectivity of the epic: they merely present a de facto ideal society in which to explore personal relationships. It is a more comforting format for the viewer and, of course, less challenging. It can be argued that *Babylon 5*'s representation of the mundane within the station itself does precisely this: the continuation of recognisable human activities such as buying and selling denies the potential of sf. However, as we noted earlier from Suvin's identification of sf's efforts to show us 'how we got there', it is the necessary linkage of the mundane reality of the present *and* of the future in juxtaposition with the extraordinary, which creates an effective degree of cognitive estrangement. A door will always be a door, but the manner in which it is presented, perceived, and thus experienced, will change across time.

HISTORY AND SCIENCE FICTION AS CONTEXT

If some sf series isolate themselves from history, *Babylon 5*, as I am beginning to demonstrate, is all about history and context. *Babylon 5* underlines a need to remember how the history that it is writing is interconnected. It also refers constantly to human history and to the history of science fiction. We have already mentioned the more obvious significance of its name via its associations with the battles of unification in ancient Babylonia and the Shadows and the Vorlons as entrenched cold warriors. Piled on these is example after example, each cast in a different light because each is stripped of its usual context. 'Nightwatch' recreates the danger of a Nazi Holocaust, the mass-driver attack on Narn is a devastating reminder of the carpet-bombing of Vietnam and the Battle of the Line reminds us of the flotilla of little ships at Dunkirk or perhaps the Spitfires and Hurricanes of the Battle of Britain. Clark and Cartagia's ghastly vision of the destruction of Earth and Centauri Prime are terrifying global echoes of General Sherman's Scorched Earth campaign in the American Civil War[24] and the killing fields of Pol Pot's Cambodia. These are all examples of action; more frightening is the ideology behind them and how the words 'of somebody we are taught to admire, such as Thomas Jefferson, find their way into the mouth of a member of the Nazi-like Nightwatch ('Eternal vigilance is the price of freedom': 'Messages from Earth'), and force us to consider the real meaning of liberty.'[25]

In 'Voices of Authority', Sheridan's temporary and unwanted 'political advisor', Julie Musante, makes a casual remark about the dictionary being 'rewritten'. She later also makes chilling speech, which is Orwell's *Nineteen Eighty-Four* made manifest, espousing the dictates of totalitarian regimes and individual extremists from across the twentieth-century world:

> In the coming months, certain individuals will be purged from their government positions on charges of sedition, immoral conduct, even spying for alien governments. With our basic freedoms at stake no response can be too extreme. There may be some minor and temporary abridgements in the traditionally protected areas of speech and association, but only until the crisis is over. We have been betrayed at nearly every level. It is going to take the efforts of every loyal citizen to keep Earth safe and ideologically pure.

In its diegetic and ex-diegetic fight against such tyranny, *Babylon 5* offers countless warnings of the dangers alongside examples of more honourable paths. 'In the Shadow of Z'ha'dum' sees Sheridan refer to the breaking of the Enigma Code, the subsequent bombing of Coventry and the apocryphal tale of the sacrifice Churchill was prepared to make in order to win the war, not just the battle. Sheridan draws a direct parallel with his enforced decision to release Morden.

He realises that Morden may be able to tell him what happened to his wife Anna, missing, presumed dead, after the Icarus' journey to the Z'ha'dum, but knows that the needs of the greater battle, against the Shadows, cannot be sacrificed. The name of the Icarus is portentous: if the Icarus of legend flew too close to the sun, the Icarus' exploration to the Rim took its crew too far – to where they did not belong. The Ikkarans in the early episode 'Infection' are little different, the name also redolent of rash adventurism; their crime, however, was to place their trust in the purity of their race and the logic of defensive machinery. Like Colossus in *The Forbin Project* and Skynet in *The Terminator*, the logically based technology decided to destroy the Ikkarans themselves, thus ensuring their preservation and purity. The spectre of the solution for countless My Lai massacres echoes chillingly through these stories: the village had to be destroyed in order to be saved.

The most familiar phrase in *Babylon 5*, the 'last best hope' of the early title sequences, also has American connections. Part of Sheridan's introductory speech in 'Points of Departure', it actually comes from Lincoln's second address to Congress in 1862:

> It was an early Earth President, Abraham Lincoln, who best described our situation. He said: 'The dogmas of the quiet past are inadequate to the stormy present. The occasion is piled high with difficulty and we must rise to the occasion. We cannot escape history. We will be remembered in spite of ourselves. The fiery trial through which we pass will light us down in honor or dishonor to the last generation. We shall nobly win or meanly lose our last best hope of Earth.'[26]

Superficially, it is a wise choice, given that Lincoln is viewed historically as being responsible for a desire to reunify the United States of America and for the ending of slavery. The souls of the nation were to be brought together, so to speak – and this is one of the quests in *Babylon 5*: not just unification and equality but, for the Minbari in particular, a bringing together of Minbari and human souls. In 'Points of Departure', Lennier explains the Minbari surrender at the Battle of the Line, telling Sheridan that Minbari souls are being reborn in humans: in a way the Minbari and humans were killing their own. The marriage of Sheridan and the transformed Delenn is a manifestation of this symbolic linkage of the souls, as are their similar experiences as leaders. Perhaps more importantly, the choice of Lincoln offers an example of how political history creates its own myth. James and Mendlesohn suggest that whilst Abraham Lincoln issued an edict and freed slaves, in his inaugural address he also said "'If I could save the union without freeing any slaves, I would do it; and if I could save the union by freeing all the slaves I would do it." Fortunately for African-Americans, the latter proved to be true, but the emancipation edict of 1862 freed slaves only in the rebel-held territories and was an attempt to create a fifth column, not a generous and humanitarian gesture. Slavery was maintained in the four Union slave states until the end of the war. A better choice might have been Harriet Tubman or Oskar Schindler.'[27] *Babylon 5*'s 'Deconstruction of Falling Stars' examines this very issue. An archive episode, set in the far future, it travels through time via historical records, examining how the story of Sheridan and Delenn's new Alliance has been interpreted, reinterpreted and rewritten by historians, politicians and the media. History is a matter of perspective. It points out in no uncertain terms how *Babylon 5* is fundamentally about knowing your own history, being true to it, and learning from it, lest you be condemned to repeat it – or lest it be used against you.

'In the Shadow of Z'ha'dum' provides Delenn and Kosh with an opportunity to teach Sheridan part of the galactic history of which he knows so little – but which he must learn if he is to understand the great battle ahead. Delenn says, in typically marked poetic language:

> There are beings in the universe much older than either of our races ... Once, long ago, they walked among the stars like giants, vast and timeless, they taught the younger races, explored beyond the Rim, created great empires. But to all things there is an end. Slowly, over a million years, the First Ones went away. Some passed beyond the stars, never to return. Some simply disappeared ...

> The Shadows were old when even the ancients were young. They battled one another over and over across a million years. The last great war against the Shadows was ten thousand years ago. It was the last time the ancients walked openly among us. But the Shadows were only defeated, not destroyed. A

thousand years ago the Shadows returned to their places of power, rebuilt them and began to stretch forth their hand. Before they could strike, they were defeated by an alliance of worlds including the Minbari and the few remaining First Ones who had not yet passed beyond the Veil. When they had finished, the First Ones went away – all but one.[28]

The remaining 'one' to whom she refers is Kosh. Her speech tells Sheridan the history she believes to be appropriate for him to hear, she is tailoring it to suit her needs, and only when pressed by Sheridan does she admit 'not all of the First Ones have gone away. A few stayed behind, hidden or asleep, waiting for the day when they may be needed – when the Shadows come again.' Kosh stays hidden, and we understand only once he is perceived differently, angelically, by a variety of races, rescuing Sheridan in 'The Fall of Night', that he too is participating in ideological and historical manipulation.[29]

Delenn's words about the Ancients echo those she utters to the Grey Council in 'Babylon Squared'. She declines to lead the Minbari, asking to be allowed to remain on Babylon 5. Paradoxically, in the very qualities her fellow Minbari see as human weaknesses, she finds great strength. Echoing her words about the Ancients, she says that humans:

> do not seek conformity, they do not surrender ... the passions we deplore have taken them to their place in the stars, and will propel them to a great destiny. They carry within them the capacity to walk among the stars as giants. They are the future, we have much to learn from them.

This is repeated in her demands for unity in 'Between the Darkness and the Light'. When the new synthesis is commented upon by the former remaining leaders of the old Council, G'Kar's words are most telling: 'In the past we had nothing in common, but now the humans have become the glue that holds us together.' Despite the obvious human divisions and frailties throughout the series, through Sinclair and then Sheridan, the humans are the ones who keep the new alliance on track – they are the nexus. The human we see in the final sequence of 'The Deconstruction of Falling Stars' epitomises the recognition of this need for unity, the unity created through the

10. *BABYLON 5*: DELENN AND MINBARI ACOLYTE
OF THE RELIGIOUS CASTE, IN 'LEGACIES'
(SEASON 1).

humans, and the future. The similarity between the encounter-suit we see and the encounter-suits worn by the Vorlons is perhaps more than coincidence – the once mysterious and god-like Kosh guided Sheridan into seeing things in a new light, freeing him to 'fight legends' with the aid of the First One, Lorien; now at the death of the Sun and solar system, a future human takes on a Vorlon-like cast. Thus, in *Babylon 5*, the history we see is shown to have a pattern, one that repeats itself, and many of the little asides and comments within the series become glaringly obvious in retrospect. Asked by Elric the Technomago (in the 'Geometry of Shadows'), whether or not he believes in magic, Sheridan replies, 'If we went back in time a thousand years and tried to explain this place to people, they could only accept it in terms of magic.' As Andy Lane points out, Babylon 4 *is* taken back a thousand years[30] and presented to the Minbari by Sinclair, magically transformed into Valen ('a Minbari not of Minbari born') by the same device that transforms Delenn.[31]

POPULAR   CULTURE   AS   CONTEXT

Babylon 5 does not just use social and political history as context, it also refers to science fiction literature, film and television, a marked contrast to most sf/fantasy series – unless they veer towards pastiche like *Farscape*, which plays fast and loose on every level, use some comedy on a regular basis, like *Stargate SG-1*, which relies chiefly upon O'Neill's latter-day Shakespearean fool, or are comedies themselves and far less concerned with sf per se – like *Third Rock From the Sun* and the animation *Futurama*. The initially lightweight *Andromeda* makes several jokes about its star Kevin Sorbo – of *Hercules* fame – in its first episode: 'Who does he think he is, some kind of Greek god?' for example. In total contrast, most non-comedy sf series seem fearful of fracturing their reality by self-reflexivity. In *Babylon 5*, however, there are frequent, ironic comments about 'Deep Space' franchises, and wry acknowledgements from the Command staff that *everything* seems to happen *all* the time on Babylon 5. In 'Sleeping With Light', the Hugo Award (for Science Fiction Achievement) writer/ producer Straczynski received for 'The Coming of Shadows' is on General Ivanova's desk, and during Musante's attempted seduction of Sheridan in 'Voices of Authority', Ivanova's hologram appears from Epsilon 3 to cheekily parody *Star Trek*'s opening voiceover (and Kirk's penchant for seduction). 'Good luck Captain,' she says, 'I think you're about to go where *everyone* has gone before.'

More seriously, commercial and military vessels use authors' names (the Asimov, the Spinoza) as well as names from mythology (the Agamemnon, Achilles, Heracles, Hera) and history (the Roanoke, the Churchill). The alien race who kidnap Sheridan in 'All Alone in the Night' are the Streib, a subtle play upon the surname of Whitley Strieber, the author of *Communion* and other tales of alien abduction. Sharing a name from Michael Moorcock's *Elric* stories, Elric the Technomage quotes Tolkien's *Lord of the Rings* in 'The Geometry of Shadows' when he warns 'Do not try the patience of wizards, for they are subtle and quick to anger.' Rabkin's transformed language is represented well by the stately Lorien, who also recalls Tolkien – this time, the Elf-realm of Lórien. The pit at Z'ha'dum into which Sheridan jumps is a parallel to Khazad-dûm (a reversal of the first two syllables) and the mines of Moria, where Gandalf the Grey fell, only to be resurrected as Gandalf the White – in similar fashion to Sheridan. Likewise, the apparatus of the great machine on Epsilon 3 is remarkably similar visually to the massive Krel machinery in *Forbidden Planet* (1956). The blue spacesuit used in 'Babylon Squared' and 'War Without End' Parts 1 and 2 is from the film *2010*. References abound: the most obvious is that of Psi-Cop Alfred Bester, presumably named after the author of *The Demolished Man*, one of the best known novels about telepathy. Even security officer Zack Allen is blessed with a heritage; as Andy Sawyer suggests in his essay on Lovecraftian influences in *Babylon 5*, his name is reminiscent of the town drunk, Zadok Allen, in the H.P. Lovecraft story 'The Shadow over Innsmouth'.[32]

The act of cultural referencing is one of *Babylon 5*'s great strengths and it extends to great depths. Today we still use things from the past which are considered outmoded or obsolete – record players, typewriters – yet we do not necessarily find them redundant, or even antiques. They may simply be part of retro-styling or they may have personal resonance. *Babylon 5* assumes precisely this, so in 2258, we find everyday objects featured, and attitudes and associations are made that we can easily recognise from present culture. The series even mocks its own medium in the appropriately named 'Between the

Darkness and the Light', when an Earth Force security guard scorns: 'I don't watch tv. It's a cultural wasteland filled with inappropriate metaphors and an unrealistic portrayal of life created by the liberal media elite.' When Garibaldi watches *Daffy Duck* and eats popcorn in such a place of constant confusion, it creates a sense of continuity, not awkwardness. When Ivanova grows an illegal coffee plant in the hydroponics bay, we can sympathise with her desire for 'fresh' coffee. *Babylon 5* also relates wittily to the more bizarre aspects of sf culture. For instance, in a throwaway introductory scene we watch part of a court case where a human is suing an alien's great grandson for abducting his great grandfather. In direct contrast to all other aliens in *Babylon 5*, this alien looks like the alien 'grey' so strongly associated with Roswell and countless UFO/abduction cases. *Babylon 5* does what sf needs to do: it shows us the future and it shows us how we got there.

Humour, mostly observational, is used to great effect to connect our present with *Babylon 5*'s vision of the future – imperialism, sexism, capitalism, etc. are all targets, and Ivanova offers her opinion on most of them. Told to eat a higher calorific diet, the Russian commander responds: 'Figures. All my life I've fought against imperialism. Now, suddenly, I *am* the expanding Russian frontier.' (Franklin daringly suggests that she has 'very nice borders'.) In 'Believers', she despatches with a hint of sexism by suggesting with heavy irony that she could always 'knit something' to keep herself busy. G'Kar, his people subjected to hell by the occupying Centauri regime and, more specifically, tortured by Cartagia, can eventually say to Londo in 'The Paragon of Animals': 'Oh, go away. Repress someone else.' Vir too, in 'Movements of Fire and Shadow', remarks glibly that the Centauris' 'biggest losses have been in Drazi space. They are real good fighters – not terrific conversationalists, and their table manners can make you go blind in one eye, but – *real* tough behind the weapons console.' Again, this is something many other series avoid, choosing only to comment wryly about their immediate situation. In 'And the Rock Cried Out, No Hiding Place', Sheridan despairs of sleeping after Kosh's death, remarking to Delenn that his dreams were enough to 'make your hair stand on end'. 'That explains the Centauri, at least,' quips Delenn. With a whole year of study in temple devoted to humour, Satai Delenn also has a sense of fun. On one level, this ensures that *Babylon 5* does not offer its aliens as exotic, or enigmatic and humourless creatures. There is nothing of Bierstadt or Fenimore Cooper's noble or natural savages here, no hint of primitivism so associated with the eighteenth-century Romance. There is no room even for *Star Trek*'s inferior/superior unknown species. Aliens and humans alike are alternately witty and serious, busy or indolent, successful or a failure, selfish or selfless – they are believable, rounded individuals. In the novelistic sense, this helps us to connect with the characters and their situation, an important balance in a genre where to understand even one's environment is a constant challenge.

THE CONFUSED CITADEL

During the Shadow War and the battle with Clark's forces, Babylon 5 occupies a military role, protecting those within its walls. However, more importantly, it functions throughout the five seasons as a citadel, truly the 'home away from home' described in the opening voiceover to the first season. The city as dystopia or utopia has long been a favourite of futuristic writers and film-makers, and more often than not becomes a place of frightening social stratification or confused locality. Worse still, its increasingly alienating environment brings about questions of what it is to be human, and problematises the increasing fusion of humanity with the cold machinery of technology. Bukatman suggests that:

> the rise of the [sf] genre remains bound up in the same technological revolutions which produced the complex industrial urban environment, with all the commensurate ambivalence towards the idea of progress that might imply. The city was most frequently projected as a negative entity, while utopian aspirations were focused instead upon an agrarian existence.[33]

Published in 1888, Bellamy's *Looking Backward* promoted the industrialised utopia and, in *The Shape of Things to Come* (1936), the vision was realised in film (its dystopic opposite having already arrived in the 1926 film *Metropolis*). In the real world, the city as micro- and macrocosm emerged in the aftermath of the Second World War, in the shape of 'new towns' like Stevenage or Harlow in

England and buildings such as John Portman's Bonaventura Hotel in Los Angeles. More commonly, it appeared in the form of the modern, monadic shopping mall, which has 'no windows and no weather, while points of egress are hidden off to the sides'. Carefully denying exterior and interior, with mirrors, glass, water, and airy spaces, these malls have streets containing:

> carefully planted and nurtured trees; a central 'food court' mimics the piazzas and plazas of a more traditional urban space. This imploded urbanism, reconciling the irreconcilable differences between public and private, or inside and outside, is insistent upon its status as a 'total space'.[34]

It is everything, all at once.

In sf, the city often becomes what Bukatman describes as 'an intolerable space',[35] one which lacks the social and moral space of older cities, and becomes instead a challenge, a topographical morass to be comprehended in order to survive. *Babylon 5*'s Production Designer, Ron Thornton, repeatedly acknowledges the influence of *Blade Runner*,[36] whose influence upon much post-1980s sf should not be dismissed lightly. It provides an excellent example of a postmodernist combination of film noir narrative and Gothic imagery, a gloomy, fractured future replete with cyborgs (replicants).[37] Beneath *Blade Runner*'s superficial Gothic gloom and decayed decadence lurks a fine array of sf subject matter. The futuristic Los Angeles of 2019 is an urban melting pot, a heady concoction of a semi-recognisable present-day LA amid the hardware and argot of tomorrow. The City of Angels is in decay, a projected manifestation of rotting consumerism. It is dark; its buildings are in ruins, the rainfall is almost constant, and the overall gloom is interrupted only (and constantly) by advertisements whose penetrating verbal sales pitches are matched only by the garish colours of their neon hoardings. The modern city is directionless, constructed three-dimensionally; flying cars zoom above the streets, and advertisements appear on the sides of tower blocks. They deny the substance of the building and turning it into a mere screen – exhorting the viewer to travel further – to the off-world colonies. The very walls of the apartment blocks become sites of projection, not habitation.[38] We are denied any means of locating or mapping ourselves within this urban jungle.

In turn, Babylon 5 ought to be easily charted – there are colour co-ordinated corridors and zones, with information points at every turn – but it is a fractal city, a postmodern location where we cannot map ourselves, and therefore cannot know ourselves. It offers a confusing myriad of impossible locations within its spinning station shell, functioning firstly through the dislocated sense of the station itself (the audience has no sense of where this neutral territory is actually located) and secondly through the temporally confusing visions and predictions we encounter throughout the series. Although it is not a city in the sense of the luminous crystal-carved arches and lofty towers of the Minbari capital, nor the elegant Sun-King courtyards and Roman palaces of Centauri Prime, it is more of a home. Narn is devastated and a howling post-apocalyptic shell of its former agrarian self, and we seldom see Earth, apart from the grim concrete block of EarthGov in Geneva, a brief glimpse of the San Diego wastelands or the sterile Psi-Corps headquarters. Mars too, the other chief area of human control, offers gleaming domes linked by fragile networks of travel-tubes, the cramped luxury of William Edgars' domicile but, beyond them, there are only the collapsing tunnels and caves of No. 1's resistance cells. The red planet is as hostile and unforgiving as the concrete of Earth is unwelcomingly uniform and staid.

In contrast to the static edifices of the planetary capitals, Babylon 5 is in perpetual motion, light glinting off its blue-metal tiles and gleaming forward-stabilisers. Its interior recalls Jameson's descriptions of the monadic shopping mall and Portman's LA Bonaventura Hotel. It is a self-perpetuating city turned outside-in, and we frequently see examples of this at its core: the trees and plants along the walkways, the gardens and lakes, sometimes above us, visible from the monorail, ambassadorial apartments and offices, the shops and bars of the Zocalo. There are plenty of ways through and across the station, but exits and windows are not readily visible: the only clue to their existence is the security/customs hall where identicards are checked. From the outside, access is equally limited: the only way in lies through the brutal steel jaws of the docking bay. In the same way, the various levels of the station are hard to locate precisely. 'Down below', where the Lurkers go, reminds us that this future is riddled with the same social problems we face today – ones notably denied by the future politicians we encounter. On Earth, under Clark, there are no homeless, displaced or unemployed people, says Julie Musante in 'Voices of Authority'; if there are any, they 'choose to be', or are 'criminally insane'. People come to Babylon 5 looking for a new start, use up all their money and end up in the miserable ghetto that is 'down below', eking out a living, falling on more and more difficult times until they can barely exist. The fascist and racist ISN reports in 'And Now for a Word' and 'The Illusion of Truth' may appeal shamelessly to the isolationist movements on Earth with their scurrilous tales of alien influence and alien depravity, but the images themselves are based in truth: the poverty and misery of 'down below' is not a lie.

Whereas the fluctuating state of Dabylon 4 in 'Dabylon Squared' and 'War Without End' offers a permanent if hazy warning that time and space 'don't work right', two other episodes identify more precisely the problem of locating oneself. In 'Day of the Dead', a whole sector of the station goes missing. Bought by the Brakiri Ambassador for a set period of time, it becomes a physical and spiritual part of the Brakiri homeworld, cut off from the rest of the station from Brakiri dusk until dawn. In 'Grey 17 is Missing', Garibaldi checks through the station's various 'levels' after the extraordinary disappearance of a maintenance engineer. He discovers an entire level of the station has vanished. It *is* there, of course, but the lift doesn't stop at it, and only by counting the three-second elevator journey between all the other levels, in the time-honoured detective tradition, can Garibaldi identify the problem and gain access by stopping the elevator in the 'wrong' place – the missing deck. His search enters into a fractal space, a two-dimensional geometrical impossibility according to everyday reality and the maps, but a reality once he is there to solve the crime. It is a netherworld, with its own hierarchy, an alternative station within the station itself, neither part of the diplomats' and crew's living quarters and commercial station life, nor 'down below'.[39] But of course there is no 'down below' in a rotating, cylindrical station. So the question of location is further complicated by the presentation of the station's interior. *Babylon 5* has sets with which we become familiar – the Zocalo, the Japanese garden, the command centre – but their actual location and the corridors linking them are a mystery. The abundant maps are of no actual use despite their apparently helpful intent, they serve rather to confuse; blue sector, red sector, level 10, grey sector, level 14 …

The view from Sheridan's office showing the station core and, most obscurely, its maze,[40] only furthers the sense of disorientation and estrangement. In the darkness of 'down below' we find the hidden depths of the station, yet where *is* 'down below'? When Sheridan falls from the monorail he falls slowly, because he is close to weightless, yet he must be caught before he hits the rotating station floor at over 60 miles per hour.[41] We do not know where he and Kosh will land: the station is a conundrum, at once mapped and delineated and yet also cognitively unmappable: a mystery. In direct contrast, although we do not know the route from the bridge to sick bay, or from sickbay to Ten-Forward, or from the Promenade to Sisko's quarters, in the *Star Trek* series, the turbo lift takes us to where we wish to go. The crewmembers step inside, state their destination and are magically whisked away and neatly delivered to the appropriate location: there is no confusion. In *The Next Generation*'s 'Disaster' and *Voyager*'s 'Twisted', the breakdown of a turbo lift or the warping of the ship's corridors respectively form the core for an episode of drama, so traumatic is it for the Starfleet crews. In the universe of *Babylon 5*, the only thing that can be relied upon is that confusion is constant, and constant renegotiation is essential. 'No-one here is exactly what he appears to be – not Mollari, not Delenn, not Sinclair and not me,' says G'Kar to Catherine Sakai in 'Mind War'. Indeed, they are not, and the same is true of the universe they inhabit.

FORESHADOWING

This aura of confusion is partially a feature of postmodern texts in general. For Babylons 4 and 5, this confusion provides a loss of direction and place – not only in the three dimensions of space, but also in the fourth dimension: time. A major means of creating mystery and temporal confusion in *Babylon 5* occurs not just through foreshadowing, but also via flash-forwards. This is highly unusual in serial television and, without a clear story arc, impossible over the long term. Flashbacks are easy to incorporate, the material is already to hand, but flash-forwards, which occur frequently in *Babylon 5*, not only between episodes, but also between seasons, simultaneously articulate and require a clear sense of context on the behalf of the storytellers – although the audience is necessarily deprived of that knowledge. Visually, their effect is enhanced by flash-forwards being in colour while flashbacks, whether as personal memories or narrative events, are in black and white, whilst predictions and visions are shown according to their type. The sequence is repeated when the event is actually reached, but it is enhanced by other scenes which explain and make clear the context – such as the destruction of the station or Londo's repeated vision of Shadow ships flying over him on Centauri Prime.

The flash-forwards do not just occur in the time-travel episodes, although they are most common there, and we see glimpses of possible futures for Garibaldi, Sinclair, Delenn and Sheridan. Nevertheless, rather than repeatedly playing on time travel, *Babylon 5* uses it sparingly, and those who experience it do not have the power to completely control it – hence Sinclair and Garibaldi's experience on Babylon 4, and Sheridan and Delenn's journeys through time in 'War Without End' Parts 1 and 2. The stabilisers worn in the time rift are clearly established as a necessity, yet explained only briefly by Zathras, who has brought them from the Great Machine on Epsilon 3. This non-technological approach leaves development room for other areas of interest through mystery, prediction and oracle. Uniquely in sf television, the *Babylon 5* universe ordains, predicts, warns and foreshadows, and the audience can attempt to extract meaning through extrapolation, but is never allowed a full context.[42] It functions like an oracle responding to someone's request about the gender of his or her unborn child by saying 'Boy – no girl.' But does it mean there will be a boy, but no girl, or an apologetic 'it'll be a boy, sorry – no, actually it'll be a girl'? Like Kyle Reese's post-apocalyptic nightmare world in *The Terminator*, we are given visions of 'a possible future' and, just like Reese, we 'don't know Tech stuff.' – things are not explained in technological or chronological terms so we cannot be confident of knowing how or why this future may occur. Like Data and Troi in *The Next Generation*'s 'Darmok', we are given the information, but are denied any context, and thus any reliable meaning. The frustration is immense, human curiosity is aroused and we watch, caught helplessly in a narrative web, knowing that we dare not miss any information that might provide the context necessary to understanding. Given our conceptual linkage of time and space, and our reliance upon temporal linearity, this is a significant problem for the viewer's understanding. The sense of confusion in *Babylon 5* is exacerbated in the three time-travel episodes, 'Babylon Squared' and 'War Without End' (Parts 1 and 2), where the characters are not only confused as to *where* they are, but *when* they are. The impact of these episodes reverberates throughout the series.

NARRATIVE COMPLEXITY

If *Babylon 5* poses questions which contribute to a story arc lasting for five seasons, it must also at some stage answer them. As we have seen, 'Babylon Squared' and 'War Without End' explain what happened to Babylon 4 and why Babylon 5 is so vital – Delenn's admiration for the ability of humans to build communities is all the more practical in this light. However, there is another episode which demonstrates very clearly the narrative strategies employed by *Babylon 5*: 'Signs and Portents'. It establishes the overall arc of the series and poses many more questions than are answered by either 'Babylon Squared' or 'War Without End'. If Londo's introduction to 'The Gathering' establishes the sprawling, historical nature of the series, and the constant recourse to ISN and newscasters reminds us of the influence of perspective, in turn 'Signs and Portents' stresses both the epic and romantic nature of the narrative, whilst its focus is upon the station itself. The continuing exploration of the lives, loves and experiences of those inhabiting it ensure the familiar romantic, novelistic approach which we associate with television, while the epic nature is underlined by the ethical and moral struggles articulated later in 'War Without End', 'Z'ha'dum' and 'Into the Fire' in particular.[43]

'Signs and Portents' is a profoundly arc-related episode and offers more clues to the past and future direction of the series' universe than either 'Babylon Squared' or 'War Without End', although they are more action-orientated and thus appear more explicit. When the deceptively charming Morden arrives on the station, he tells the entry officer that he has been out on the Rim. The Rim is a mysterious area in *Babylon 5* terms – the equivalent of the very edge of the frontier, perhaps, because it is also where we can find the Shadows' planet, Z'ha'dum. It is also the gateway to the mysterious 'whatever' that lies beyond, a place to which the Technomages and the First Ones depart

– and the place from which Lorien returns for Sheridan. Certainly 'the Rim' is mentally allied to Mather's 'Devil's territories'. Asked by the entry officer if he found anything interesting out there, Morden's response is a cryptic 'Yes'. It transpires that his mission is to ask each of the Ambassadors the same, deceptively simple question: 'What do you want?' – the Shadow's equivalent to the question with which Vorlon Kosh confounds everyone in turn: 'Who are you?'

The replies Morden obtains from G'Kar and Londo are the most interesting, and each can be split into two segments. Their initial replies are the same, expressing a personal desire for him to leave, but the second parts of their responses both answer Morden's question and articulate a political ambition. Ultimately, like Vir's desire to see Morden's head on a pike, their words impact upon what finally happens to them personally and politically. Londo Mollari initially considers Morden a harmless madman and tells him to go away, but is worn down by Morden's inane, grinning insistence. 'I want to be left alone,' he says – and he is, as the Drakh's puppet Emperor in the final episodes of the last season, he is a tragic figure of solitude – no one is more alone than Centauri Emperor Mollari. The rest of his answer echoes Delenn's warning about the Shadows' ambitions, giving Morden the response his masters have been waiting for:

> Do you really want to know what I want? Do you really want to know the truth? I want my people to reclaim their rightful place in the galaxy. I want to see the Centauri stretch forth their hand again and command the stars. I want a rebirth of glory, a renaissance of power. I want to stop running through my life like a man who is late for an appointment, afraid to look back or look forward. I want us to be what we used to be. I want – I want it all back the way it was. Does that answer your question?

G'Kar initially tells Morden, 'I want to be left in peace.' The second half of his response is vague and uncertain in comparison with Londo's angry tirade. He wants the destruction of the Centauri Republic, nothing else really matters 'so long as Narn is safe'. G'Kar is, of course, left in peace – finding over time, a new spiritual depth and comfort in his life for a period. His other wish comes true: the Centauri Republic is destroyed and despite its appalling sacrifice in the Narn-Centauri war, Narn *is* safe. As he greets Garibaldi in the fourth season 'Epiphanies', G'Kar is ecstatic: 'Narn is free'. Nothing else matters – including the loss of his eye and later, locked in final combat with Mollari, his life. Fittingly, although both travel some distance spiritually (especially G'Kar), these two final representatives of the old way of thinking die together, along with their races' eternal hatred.

Morden's encounters with Delenn and Kosh are more limited but equally revealing. Delenn challenges his question, already more philosophically aware of its complexities than her fellow ambassadors. As he speaks to her, the Triluminary sign (spiritually associated with Valen and thus central to the Minbari Religious caste) appears on her forehead, warning her, although at the time we are unaware of its significance – to both her and Sinclair.[44] As she looks at Morden, he is cast into shadow and, clearly shaken, she tells him to go: he does so. The meeting with Kosh is accidental, but the Vorlon's ship arrives in time for Kosh to instruct him: 'Leave this place, they are not for you.'

The later episode 'In the Shadow of Z'ha'dum' demonstrates that Morden is never alone. Talia telepathically senses the (invisible) Shadow creatures accompanying him, we hear a strange transitory sound, and the camera in Morden's cell permits us the briefest glimpse. The Vorlons are ever cryptic, so it is uncertain whether Kosh is speaking to Morden or the Shadows in 'Signs and Portents'. In either case, if 'they' are not for him, then for whom? Only when the intentions of the Vorlons and the Shadows become clear in the fourth season do we realise that this was a matter of selecting sacrificial pawns for the battle ahead. Nevertheless, the words of both Kosh and Delenn are prophetic, this time for Morden. He and, by default, the Shadows are told: 'Leave. Go now.' Ultimately, with the exception of Londo, those living on Babylon 5 refuse to be used as pawns for the Shadows or Vorlons. Even Londo, recognising his error is the same as that which he accuses Sheridan of in 'War Without End' (the crime of convenience), is given three chances to redeem himself by the prophecies of Lady Morella in 'Point of No Return', and perhaps does so.[45]

'Signs and Portents' also marks the brief first appearance of a terrifying spider-shaped Shadow vessel, although we have no idea of what it is – only that it is connected to Morden in some way. Londo has been dealing with a questionable art-trader and has obtained a precious artefact: an ancient symbol of Centauri authority – the Eye. It has been missing for over a century, and echoes Londo's verbal longing for everything to be the way it used to be. Londo lives in the past. Lord Kiro and his aunt, Lady Ladira, come to Babylon 5 to collect the Eye but rather than returning it to the Centauri Emperor, as intended, Kiro begins to express his desire for power. En route to his ship with Londo and Ladira, Raiders take him hostage, apparently stealing the Eye. Once on their ship, Kiro is shown to be in league with them – and left with Londo, the Lady Ladira repeats a warning she gave to Kiro when he was an adolescent: 'The Shadows are coming.' This time, she says, 'the Shadows have come for us all.' No sooner have they set out from Babylon 5 than the Raider ship, its crew and the devious Kiro, are destroyed by the mysterious spider-like vessel. Talking to Sinclair later, Ladira shares her vision of Babylon 5's possible fiery demise, an image we see repeatedly in the series.

The other important strand of the episode deals with Sinclair's loss of memory. He is missing twenty-four hours from his life during the Battle of the Line, beginning when he is taken aboard the Minbari vessel on Delenn's command. When he regains consciousness, he is drifting in his Starfury. It is mentioned in 'The Gathering' and in 'And The Sky Full of Stars', where he is interrogated by renegade officers from Earth Force who believe he made a deal with the Minbari. In fact, 'And the Sky Full of Stars' shows that when Sinclair is taken prisoner, the Minbari interrogate him. The glowing Triluminary reveals to them the secret that Lennier discloses to Sheridan in 'Points of Departure – that Minbari and humans souls are linked in some way. Under instruction from Sinclair, Garibaldi discovers that everyone short-listed for the post of station Commander was rejected by the Minbari – until his name was reached. This is an apparently minor storyline in 'Signs and Portents', but it establishes one of the factors necessary to 'Legacies' where the Minbari warrior Neroon tells Sinclair that he 'talks like a Minbari', justifies Sinclair's posting to Minbar as Ambassador in 'Points of Departure' and in 'War Without End' Part 1 clarifies the Vorlon's comment to Rathenn, on Minbar, that Sinclair 'is the closed circle. He is returning to the beginning.' It establishes an undeniable link between Sinclair and the Minbari. So the episode plays a major role in the story arc without using time travel, but by creating the same narrative effects. It picks up themes established in the pilot and previous episodes and, out of them, creates further mystery and impetus.

SHERIDAN AND DESTINY

This narrative technique occurs several times, but the most important example concerns Sheridan. Just as the roles of the other major characters are established in the first series, so Sheridan's character and destiny must be articulated soon after his arrival in 'Points of Departure'. His frustration at being assigned to Babylon 5, initially allegedly to deal with the renegade Minbari cruiser Trigati, but also to aid General Hague's plans to curb Clark's illegal actions, is further explored briefly in 'A Distant Star'. However, the greater role he (and others) will play is better, albeit implicitly, explored in 'The Coming of Shadows'. Here, the dying Centauri Emperor, Turhan, visits the station, because he admires its work for peace. Turhan's intention is to apologise to G'Kar and the Narn people for the atrocities carried out by his ancestors. Meanwhile, G'Kar, consumed with hatred, plans to assassinate him, but the Emperor collapses before G'Kar can do so. The devious nature of Centauri politics is revealed by the Emperor's unwillingness to trust his people to deliver his message of reconciliation: it is Franklin who visits G'Kar to say 'I'm sorry' on behalf of Turhan. Centauri deception is further clarified by the conspiracy between Lord Refa and Londo – a conspiracy in which Londo ominously involves Morden and the Shadows. Musing on Morden's earlier offer – 'Just name a target' – and ignoring Vir's horrified pleading, Londo has the Shadows destroy a Narn colony/listening post in Quadrant 14. It results in a new Narn-Centauri war, creating the conflict and chaos that is the Shadows' ultimate goal. Even as Turhan draws his last breath, Mollari is manufacturing history, a crime of the highest order in *Babylon 5*. To the people assembled in the medical centre, Londo says the Emperor has told him: 'Continue. Take my people back to the stars.' In the corridor, Refa asks what he really said. Londo replies, 'He said that we are both damned.' Time and the universe prove him right.

Prior to his illness and official speech, Turhan asks to see Sheridan; their conversation foreshadows Sheridan's destiny. It also refers to Sheridan's love and respect for his father (the significance of which explains why Kosh is initially drawn to using him, as he is to Delenn, equally observant of her elders) – and is worth repeating in full:

Emperor   Why are you here? In this place, in that uniform? Was it your choice, or were you pressed into service?

Sheridan   It was my choice. The planetary draft didn't start until the war, a few years later. I guess I wanted to serve something that was bigger than I was, make a difference somewhere, somehow. You seem interested in why people chose to be here.

Emperor   It has occurred to me recently that I have never chosen anything. I was born into a role that had been prepared for me. I did everything that I was asked to do because it never occurred to me to choose otherwise. And now – at the end of my life – I wonder what might have been.

Sheridan   That's why my father taught me to live each second as though it were the last moment of my life. He said: 'If you love, love without reservation, if you fight, fight without fear.' He called it the Way of the Warrior.

Emperor   No regrets then?

Sheridan   A few, but just a few. You?

Emperor   Enough to fill a lifetime. So much has been lost, so much forgotten. So much pain, so much blood, and for what, I wonder? The past tense, as the present, confuses us, and the future frightens us, and our lives slip away moment by moment, lost in that vast terrible in-between. But there is still time to seize that one last fragile moment, to choose something better, to make a difference, as you say. And I intend to do just that.

Sheridan's encounter with Turhan tells implicitly of his plunge into the abyss at Z'ha'dum, and the test he faces whilst there. This is also foreshadowed and paralleled in 'There All the Honor Lies'. Here, harassed by his home officials, subjected to unreasonable demands, Vir tells Londo he spends his life trying to do 'what they want, what you want – I don't even *know* what *I* want'. He speaks of 'falling into a pit where there is no way out'. At the same time, Sheridan is framed, accused of murdering a Minbari, and faces the same dilemma. Kosh, in the process of teaching him 'to fight legends' – 'Hunter, Prey' – insists that Sheridan keeps his appointed lesson, far down in the depths of the station, despite the apparent desperation of his current situation. Kosh shows him 'one moment of perfect beauty', which Sheridan later describes to Ivanova as 'beauty – in the dark'. Notably, she responds by saying Kosh's lessons must be working – 'You sound just like him' – retrospectively fascinating, given that part of Kosh is inside him at Z'ha'dum. Kosh has led Sheridan far into the bowels of that unchartable area 'down below'. Sent into a sector where he must stoop to proceed, Sheridan finds what seem to be piles of sackcloth, which inflate into figures. He is asked for a token, and apologetically offers his gold 'stat bar', a symbol of the pride associated with his uniform and role. The figures begin a Gregorian chant, part of the Christmas Mass: while Sheridan experiences this perfect moment, he also learns about himself.

This descent into an abyss (metaphorical or physical), after which self-knowledge is obtained, is a motif common to the Gothic and to sf,[46] and common also is the Sublime. Whilst 'The Coming of Shadows' reveals much about the story in seasons to come, Turhan's questions foreshadow Sheridan's conversation with Lorien in 'Whatever Happened to Mr Garibaldi?' in the depths of Z'ha'dum. At Z'ha'dum, Sheridan is in precisely the situation Turhan remarks upon. He is caught 'between seconds, lost in the infinite possibilities between tick and tock'. He dreams of being held by an extraordinary being of light (Lorien), and the scale, composition and lighting of these scenes underscore *Babylon 5*'s use of the Sublime discussed in previous chapters, that identified by de Chardin and Robu. The vast creature of light (the immense), holds Sheridan (the complex) whilst tiny molecules (the minute), swirl and spiral around its non-corporeal 'limbs'. Lorien asks Sheridan the same questions posed by the Vorlons and Shadows: 'Who are you. What do you want?' But he also poses another, one which vitally links the other questions: 'why are you (here)?' – the same question Turhan asked of Sheridan. Lorien warns Sheridan that he:

> can't turn away from death simply because you are afraid of what might happen without you. That's not enough. You're not embracing life, you're fleeing death. And so you're caught in between, unable to go forward or backward. Your friends need what you can be when you are no longer afraid, when you know who you are and why you are, and what you want. When you are no longer looking for reasons to live, but can simply be ... You must let go. Surrender yourself to death. The death of flesh, the death of fear. Step into the abyss, and let go ... It's easy to find something worth dying for – do you have anything worth living for?

At first, Sheridan cannot answer; repeatedly he responds with 'I can't', or 'I don't know how', or 'What if I fall?' But as Lorien continues talking, he begins to understand the question. Sheridan quotes Kosh: '"Understanding is a three-edged sword" – your side, their side, and the truth in between.'[47] The two questions the Vorlons and Shadows pose are linked here by Lorien when he says Sheridan must know 'why you are' – only this can give the real answer, and the answer that will allow Sheridan to escape from in between – to death or to life. When Lorien tells Sheridan to take a chance, to jump once more into the abyss, he says that he may be able to save him, 'I caught you before', but also that it 'might not work'. Sheridan utters the words that allow his return: 'But I can hope.' Lorien's response articulates a foundational belief in *Babylon 5*: 'Hope is all we have.'[48]

Lorien's speech also echoes G'Kar's previous season's end voiceover about the death of hope. In his experience in obeying Kosh and exploring 'down below', jumping from the monorail and jumping into the pit at Z'ha'dum, Sheridan confronts respectively his own power, his mortality and his death.

In each instance, in the darkest moment he discovers that the worst of places still offer wonder. In the darkness of Z'ha'dum, we see his stat bar lying on the floor in a direct reminder of the previous occasion he relinquished it. At the third time of sacrificing himself, he is resurrected. The messianic scene from 'There All the Honor Lies' provides a 'pastiche of the nostalgic and the devout, with the alien and the scientific' and foreshadows Sheridan's return from the dead in 'The Summoning'.

Although *Babylon 5* avoids verbal redundancy and unnecessary repetition in a linear sense, unlike the soap opera, as we can see from these examples, it still provides careful parallels within its narrative to reiterate at different levels (physical, psychological and metaphorical) the messages it is imparting. Sheridan thus experiences his darkest moments at the same time as Vir and later Franklin and, in 'Whatever Happened to Mr Garibaldi?', is tested by Lorien at Z'ha'dum at the same time as Delenn, Garibaldi and G'Kar face the bleakest of futures. The important difference between *Babylon 5*'s narrative form and that of a soap opera is that the specific issue and its entire context shifts, unlike in a soap opera where a generally static issue is continually worked through from a variety of perspectives. So although there is a lack of overt redundancy, the major concepts of the series *are* presented in a variety of forms and with minute differences in repetition.

There is a strong parallel between Sheridan's revelatory experience and Franklin's more personal revelation in 'Shadow Dancing', and it helps to mark out the epic and novelistic functions of their respective characters. Sheridan's romance with Delenn may seem novelistic, in the sense that it is primarily about them and not the 'bigger' picture, but its significance and their subsequent actions, dictated for so long by others, are primarily epic. In contrast to this is Dr Franklin, who is not manipulated by external forces; his experiences are personal and novelistic, dictated only by his own weakness and addiction to 'stims' (stimulants). However, Franklin's actions are also shown as an exercise in self-indulgence, not an exercise of willing self-sacrifice as Delenn and Sheridan experience, particularly in 'Comes the Inquisitor', 'Z'ha'dum', and 'Moments of Transition'. One of Franklin's first actions on the station is to go against the orders of his commanding officer, Sinclair, and the parents of a child he wishes to save by operating – because he refuses to accept their religious belief above his ability as a physician ('Believers'). He offers to resign: Sinclair refuses to accept it. In 'A Race Through Dark Places', he establishes an underground railway for telepaths; instead of trusting others, he again 'goes it alone' and jeopardises the independence of the entire station. At a time of immense pressure, in 'Interludes and

Examinations', he resigns and goes 'walkabout'. Addicted and in need of cleansing, in 'Shadow Dancing' he 'meets himself' just as he had hoped, but the meeting is far from comfortable. Trying to help someone who is being attacked by a thug, Franklin is stabbed and left to die. As his blood pressure drops and he weakens, a uniformed Franklin appears, to carry out what Gareth Roberts calls a 'brutal' attack on the reasons for his resignation:

> You finally had it all, didn't you? A good job, people who cared about you, and you messed it up. 'I have to leave before they fire me.' 'I have to find myself.' What a bunch of moaly-mouthed self-indulgent Foundationist crap ... Take responsibility for your actions, for crying out loud.

This, says Roberts, 'is the subversion. The trite "I have to find myself", trotted out with all seriousness so often in American drama, is debunked and dismissed'.[49] The incident takes place as the Alliance faces its first open conflict with the Shadows, in 'Shadow Dancing', and only shortly after Garibaldi's lecture to G'Kar about his responsibility as a leader, and about the need for working together in 'Walkabout'. Like Sheridan, Franklin is in his own abyss, not just the mental one into which he has retreated, but also physically: not only is he 'down below', but he has to climb a ladder to escape from the pit in which he literally 'finds' himself. Like Sheridan, understanding, and sheer force of will, a determination to live for something – not to die for something – allows him to escape. But worse is still to come. When he comes round in Med-Lab, through the window to his room he can see the dead and wounded from the battle with the Shadows. At the very time he was needed most by the others, he was not there, too engaged in the little picture, himself, to remember the big picture, those around him. He later tells Sheridan he finally understands: the stims might have kept him going, allowing him to do more, but he needs to 'do better', not more. Just like Sheridan, and at the third time of asking, Franklin accepts his duties as a doctor, but his resurrection is purely personal.

DIFFERENT CHOICES

So, while Franklin occupies an important and engaging role as a novelistic character, Sheridan embodies the epic at the heart of *Babylon 5*. His life force replenished temporarily by Lorien in 'The Summoning', he also needs to do not more, but better. He returns from Z'ha'dum harder, grown in stature – matured. Z'ha'dum is his rite of passage: the warrior that he was and the spiritual teachings of Delenn, Kosh and Lorien have combined to create a new way, another choice. In a universe of elders who offer only order or chaos, under Sheridan and Delenn's leadership, the younger races choose to reject the binary ideology and embrace the new. The voiceovers from the first two seasons begin to make sense: 'It was the dawn of the *Third* Age of Mankind.' Evolution will take place, but natural evolution, not one created through the perversions of the Vorlons' genetic intervention or the Shadows' psychological games. It is significant that the Vorlons are insubstantial, non-corporeal beings of light and the Shadows are skeletal. The Shadows do not change, using intangible, psychological techniques for their manipulation (the alluring desire for power, glory and victory), whilst the Vorlons use physical ones (appearing as angelic figures from religion and myth and seeding various worlds with telepaths, as we see in 'The Fall of Night' and 'Dust to Dust'). Both aim to create the situation most advantageous to themselves in the next great war, with no concern for the younger races who will carry out their will.

A prime source of this deception occurs through an unwitting Delenn, and more questionably, through the first Ambassador Kosh, who ultimately demonstrates his selflessness and foresight and is prepared to sacrifice himself for the good of the younger species. Delenn is for a long time unaware that she is being manipulated by the Vorlons into using the Rangers and Sheridan in a fashion just as cynical as the Shadows' use of Morden and, through him, the Centauri Ambassador, Londo, and the courtier Lord Refa. Like the characters, the audience is asked to constantly renegotiate its readings, until ultimately we recognise the situation for what it is, not what we have presumed it to be. When we see the two ancient races in their natural form, unsurprisingly, they are not so different. The second Kosh may be non-corporeal, but enraged in 'Falling Towards Apotheosis', its fluctuating light-features are not dissimilar to the overall appearance of the more substantial Shadows: they are, like their ideologies, simply two extremes of the same thing. McMahon refers to Goethe in his demonstration of how equal and opposite the two older races are, when he says, 'There is strong Shadow where there is much Light.'[50] Sheridan is drafted to fight on the 'side of light', as Zathras calls it, but in time we realise that the light of the Vorlons is just as blinding as the darkness of the Shadows. When Sheridan suggests that he has to 'think like them' in order to defeat them (in 'And the Rock Cried Out No Hiding Place'), an appalled Delenn drags him away from the command centre: she had already realised that no answer will be found in such polarised binary logic.

Babylon 5's inherent challenge to binary ideology sometimes occurs in more explicit ways. For example, the idea of the flag, the uniform, the symbol of a nation to be honoured without question and above all else is challenged in 'The Geometry of Shadows'. Every so often, according to tradition, the Drazi enact an arbitrary ritual. They put their hands in a barrel and take out a coloured sash – green or purple. They fight to the death, if necessary, until one side has the upper hand and takes control. Asked by Sheridan to practise her diplomacy by dealing with the ever more flammable situation between the Green and Purple Drazi on Babylon 5, Ivanova is astonished at their explanation for fighting. But her argument that at least human flags 'are worth something' sounds hollow in this context. Ultimately, as Stephen Clark says, we are 'uncomfortably aware that birth and circumstance dictate allegiance just as arbitrarily'.[51] The title of the episode gives a clue to the importance of this seemingly amusing encounter – while the Vorlons and the Shadows are setting up the younger races to fight for them. Sheridan and Delenn initially and unwittingly act on behalf of the Vorlons, battling the Shadows and create a universe of perfect Vorlon order. At the same time, the Shadows through Morden, Emperor Cartagia and President Clark are creating chaos and mistrust on Babylon 5, Centauri Prime and Earth respectively, and dozens of other worlds into the bargain. Each power offers its own twisted version of history and evolution to the younger races.

Manufacturing history is a crime in the world of *Babylon 5*. The Vorlons and the Shadows have done it for centuries, the Narn and Centauri and, to a lesser extent, the humans and Minbari do it before our eyes. For instance, Delenn, in league with Kosh, allows Sheridan to believe that Anna, unwilling to serve the Shadows, must be dead. She and Kosh do not know, they merely presume, but they are wrong. In effect, they deny Sheridan the opportunity to find out for himself, and Delenn faces humiliation for this in 'Z'ha'dum' as Sheridan berates her for not trusting him enough: 'You "couldn't allow it". You'd deny me the right to choose.' Her sin parallels that of the Vorlons, parents who choose for their children, expecting obedience without question. In 'Interludes and Examinations', Kosh has earlier revealed his 'true colours' when he lashes out at Sheridan, calling him 'disrespectful' and 'impertinent'. Later, as he is about to be torn apart by the Shadows, Kosh appears to Sheridan as his father in a dream, admitting that he was wrong: 'You have to fight your way ... I knew what was ahead, I guess – I guess I was afraid.' He is thus distanced from the other Vorlons, who after his apparent death display no concern for the lives of the younger races. In 'The Hour of the Wolf', after Sheridan vanishes at Z'ha'dum the new Vorlon Ambassador tells Delenn, casting around for solace in her grief and frustration, that 'respect is irrelevant'. Lyta Alexander, acting as his ambassadorial aide, suggests that the 'picture just got bigger', and we are forced once more to reconsider what we understand of the Vorlons and their ambitions. The answer is very little.

ORDER AND STRUCTURE

The metaphorical comparison of parent-child relationships and the two older races' control of the younger races are paralleled in some of the actual relationships and their hierarchical structures. The love, or the rift, between parent and child is alluded to frequently. Delenn and Sheridan speak constantly of their love for their parents and their good relations with them. Yet their parents are absent – Delenn's father is dead, her mother in a convent, while Sheridan's father (a retired diplomat) and mother, are on Earth, far from the conflicts in which Sheridan is embroiled, yet supportive of his actions. Delenn and Sheridan thus come to Babylon 5 with no explicit reason to rebel. Delenn initially falls foul of learning her lessons too well: once the prophecy has been fulfilled (that is, the knowledge that Sinclair could offer from taking Babylon 4 back in time and becoming Valen), she is at a loss, her philosophy temporarily challenged by the capricious second Kosh. But Delenn is rebellious and outspoken. She learns a hard lesson from her hasty, angry words in the Earth-Minbari War, for we learn in 'Atonement' that she was the one who cried out 'Strike them down. No mercy. No mercy!' after the tragic death of Dukhat. Now she thinks when she speaks, she considers the consequences. In 'Comes the Inquisitor', the Vorlon emissary, Sebastian, tells her, 'Your only destiny is to be the nail that gets constantly hammered down. Bang, bang, bang.' He instructs her to 'be a nice Minbari, conform, be quiet'. She will not. She refuses to accept the post of leader of the Grey Council, she enters the chrysalis and transforms herself into half-human half-Minbari without the approval of the Council. She flies in the face of tradition when it suits her, electing to marry Sheridan, and she accepts the role of *Entil'za*, leader of the Rangers, despite the rejection of others, most notably Neroon – who later becomes a convert and sacrifices himself to her cause: life.[52] No wonder Dukhat is driven to remark that the truth and Delenn are seldom convenient.[53]

Like Delenn, Sheridan initially acts merely as a convert to the idea of order and structure – as a military man it is unlikely he would appreciate much else. But, like Sinclair before him, Sheridan spends much of his time *not* obeying orders. When he and Ivanova are asked to pay a token fee for their quarters, Sheridan will have none of it and they spend an uncomfortable night in his office, made no better by his terrible jokes. When EarthGov signs a non-aggression pact with the Centauri and refuses to give emergency aid to the Narn, Sheridan still harbours a Narn warship. When President Clark issues an order declaring martial law, Sheridan struggles to delay it – until he realises that the instruction itself is illegal and thus contains its own means of escape. Nevertheless, eventually he announces Babylon 5's secession from the Earth Alliance. So when he feels Kosh is not supporting him in the work against the Shadows, Sheridan rebels, and although that rebellion ultimately, apparently, costs Kosh's life and significantly shortens his own, it also signifies the maturity of the younger races – at least in their leaders. Again, Sheridan takes a third way, not the anticipated selection: he opens 'an unexpected door'.[54]

In 'War Without End' Part 2, pointing out Sinclair, Delenn, and Sheridan in turn, Zathras not only highlights the importance of their roles, but also summarises the key aspects of *Babylon 5*'s narrative. He articulates the importance of remembering that there are not just two rigid binary options, there is a whole range of alternatives. He draws them together in the personifications of Sinclair, Delenn and Sheridan, in a rejection of binarism and old hierarchical structure and orders, reminding Delenn in particular of how Valen had established a tripartite balance in Minbar a thousand years ago (not the religious/warrior dominance of their present time), saying:

> I know you, and I know you, and I know you. All Minbari belief is around three. Three castes: Worker, Warrior, Religious. Three languages: Light, Dark, and Grey. The Nine of the Grey Council – three times three. All is three, as you are three, as you are one. As you are *the* One. You are the One who was. You are the One who is. You are the One who will be. You are the beginning of the story, and the middle of the story and the end of the story that creates the next great story. In your heart you know what Zathras says is true.

The number three is indeed an important figure in *Babylon 5*. It is the manifestation of balance, an alternative path of compromise and sacrifice between intransigent ideological polarity. As Zathrus explains, Sinclair, Delenn and Sheridan form a trinity – each 'the One' as their stars come into ascendancy – but each reliant upon the others, and occupying the same space and time. In the same episode, just *who* is wearing the blue spacesuit *when* becomes an issue – we know Sheridan and Sinclair have worn it, but 'the One' of whom Zathras speaks, is Delenn, who has switched time stabilisers to save Sheridan and appears in time to save Zathras. The three are thus interchangeable and easily confused, yet what they symbolise is clear. They offer an unexpected alternative at a time when alternatives seem extinct.

We can identify the value of 'three' in the Minbari system of which Zathrus speaks – and the Grey Council was notably established by Sinclair, who learns from Delenn and the Minbari of 2059, who follow the practices established by Valen (who was Sinclair). This creates a crucially circular development, which depicts no single person as responsible for the belief system. Three is also a significant number in the transformation of Delenn and Sinclair from Minbari and human to Minbari-human hybrids, and in the result of the blending of Sheridan's military pragmatism and Delenn's spiritual idealism, represented physically by the news of Delenn's pregnancy in 'Wheel of Fire'.[55] Finally, and vitally, the number three also represents the Sublime, as Pascal and de Chardin would have it – the Minute (molecular) and the Immense (the universe), contemplated by the Complex (life). This is articulated by Delenn on many occasions, most notably by her descriptions of the universe, and by Sheridan's experience with Lorien, and it is also visualised repeatedly in *Babylon 5*'s dynamic use of markedly different planes, perspectives and dimensions as part of its active and narrational *mise-en-scène*.

The danger of failing to make use of a third option is also made clear. When Sinclair takes Babylon 4 back in time, he takes with him Zathras – an alien who functions as a beast of burden. With the influence of Valen (and Zathras' words to Sinclair/Valen), the spiritually wise Minbari have understood and recognised the need for a third option, the power of three over the past thousand years. Along with the Warrior and the Religious castes are the Minbari Workers. The Civil War occurs because, as Delenn argues, for too long the Workers were forgotten, while the Warrior and Religious castes held sway. The Minbari temporarily forgot the third option, and reverted to polarised binary politics, resulting in Civil War. Delenn's intended self-sacrifice and Neroon's martyrdom in 'Moments of Transition' remind us all of the dangers of this. Re-forming the Grey Council, Delenn says it will no longer float in the stars, set apart from its people, but will instead be rooted firmly amongst them. The Worker caste has four representatives while the Religious and Warrior caste only have two each. The final place is 'reserved in memory of Neroon, until the day it is taken by the One that is to come'. This is an updating of the traditions we have seen throughout the series, where a place is frequently reserved for the return of Valen (such as the ritualistic preparation and eating of 'Flarn'). The Worker also serves as a link between the Warrior and the Religious caste, the necessary link between the action and the philosophy. Delenn is looking forward here, not backwards, reaching to the future, not trapped by the past.

Interwoven within the very fabric of *Babylon 5* is a central denial of binary ideology, and a demand for an awareness of the interconnectedness of life through actions, thoughts, and words, across the universe. The series can function in this manner because of its strong, preordained epic story arc and although the uncertainty of renewal compromised a smoother narrative flow towards the end of season four and into season five, the story was not overtly compromised. It still utilises long, arc-related threads — the establishment of the new Alliance, the telepath crisis, the Drakh and the fall of Centauri Prime — their ordering and complexity is merely adjusted. The original ability to preordain, foreshadow and, more importantly, flash-forward as well as into the past, creates and maintains a link and a hook, much like Sinclair's 'closed circle', drawing its audience back until a satisfactory resolution to all levels of the story is achieved.

This is how *Babylon 5* turns what can be a weakness of the soap opera format into a considerable strength, whilst simultaneously suffering from a problem unique to its narrative form. Soap opera is driven by the need to multiply incident, the complex multiplicity of plots means that character coherence is secondary to incident, and so participants are forced to act 'out' of character as often as 'in' character: one month, someone is unrepentant over having an affair; the next month, they lead the condemnation of someone else for an identical act. Because soap operas debate and 'work through' current events through discussion from a variety of perspectives and therefore respond to outside, non-diegetic influences, their characters can appear inconsistent or implausible, especially to the casual viewer. Equally, the complicated narrative of *Babylon 5* is likely to be incomprehensible to the casual viewer precisely because its narrative avoids the redundant and arbitrary tendencies of traditional long-term television soap opera, whilst simultaneously exploiting its fundamental elements. It relies upon continuous incident to draw back its audience, but that incident is planned and thus entirely coherent, and in that sense, discrete. It (re)considers actions from various, alternative perspectives at different times, and has an array of potentially malleable characters, from Sheridan and Delenn to the ISN reporters and minor alien delegations. However, these characters are not inconsistent; instead they are evolutionary, changed by both action and circumstance. The complex story, our understanding of both it and of the characters themselves, is directly linked to the degree of knowledge they and we possess of the unfolding arc. The actions of the characters change according to this knowledge. Thus, just as *Babylon 5*'s universe is continuously interwoven with the actions of its characters, so the understanding of that story is interwoven with the attention of its audience. Equally, *Babylon 5* integrates its narrative into our lives, through recognisable social and historical issues from our own cultures, especially from science fiction, but sufficiently distanced for us to encounter them as if anew.

Babylon 5's narrative adheres to the segmented nature of commercial television – writers for American television are well accustomed to five or six commercial breaks within their programmes. However, one of *Babylon 5*'s most daring episodes, 'Intersections in Real Time', sums up the narrative strategy of the entire series. The very pattern of commercial television is used in order to subvert audience expectation and enhance the narrative situation. Here the 'real time' is the narrative of the episode, the interrogation and torture of Sheridan, while the 'intersections' are the uneven commercial breaks. As a result, we lose our sense of time as much as Sheridan does. When the interrogator tells him it is morning, we can only wonder whether or not he is telling us the truth: we have no frame of reference. The segmented narrative is a key feature of television, yet here the use of it superficially destroys our ability to be reassured by reading it. This is a key feature of sf: our frame of reference, our ability to contextualise, is constantly challenged in some manner. In the case of this episode, *Babylon 5* even subverts the actual format of the television episode by using the commercial breaks as structural absences.

VERBAL AND VISUAL IMAGERY

In *Babylon 5*, people carry out extraordinary acts of epic proportions and, as Ivanova's voiceover from 'Sleeping in Light' recognises, sometimes 'true strength comes from the most unlikely places', such as the once indecisive Zack and timid Vir. Yet importantly, all the characters base their lives around very ordinary things. They still eat out, dress up, buy trinkets, have small ambitions and daily desires, personal problems and personal relationships. Garibaldi is a struggling reformed alcoholic, Zack has a questionable past, Sheridan is still mourning the death of his wife Anna (season two), Lyta has financial troubles (season five) and the transformed Delenn in season two has no concept of how to wash her hair, and turns to an aghast Ivanova for help with that and other more personal issues. Trying further to explore her human side, Delenn emerges in a black evening dress, 'which will turn heads', to dine with Sheridan.

Sheridan reciprocates by eating Flarn and engaging in the lengthy associated ritual of meditation and contemplation. G'Kar inexplicably develops a love of Swedish meatballs; Lennier helps Garibaldi build a motorcycle, but adds a clean Minbari fuel source. Ivanova wakes up wondering why her mouth tastes like carpet. Everyday life is at times painfully similar to life as we recognise it today. There are no magical transporters or food replicators in *Babylon 5*, people still eat pizzas and order takeaways. Until after the Earth-Minbar war, Earth Force did not have artificial gravity in its ships, and they bought 'jump-gate' technology from other races. Human expertise has not been enough in isolation, and there are no grand pseudo-scientific explanations of the technology possessed by any race. In *Babylon 5*, technology is used the way we use technology today – we don't sit in awe of a computer, we just use it – like the crew of actors in *Galaxy Quest*. Even if we don't quite understand what *makes* it work, we understand what it *does* and (mostly) how to make it function. If we are confused, aliens are no better. Looking at the control panel in an unfamiliar shuttle on the descent to Epsilon 3 in 'A Voice in the Wilderness' Part 2, Londo muses, 'If I were a landing thruster, which one of these would I be?'

The effect of this careful juxtaposition of the ordinary with the extraordinary establishes a vital connection. It means that the sense of wonder is directed away from technology and out into the sublime universe, into our experience of it – what we see and what we hear. It is underlined by the very ordinary areas of the station the characters frequent, the very ordinary comments they make to each other. We see nondescript docking bays, the customs areas, the security area, the living quarters, the command room and the war room, the chaos of the Zocalo, the bars. Television screens are everywhere – news, information, and entertainment are at a premium. People come together off duty to party, to talk and to watch. Ivanova's illegal coffee plant and Garibaldi's *Daffy Duck* poster only accentuate this very average reality. The interior of Babylon 5 seldom resembles a space station; it is just a place where people live and work, with all the communalities and misunderstandings of mundane life today. Lennier and Vir regularly meet to bemoan their status as aides; in 'The Hour of the Wolf', when G'Kar asks naïvely if Daffy represents one of Garibaldi's household gods, Zack wickedly tells him, 'It's sort of the Egyptian God of Frustration.' Juxtaposed with this everydayness, however, is not just the apparently endless variety of aliens who live and work on the station, nor the mystical turn of phrases we hear from them – Delenn, G'Kar and Kosh in particular. There are also the incredible visions we see outside the station – the beautiful, stark universe, a dynamic vision of the cosmos, full of secret wonders. Mapped and charted it may be, and the life within integral and eternally connected, but mysteries and conundrums abound. Even as Sheridan and Delenn regard Babylon 5, Epsilon 3 and the nebula behind it, in 'Into the Fire', Sheridan remarks that, with the First Ones, the Shadows and the Vorlons gone, the magic has also gone. But Delenn corrects him: 'Now we make our own magic,' she says.

Matte artist Eric Chauvin confirms that he did considerably more work per episode on *Babylon 5* than on *Star Trek: Voyager*.[56] Certainly, *Babylon 5*'s frequent images of space and space travel utilise depth and mobility in a remarkable manner, shifting between planes and perspectives, spinning, swirling and rotating. The departure of the Imperial Centauri vessels following the death of Turhan in 'The Coming of Shadows' is a fine example of how this occurs in even the briefest of scenes. Epsilon 3 and the nebulae form the background, closer is Babylon 5, and alongside (but closer for the viewer) are the Centauri vessels. Maintaining the rotating station as its central focus, the 'camera' turns from left to right as the ships depart to the left. The result is not only powerfully dynamic, but also three-dimensional, because the different planes of action and their various movements are highlighted. Paralleling the advances made by the American landscape artists Bierstadt and Church in the late 1800s, our gaze is mobilised through the judicious use of new technology. *Babylon 5* creates dynamic composite vistas, channelling incredible depth and vibrant motion into its television images, creating a narrative *mise-en-scène* of intense power.

Except for the rarely used observation deck and Ivanova's limited view from the command centre – both with rotating backgrounds – *Babylon 5* has nothing akin to the *Star Trek* view-screens. A journey into hyperspace, the equivalent of the quiet, unflickering starlight of *Star Trek*'s warp speed, resembles a trip through hell. Angry, glaring vortices of red and black swirl in constant flux around the ships, and the danger of losing contact with the navigational beacon is made repeatedly clear ('A Distant Star', 'The Fall of Night', and 'Movements of Fire and Shadow'). When we emerge into normal space, incredible vistas, many from images captured by the Hubble telescope,[57] open up before our eyes. In normal space, the background is never static or empty. Planets have recognisable features, and the ships of the various League and Alliance members appear in a variety of designs: elegant and functional, yet aesthetically colourful and extraordinary. Whereas vessels' outer hulls in many series appear a uniform colour, in *Babylon 5* the ships are as diverse in size, shape, colour and form as the beings operating them. The First Ones' ships are massive, brilliant manifestations of light and movement, dwarfing and diminishing the flamboyance of the Alliance vessels as they enjoin battle. The organic Vorlon ships are squid-like,[58] incomprehensible hieroglyphs appearing on their hulls as they move; the Shadow vessels are obsidian, the light sliding off their spidery outline, an inchoate scream reverberating as they pass by.

The White Stars at Sheridan's disposal move in all directions possible, bird-like in their appearance and motion. The Starfuries don't turn, they twist, switching direction almost instantly; larger ships rotate or turn in the smallest circle possible, whilst the Shadow vessels utilise a strange uncertain trajectory, in keeping with their semi-organic nature. Their laser weapons slice through other vessels in nanoseconds. They do not launch fighters or missiles, but disgorge them in a shuddering orgasmic travesty of ejaculation, conception and birth. In turn, these explode into swarming clouds of arachnid weaponry. Larger vessels, notably the White Stars and the elegant angelfish Minbari warships (the less developed progenitors of which we see in 'War Without End' Part 2, when Valen/Sinclair takes Babylon 4 a thousand years back in time), have view-screens, but more frequently use three-dimensional hologrids, which cascade down from the ceiling. During the terrible battle in 'Shadow Dancing', Sheridan and Delenn command their fleet with a view of the entire arena: the conflict surrounds them, encasing them. The magnitude and final cost of the event is plain to see: fragments of shattered hulls drift all around, and the narrative shifts from epic to personal to epic as we see the conflict run its course, and the cost to those involved.[59]

Danger and terror, wonder and joy await us in the universe of *Babylon 5*. If we haven't realised this constant flux through the marvellous, omni-directional visuals, we have smaller visual signs: the costumes. Elaborate and diverse, their use is one of the simplest and clearest things differentiating *Babylon 5* from other sf series, altering according to the evolving characters and situation. Each racial grouping has an identifiable style of clothing, but it does not remain constant. The starchy blue and brown Earth Force uniform of the first three seasons gives way to the stylish black and silver outfits Delenn offers Sheridan, Ivanova, Franklin, and Garibaldi in 'Ceremonies of Light and Dark', symbolic of their movement away from Earth towards independence. Morden's flashy jewellery and designer suits become less ostentatious as the Shadow war develops, and positively minimalist as the war ends. Delenn's initially harsh appearance softens as she undertakes a change to become partly human. Her ridged head-crest bone becomes tiara-like (albeit reversed), and whilst her dresses retain their kimono-like Minbari origins, they become more flowing and elegant, reminiscent of a fairy-tale princess. When she is called into action, she wears a simpler, more practical outfit – but often has a cloak – again reminiscent of disguised princesses. Sheridan changes from youthful leader to sober statesman, his uniforms and business suits reflecting this transition, whilst Londo's colourful and flamboyant waistcoats and jackets become darker, more sober, as his character descends into a personal abyss, and he oscillates between drunken clown and Shadow puppet.

Alongside the visual imagery, we also have the verbal imagery of neologisms and transformed language identified by Rabkin to remind us of *Babylon 5*'s magic.[60] Kosh offers us the most examples of transformed language: in 'Deathwalker', he requests a meeting 'at the hour of scampering', suggesting that Talia 'listen to the music, not the song', and in 'Believers' he notes that if 'the avalanche has already begun, it is too late for the pebbles to vote'. The use of the Minbari and, to a lesser extent, the Narn languages creates adequate neologisms to underline the alien environment. Delenn is still learning English, and her attempts to speak more colloquially are somewhat embarrassing – 'abso-fraggin-lutely, dammit' in 'The Long Twilight Struggle' – but also quite natural. The everyday nature of conversation and avoidance of technical jargon juxtaposed with the exotic and alien removes the mundanity enforced by *Star Trek*'s universal translator, or *Stargate SG-1*'s basis of alien tongues in ancient human languages. In 'War

Without End' Part 1, we are denied knowledge of *all* of what Sinclair says to Delenn after Sheridan is snatched out of time. Only part of it is translated by subtitles – thus creating additional questions. In *Babylon 5*, visual and verbal language, juxtapositions and hiatuses perpetuate the mystery of existence.

When Sheridan confesses that he is uncertain about his posting to Babylon 5, Delenn lapses into poetic language, mystical and enigmatic. She tells him that:

> The universe puts us in places where we can learn. They are never easy places, but they are right. Wherever we are is the right place and the right time. Pain sometimes comes – it is part of the process of constantly being born. We are both, I suppose, going through transitions, but the Universe knows what it is doing.

> ... Then I will tell you a great secret, Captain, perhaps the greatest of all time. The molecules of your body are the same molecules that make up this station and the nebulae outside. They burn inside the stars themselves. We are starstuff. We are the universe made manifest, trying to figure itself out. As we have both learned, sometimes the universe requires a change of perspective.[61]

THE SUBLIME

Delenn does not only wax lyrical and philosophical: her connection of the minute and the immense performs that powerful function of the Sublime identified by Pascal, de Chardin and Robu. This is one of Delenn's main character functions: it is she who creates the impulse, the necessary connections, the link between the one and the three and the impetus for change, through her own actions towards her great cause – life.[62] Distracted elsewhere from the ordinary and mundane, her words encourage us to locate the smallest molecules, moving to complex contemplation of our place in the universe and to the immense majesty of the universe around us. This is rare in sf television, but it is common in sf literature, as the opening paragraph to Arthur C. Clarke's 'Who's There?' (1958) demonstrates:

When Satellite Control called me, I was writing up the day's progress report in the Observation Bubble – the glass-domed office that juts out from the axis of the Space Station like the hubcap of a wheel. It was not really a good place to work, for the view was too overwhelming. Only a few yards away I could see the construction teams performing their slow-motion ballet as they put the station together like a giant jigsaw puzzle. And beyond them, twenty three thousand miles below, was the blue-green glory of the full Earth, floating against tho ravolled star clouds of the Milky Way.[63]

It is this poetic articulation of the Sublime in juxtaposition with the mundane that allies *Babylon 5* to literary sf, simultaneously distancing it from so much science fiction television. It is also part of how the series best articulates its epic nature: the universe is a place of natural wonder, and we are but a tiny part of it.

The Sublime also occurs in depictions of Babylon 5 itself. The last of the Babylon stations is an impressive five miles long, a complete city in space, encased in 'two million five hundred thousand tons of spinning metal – all alone in the night'. The station, which appears in a different manner in all five seasons' opening credits, is remarkable, akin to those 'vast, magnificent and obscure' objects which 'evoked sublime emotions'.[64] Writing of the Sublime in general, Fred Botting suggests that:

loudness and sudden contrasts, like the play of light and dark in buildings, contributed to the sense of extension and infinity associated with the sublime. While beauty could be contained within an individual's gaze, sublimity presented an excess that could not be processed by a rational mind. This excess, which confronted the individual subject with the thoughts of its own extinction, derived from emotions which ... produced a *frisson* of delight and horror, tranquillity and terror.[65]

Certainly, the use of light and dark (inherent to the story) is freely expressed in visualisations of Babylon 5. During the five-season run, we see it from a remarkable variety of angles and perspectives, many designed as more than mere establishing shots, although these are of course used between acts. A fine example of light and dark occurs in the second-season title sequence. As Epsilon 3 eclipses the light of its star, it casts the shining blue rotating station into darkness – until its own lights come on to illuminate it in almost chiaroscuro fashion against the backdrop of the planet and vast nebulae. Undoubtedly, the station is 'a shining beacon, all alone in the night'. As previously noted, the importance of scale identified by Pascal and de Chardin is reiterated by Delenn in her mantra: 'We stand between the candle and the star.' Her much-loved linkage of the smallest molecule to ambulant life, to the nebulae outside, is also drawn to our attention. Visually, it also occurs repeatedly, often in establishing shots, where the tiny maintbots' continual engineering work, and ships in their vicinity, create a grand impression of scale. It is articulated most firmly during the same title sequence, which draws us out from the helmet of a space-worker, reflecting the blue-white stars around it, to the station itself, to the planet and nebula beyond. Babylon 5 itself stands literally 'between the candle and the star', and metaphorically, as a fortress 'between the darkness and the light'.

TITLES AND MUSIC

So, *Babylon 5* establishes an ideology and narrative pattern which visually, verbally and intellectually creates a challenge to its viewers. There is another means of ensuring familiarity does not set in at every level. Just as epics rely upon continuity and multiplicity of incident, so sf must also continue challenging its viewers. As noted earlier, *Babylon 5* changes its title sequence and theme music every season as part of a strategy to ensure familiarity does not settle in too quickly: the voiceover introduction also changes each season. These sequences offer dynamic glimpses of the marvels within the programme and also a guide to the mood of each season, which changes dramatically. The titles are mysterious and anonymous in season one, showing images of the station's construction and its inhabitants to Sinclair's voiceover and then the cast's names, merely captions set against a rotating background of the nebula outside Babylon 5, while the relatively nondescript theme builds gradually. In season two, the characters are more accessible, the cast is shown in pleasant, full-screen shots, the music is louder, more flamboyant. With the impending war in season three, Ivanova's voiceover announces daringly that the 'last best hope for peace' has 'failed'. The pictures are more determined here: the camera runs along the emphatically hard and lean outer hull of the station, with superimposed images of the cast turning as if to address their audience, whilst the music (although changing only superficially throughout the series), elevates its darker, more sombre tones. Season four is explosive: split-screen images of war and violence from the past seasons collide with images of the characters in action, while in season five the music blossoms into a celebratory anthem as images of Babylon 5's achievement give way to imagery of serious, mature characters.

The music is also non-specific, whereas the themes from *The Next Generation* and *Voyager*, etc. all have triumphant French horn and trumpet elements which are highly reminiscent of music normally associated with pioneering Westerns. *Babylon 5* eschews this, using instead far less generic, and more neutral, tonalities.[66] It does not possess the innovative alien qualities of *Farscape*'s sound design, but it is a far cry from the brass triumphalism of *The Next Generation* or *Voyager*, which equates the cosmos with the Wild West. Likewise, although its title sequences contain seasonal historical introductions, *Babylon 5* is not generally prone to the use of voiceovers, or a version of the 'Captain's Log'. However, at the rare, but vital, moments in the series, when additional voiceovers do occur, they come from non-humans, confirming the purposeful egalitarian nature of the series. Ivanova may warn of the coming war in 'The Fall of Night' at the end of season two, and she continues this grim overview with her season three voiceover, but in 'Z'ha'dum', after Sheridan's presumed death, it is G'Kar who speaks in poignant anticipation of the future. As we watch Shadow vessels circling their destroyed city, and the chasm into which Sheridan plummets in his desperate act of self-sacrifice, the Narn tells us that:

> It was the end of the Earth year 2260, and the war had paused, suddenly and unexpectedly. All around us it was as if the universe were holding its breath, waiting.

> All of life can be broken down into moments of transition or moments of revelation. This had the feeling of both.

G'Quan wrote: 'There is a greater darkness than the one we fight. It is the darkness of the soul that has lost its way. The war we fight is not against powers and principalities: it is against chaos, and despair. Greater than the death of flesh is the death of hope, the death of dreams. Against this peril we can never surrender.'

The future is all around us, waiting in moments of transition to be born in moments of revelation. No-one knows the shape of that future, or where it will take us. We know only that it is always born in pain.

Delenn introduces 'War Without End' Part 2 and 'Z'ha'dum' and comments upon the next twenty years of the Alliance in 'Rising Star'. The fourth and fifth seasons' introductions are also truly intergalactic, with excerpts from previous episodes and a multi-cast introduction. Proposals for a new Inter-Stellar Alliance involving the four major planetary powers and the League of Non-Aligned Worlds are presented in 'Rising Star', not by Sheridan but by Delenn. Similarly, the 'Declaration of Principles' (for the new Alliance) is drafted by G'Kar; his literary skills have been nicely honed throughout the past two seasons, during which he wrote a book of philosophical and spiritual revelation. Thus the future is seen to belong to everyone, and to be of everyone's making, equally human and non-human. It can fairly be argued that the smaller races are too frequently demonstrated to be spineless, conniving or simply untrustworthy. Andy Lane notes a fascist tendency of the Rangers in 'Learning Curve', reminding us that they are appointed by, and answerable to, originally unelected persons such as Delenn and Sheridan, and questions the passing of the Presidency to Delenn after Sheridan's death.[67] However, both Sheridan and Delenn earn a right to leadership through their deeds as well as their promises, and the general atmosphere is overwhelmingly suggestive of positive collaboration, which will in turn lead to justice, equality and a potentially better future for everyone.

Lane's point is perhaps related to the fact that the new Alliance is not suggested by EarthGov or by any popular consensus but by an external force. Brought to its knees by President Clark, Earth is merely invited to join, although admittedly the ground-rumbling flyover by the White Star fleet as Delenn states the terms of the treaty is more threatening than welcoming. But this is not the direct threat of external intervention in *The Day the Earth Stood Still* (1951), where Sobchack sees the 'Platonic values' manifested in Klaatu's ascetic flying saucer (and his giant robot, Gort) as a cry for 'clarity, sanity and reason' in direct contrast to the chaotic *mise-en-scène* of Washington DC's human sprawl.[68] The 1950s fear of a kindly warning, or a god-like intervention in the face of adversity or human foolishness, was not far from the fear of pure invasion – with no salvation, as *Invasion of the Body Snatchers* suggests. In *Babylon 5*, Earth is invited to join the new Alliance, not merely scolded by a paternalistic *deus ex machina*, and the Rangers, unlike Klaatu's intergalactic robot police force, are drawn from members of all the Alliance worlds. Thus an alternative partnership of human and alien (in Sheridan and Delenn's case, also of male and female, and alien/human hybridity), is made clear in these articulations, and the actions and imagery of the series further this ambition. This seasonal change and use of 'alien' voiceovers may seem minor, but it operates in direct contrast to the familiar and constant opening sequences of other sf series, which do not change, or merely enhance/amend certain aspects of their visuals.

A NEW EPIC, A NEW IDEOLOGY

In contrast to other series, then, *Babylon 5* subtly and effectively changes its titles, voiceover and music each season. Its characters not only evolve psychologically and philosophically, but their appearances also alter superficially or more fundamentally to underline this change. It works on both the epic and the novelistic levels, providing documentary observation and personal experiences. *Babylon 5* also dwells upon its images of the galaxy more than any other series, and the choice of imagery and its inherent narrative – the narrative *mise-en-scène*, as opposed to the dramatic narrative – is another factor distinguishing it from its peers. Ironically, it is partly the problematic financing of *Babylon 5* that presented it with the opportunity to use imagery in a more daring and more frequent manner. Although Eric Chauvin believes that the visual appearance of *Babylon 5* is 'the result of several factors', he unsurprisingly rates the most significant factor as money. However, echoing some of Caldwell's ideas of televisual technological innovation, Chauvin suggests that when the series started, it already 'had more visually ambitious shots than the budget could afford. A big cost saver was doing all the FX shots on a desktop computer.' So, even discounting financial reasons for numerous matte and FX shots, *Babylon 5*'s ambitions importantly combined imagery with narrative from the start. Chauvin felt that its sets:

> were very unimpressive compared to those on say the Star Trek series. To make up for their shortcomings a lot was done in the mood of lighting on the sets. The use of shadows, pool lighting and atmospherics (smoke) were used to add visual interest inexpensively. This economical approach to the show also [a]ffected the work I did on the show. Shots that were designed had high production value but didn't cost much to produce ... Once the producer caught onto how much production value they could get for the money, the amount of shots I did exponentially increased from season to season.[69]

If *Babylon 5*'s future galactic history forms the bedrock for its narrative, partially through intent and partially through financial requirements, the images of that future, its verbal articulation and the sense of destiny jointly evoked through them, are equally vital. Like everything in *Babylon 5*, they are integrated, integral, not merely pretty backdrops or exotic locations soon forgotten. But *Babylon 5* represents more than an innovative and clever use of television narrative forms and visuals by a determined author/producer and collaborative crew. It also represents that which lies at the heart of sf and yet, as we have seen, is so rarely offered consistently by television: an ideological break. As Gareth Roberts notes, this:

> is why *Babylon 5* is in such an important position. It comments upon where we are now as western culture fractures beneath the alternatives from around the world, as well as from internal pressures born of previously excluded factions of society (in terms of gender and class). We are in crisis. For too long the brutality of dichotomy, thesis and antithesis has blunted our thinking ... We have grown beyond such thinking, matured to a point were we can handle more than mere binary opposition. It served its purpose, but its time is passed.[70]

The light of destiny in *Babylon 5* is like its ideology, it is not linear: it is everywhere. Instead of the directional, binary light of the frontier – west towards the future or east towards the past – a divine illumination of a specific location ahead of us in time and place, in *Babylon 5* our destiny is where we make it, and where we find it. If the good ship Voyager vanishes into a diamond flash of light on its way home, *Babylon 5* itself *is* that light – 'a shining beacon, all alone in the night'. Only at the end does the station itself perish, in fire, as predicted by Ladira twenty-five years earlier. But the promise forged within it lives on.

Even in the final episode this wonder remains. In 'Sleeping in Light', Sheridan dreams of Lorien, who tells him that he must return to the place where it all began. We were forewarned of this in 'The Day of the Dead'. Kosh's message to Sheridan is: 'When the long night comes, return to the end of the beginning' – a typically cryptic reference to Coriana 6, the site of the final encounter between the Vorlons and Shadows. Bidding an agonised farewell, Sheridan and Delenn remind us of their connection with the universal Sublime: 'Goodnight my love, the brightest star in my sky,' he says. 'Goodnight – you, who are my sky, and my sun, and my moon,' she replies. Departing from Minbar, Sheridan visits Babylon 5. Its fate is intrinsically linked to that of Sheridan – it is about to be decommissioned. Sheridan then travels on alone to the place where the new order was finally, incontrovertibly established: Coriana 6. He tells Delenn it is better to 'end out there'. The power of myth is articulated through the mature Sheridan, as is a recognition of the need for it: just as Valen's body is never found, so in-diegesis and ex-diegesis, people will never know exactly what happened to Sheridan. Our rare omniscience, our privilege as television viewers in this scene, is to watch Lorien return in a shimmering blaze of silver/golden light, to take him beyond the Rim.

The magic and wonder of the moment is returned to at the end of the episode. Watching Delenn greeting the golden Minbar sunrise, as she did with Sheridan during their last hours, Ivanova says: 'As for Delenn – every morning, for as long as she lived, Delenn got up before dawn and watched the sun come up.' In the golden glow of the sunrise, the image of Sheridan, clad in golden brown robes, appears briefly at Delenn's side as her outstretched hand reaches beyond him, towards the future: despite its incredible sadness, the present and the past infuse the tableau with warmth and security.[71] The scene also reiterates what *Babylon 5* has dared suggest elsewhere: beyond what we can perceive lies the 'next great story', the next step in evolution. For now it remains hidden in a blaze of light, but that light is like that of the early New England Luminists – artists who created their images before America began actively to 'compose' its Manifest Destiny and thus its landscape. It is centred, not directional: it is simply beyond.

That it is sunrise, not sunset, may seem a small difference, but it is one of incalculable significance. Sunrise does not offer us the light of something past, a light which can only be chased along a narrow, linear course – futilely sought behind Yosemite's El Capitan, the western mountains, or the next star – always just beyond our grasp. Sunrise is the dawning of a new day, the promise of light all around, and its light is shared by all. It casts down tangible sublimity in the tradition of those clouds in nineteenth-century American landscape art, but that light moves towards us, not away from us. It is the promise of the future, not a dusky remembrance of what has been and is gone; in *Babylon 5* it is quite literally 'the dawn of the Third Age of Mankind'.

Fittingly, given her prophetic introduction to the third season, the words that summarise the story that begins 'the next great story' are spoken by Susan Ivanova:

> Babylon 5 was the last of the Babylon stations. There would never be another. It changed the future and it changed us. It taught us that we have to create the future, or others will do it for us. It showed us that we have to care for one another, because if we don't, who will? And that true strength sometimes comes from the most unlikely places. Mostly though, I think it gave us hope that there can always be new beginnings, even for people like us.[72]

But Ivanova's words are not the end. Even 'The Deconstruction of Falling Stars' does not show us 'the end', only the end of one portion of the story. As 'Sleeping in Light' closes, the credits (uniquely absent from the beginning of the episode) acknowledge not only the characters and the cast, but also the team behind the programme. Meanwhile, the voiceover tells us that we have been watching a 'historical document'

– an ISN 'take' on the story of the last of the Babylon stations. As maudlin grief sets in at the loss of Sheridan and the end of *Babylon 5*, the objective interrupts us yet again. We have indeed been watching historical records of epic events; the only difference is that they are not recorded *past* events but, in the fashion of science fiction, records of a potential *future*. Even in its final seconds, *Babylon 5* subverts our expectations and subverts the traditions of television and television science fiction.

Babylon 5 was created through collective boutique authorship and marketing, it is an epic that acknowledges but transcends the fractured mythology of the frontier to find a new means of ideological expression and a new hope in the same location promised to us by the Western – that 'undiscovered country' of the future.[13] Its Machiavellian politics compel us to explore our own political ideologies through the potent future histories of science fiction. Through its incorporation of the Sublime within its *mise-en-scène*, *Babylon 5* reminds us of ancient speculations and journeys of discovery. With its constant use of neologisms, alien lexicons, arcane and transformed language, its poetic and linguistic juxtapositions create and enhance a strong degree of cognitive estrangement. Its combination of the novelistic and the epic, its consistent reworking of traditional television forms, through subversion, deviation and repetition on many levels, ensures a constant renegotiation of those ontological structures and institutions so often taken for granted. Like Rilke encountering true myth in Apollo, in *Babylon 5* we face true myth. Like Apollo to Rilke, it tells us that we must change our lives.[14]

CONCLUSION

Since the earliest days of film and television, science fiction has graced the small screen in some form. Some of the best shows, like the original *Outer Limits* or *The Twilight Zone*, demonstrate repeatedly that fancy sfx are not necessary for thought-provoking television, and they offer sf at its philosophical best. However, as broadcast technology has advanced and increased, so have our expectations, and we demand so much more. Since the 1980s, television has been able to offer not just spectacular stories but spectacular visions; the old wordy expositional scenarios have been replaced by more minimalism in scripts, flashing lights and clunking computers by dazzling cgi that morgos seamlessly with analogue sfx to create impossible yet entirely plausible worlds. The previously dominant action-narrative became equalled, and sometimes surpassed, by the coexistent narrative of a vibrant *mise-en-scène*: the background could not only be seen, it could be explored — and science fiction came boldly to the foreground of television.

The peculiarly domestic location of television actually encourages that particular distanciation demanded by sf, and the result is a more adventurous, more demanding and more stimulating kind of storytelling. Science fiction can fill a half hour or twenty-minute slot; it can offer individual episodic hours of alienation or longer-term narratives that occasionally pick up on that which has gone before. Or it can provide an epic: a vast sprawling interconnected narrative demanding absolute and irrevocable attention from its niche audience. The advent of new technologies and the advent of new forms of narrative have allowed sf to mature, to go boldly where sf has not gone before – and to demonstrate to the world that it can not only work on television, it can work exceptionally well. More than this, its constant renegotiation and reconsideration of events demands that we *think* outside as well as within our subject text. Its iconoclastic scenarios actively challenge tired ideologies and concepts, easy answers and false histories. In this way, it has shown itself to be a new way forward for mythology – a free reworking and interrogation of old themes does not only breathe new life into them, it also allows them to be rejected in favour of new paradigms and new ways forward. Its possibilities are endless, its hope is eternal and it offers us infinite 'unrealised realities' in which we can not only play but we can also wonder: what if?

Genre is an on-going process; we can only capture a snapshot of it at a particular moment in time, our lens tinted by our own hopes, fears and aspirations. However, this book has tried to draw together indicators of what seem to be fascinating connections, repetitions and progressions. Ultimately, it is perhaps natural for America's myth-making faculties not just to turn from the Western, but also actively to seek the opportunities of science fiction. Science fiction television can then take on the mantle of a new kind of visual American mythos – one that necessarily draws on its past, one that is invariably indicative of its current cultural and ideological concerns, but one that can also extrapolate – and to look *forward* is surely a positive act. This is something which the elegiac Western could never actually do, time-tied as it was by the closure of a very real frontier, and limited as it is by a preconceived historical reality. The art of the frontier articulates this problem most clearly – the pictures look to the west, but invariably it is sunset, the day is gone and a sense of nostalgia already dominates. Without that temporal and directional shackle, with television now able to rival cinema in technical expertise and aesthetic spectacle (if not in size), and with a more visually literate audience whose interest in storytelling is sometimes as much about the process of telling as the story itself, the medium of the small screen can offer us the wonders of sf as never before. There is a movement away from technical fascinations towards a more contemplative and open-minded image of the future

– a place where much of what we value and treasure about our lives remains, and a place where much of what we dislike about the worst of humanity can be safely explored. Modern American sf television is neither utopian nor dystopic; it enforces a critique of the Western mythos, whilst renegotiating its finer aspects. It is a place where there is much to do and where there are many faults, but also a place where there is much hope for humanity. Most of all, this new sf is far-seeing: it is truly tele-vision.

NOTES

INTRODUCTION

1. John W. Campbell, cited in Edward James, *Science Fiction in the Twentieth Century* (Oxford: Oxford University Press, 1994), 56.
2. Reginald Bretnor, 'Science Fiction in the Age of Space', in R. Bretnor (ed.), *Science Fiction: Today and Tomorrow* (New York: Harper and Row, 1974), 150.
3. http://www.antwrp.gsfc.nasa.gov/apod/astropix.html
4. Andrew Darley, *Visual Digital Culture: Surface Play and Spectacle in New Media* (London: Routledge, 2000), 96.
5. J.P. Telotte, *Science Fiction Film* (Cambridge: Cambridge University Press, 2001), 9.
6. John Thornton Caldwell, *Televisuality: Style, Crisis and Authorship in American Television* (New Brunswick, New Jersey: Rutgers University Press), 1995.
7. Samuel R. Delany, *The American Shore: Meditations on a Tale of Science Fiction By Thomas M. Disch – 'Angoulême'* (Elizabethtown: Dragon Press, 1978), 55.
8. Darko Suvin, *Metamorphoses of Science Fiction: On the Poetics and History of a Literary Genre* (London: Yale University Press, 1979).
9. *The Epic of Gilgamesh*, translated and introduced by N.K. Sandars, revised edition (Harmondsworth: Penguin Books, 1972).

10. Edmund Burke, *A Philosophical Enquiry into the Origin of our Ideas of the Sublime and Beautiful* (Oxford: Oxford University Press, 1992); Immanuel Kant, *The Critique of Pure Reason*, translated and edited by Paul Guyer and Allen W. Wood (Cambridge: Cambridge University Press, 1997).

11. Pierre Teilhard de Chardin, *La Place de l'homme dans la nature. Le groupe zoologique humain* (Paris: Albin Michel, 1949) and Blaise Pascal, discussed in Cornel Robu, 'The Sublime: A Key to Science Fiction', *Foundation*, 42 (Spring, 1988).

12. John Hellman, *American Myth and the Legacy of Vietnam* (New York: Columbia University Press, 1986).

13. John Ellis, *Visible Fictions*, revised edition (London: Routledge, 1992); and Raymond Williams, *Television: Technology and Cultural Form* (London: Fontana, 1974).

14. Patrick Parrinder (ed.), *Science Fiction: A Critical Guide* (London: Longman, 1979); Patrick Parrinder, *Science Fiction: Its Criticism and its Teaching* (London: Methuen, 1980); Eric S. Rabkin, 'Metalinguistics and Science Fiction', *Critical Inquiry* (Autumn 1979), 79–97; Claudio Guillen, *Literature As System: Essays Towards the Theory of Literary History* (Princeton: Princeton University Press, 1971); Damien Broderick, *Reading By Starlight: Postmodern Science Fiction* (London: Routledge, 1995); Fredric Jameson, *Postmodernism, or the Culture Logic of Late Capitalism* (Durham, North Carolina: Duke University Press, 1991), and *The Geopolitical Aesthetic* (London: BFI, 1992); Steve Neale, 'Questions of Genre', *Screen*, 31, No. 1 (1990), 45–66, and 'Aspects of ideology and narrative form in the American war film', *Screen*, 32, No. 1 (1991), 35–57; and Robin Wood, 'Ideology, Genre, Auteur', in Mast, Cohen and Braudy (eds), *Film Theory and Criticism: Introductory Readings*, 4th edition (Oxford: Oxford University Press, 1992), 475–485.

15. Mikhail Bakhtin, *Rabelias and His World*, translated by Hélène Iwolsky (Bloomington: Indiana University Press, 1984).

16. Michèle Barrett and Duncan Barrett, *Star Trek: The Human Factor* (London: Polity Press, 2001).

ONE: SCIENCE FICTION IN CONTEXT

1. Brian Stableford, John Clute and Peter Nicholls, 'Definitions of SF', in Clute and Nicholls (eds), *The Encyclopaedia of Science Fiction*, 2nd edition (London: Orbit Books, 1993), 311.
2. Arthur C. Clarke, *Astounding Days: A Science Fiction Autobiography* (London: Victor Gollancz, 1989), 11.
3. Stableford, Clute and Nicholls, 'Definitions of SF', 311–314.
4. Broderick, *Reading By Starlight*, 3.
5. Vivian Sobchack, *Screening Space: The American Science Fiction Film*, 2nd enlarged edition (New Brunswick, New Jersey: Rutgers University Press, 1987), 17.
6   In Brian Aldiss and Brian Wingrove, *Trillion Year Spree: The History of Science Fiction*, 2nd edition (London: Victor Gollancz, 1986), 446.
7. Parrinder, *Criticism and Teaching*.
8. Broderick, *Reading By Starlight*, 4.
9. Kathryn Cramer, 'On Science and Science Fiction', in David Hartwell and Kathryn Cramer (eds), *The Ascent of Wonder: The Evolution of Hard SF* (London: Orbit Books, 1994), 24.
10. Fredric Jameson, 'Towards a New Awareness', *Science Fiction Studies*, No. 9 (1982), 322.
11. Guillen, *Literature As System*, 508–510.
12. Tzvetan Todorov, *The Fantastic: A Structural Approach*, translated by Richard Howard (Ithaca: Cornell University Press, 1975), 3–4.
13. See Broderick, *Reading By Starlight*, 29.
14. James Donald, *Fantasy and the Cinema* (London: BFI, 1989), 10.
15. Jameson, 'Towards a New Awareness', 322.
16. John Caughie, 'Adorno's reproach: repetition, difference and television genre', *Screen*, 31, No. 2 (Summer 1991), 127.
17. Jostein Gripsrud, *The Dynasty Years: Hollywood Television and Critical Media Studies* (London: Routledge, 1995), 20.
18. Robin Wood, 'Ideology, Genre, Auteur', 478.
19. Broderick, *Reading By Starlight*, 15.
20. Delany, *The American Shore*, 55.
21. Jonathan Culler, *Structuralist Poetics: Structuralism, Linguistics and the Study of Literature* (Ithaca: New York, 1975), 189.

22. Kathleen L. Spencer, '"The Red Sun is High, the Blue Low": Towards a Stylistic Description of Science Fiction', *Science Fiction Studies*, 10 (March 1983), 38.

23. Suvin, *Metamorphoses of Science Fiction*, 7–8.

24. Robert Stam, *Film Theory: An Introduction* (Oxford: Basil Blackwell, 2000), 48.

25. Ibid.

26. Estrangement is also common to the fairy tale and folk tale, and indeed Harry Levin asks us to consider the folklore categories established by the Formalists as 'the standard situations' of science fiction. Harry Levin, 'Science and Fiction', in G. Slusser, G. Guffey, and M. Rose (eds), *Bridges to Science Fiction* (Carbondale: University of Illinois Press, 1980), 21.

27. The rigorously aesthetic approach of the Formalists lies in opposition to the dominant Realist/Romantic aesthetic theories of the time, epitomised by the maxim that 'art is thinking in images'. Alexander Potebnya, quoted in *Russian Formalist Criticism: 4 Essays*, translated and edited by Lee T. Lemon and Marion J. Reis (Lincoln: University of Nebraska Press, 1965), 5.

28. Jurji Tynjanov, quoted in Stam, *Film Theory*, 49. See also Tynjanov, 'On Literary Evolution', in Ladislav Matejka and Krystyna Pomorska (eds), *Readings in Russian Poetics: Formalist and Structuralist Views* (Ann Arbor: University of Michigan, 1978), 66–78.

29. However, this approach does not openly consider that all language is a complicated and disparate series of discourses, varying according to context, gender, class, status and region. Thus estrangement only works against a 'certain normative linguistic background' and, if this background were to alter, the writing might no longer be literary. Terry Eagleton, *Literary Theory: An Introduction* (Oxford: Basil Blackwell, 1983), 5. So the first problem with estrangement is that its effect cannot be guaranteed. The second problem with this explanation of estrangement facilitates the type of humour so beloved of *Monty Python*. If we put in enough effort and creativity we can read almost anything as estranging. An apparently unambiguous statement like 'Dogs must be carried on the escalator' is less

unambiguous than at first sight. Eagleton asks 'Does it means that you *must* carry a dog on the escalator? Are you likely to be banned from the escalator unless you can find some stray mongrel to clutch in your arms on the way up?' (Eagleton, 6–7). Nevertheless, to read the sign in this fashion is still to read it as poetry. This is the vital distinction here – the specific and special use of language which exists not only *inside* the text, but also *outside* of it. Thus 'Literariness' is a 'function of the differential relations between one sort of discourse and another' (Eagleton, 5); it is not a permanent condition.

30. Eagleton, 136.
31. Ibid.
32. Ibid. 137
33. Roman Jakobson, 'Closing Statement: Linguistics and Poetics', in T.A. Seboek (ed.), *Style in Language* (Cambridge: MIT Press, 1960), 377. Also known as 'Concluding Statement'.
34. 'Classic Film Theory and Semiotics', in John Hill and Pamela Church Gibson (eds), *The Oxford Guide to Film Studies* (Oxford: Oxford University Press, 1998), 55.
35. Jameson, *Postmodernism*, 285.
36. Scott Bukatman, *Terminal Identity: The Virtual Subject in Post Modern Science Fiction* (London: Duke University, 1993), 10, 11.
37. Larry McCaffrey, *Across the Wounded Galaxies: Interviews with Contemporary American Science Fiction Writers* (Chicago: University of Illinois Press, 1990), 3–4.
38. Heinlein's 'Beyond this Horizon', discussed by Harlan Ellison, in Samuel R. Delany, *The Jewel-Hinged Jaw* (Elizabethtown: Dragon Press, 1977), 34.
39. Delany, *The Jewel-Hinged Jaw*, 79.
40. Delany, quoted in McCaffrey, *Across the Wounded Galaxies*, 79.
41. Delany, *The American Shore*, 60–61.
42. Spencer, 'The Red Sun is High, the Blue Low', 45.
43. Bukatman, *Terminal Identity*, 11.
44. Edward James, *Science Fiction in the Twentieth Century* (Oxford: Opus Books, 1994), 109.
45. Suvin, *Metamorphoses of Science Fiction*, 71.

46. According to Patrick Parrinder, the concept of cognitive estrangement 'assumes the dynamic interaction of its two terms, its force is clearly normative as well as descriptive. Such a definition suggests that the work in which the potentialities of science fiction are most fully realised will be that in which the "novelty" is not only significant in itself, but is developed in the most thoroughly cognitive or scientific spirit. Cognition must be understood as embracing the polarities of human intelligence; that is, it is at once logical and imaginative, rational and empirical, systematic and sceptical.' Parrinder, *Criticism and Teaching*, 21.

47. John Ellis, from notes and in discussion, 17 December 1999.

48. Spencer, 'The Red Sun is High, the Blue Low', 37.

49. Delany, *The Jewel-Hinged Jaw*, 33.

50. Parrinder, *Criticism and Teaching*, 21

51. Darko Suvin, 'On what is and is not an SF narration', *Science Fiction Studies*, V, No. 1 (1978), 45.

52. Theresa Ebert, 'The Convergence of Post-modern Innovative Fiction and Science Fiction: An Encounter with Samuel R Delany's Technotopia', *Poetics Today*, Vol. 1, No. 4 (1980), 92.

53. Parrinder, *Criticism and Teaching*, 19, 21.

54. Ibid. 21–22.

55. Spencer, 'The Red Sun is High, the Blue Low', 37.

56. Ibid. 37.

57. J.G. Ballard, *A User's Guide to the Millennium* (London: Flamingo Books, 1996), 18.

58. The interviews were screened in summer 2003 alongside the fourth and final season.

59. Spencer, 'The Red Sun is High, the Blue Low', 37.

60. Ibid. 38.

61. McCaffrey, *Across the Wounded Galaxies*, 6.

62. Bukatman, *Terminal Identity*, 6.

63. Jean-François Lyotard, *The Postmodern Condition: A Report on Knowledge*, translated by Geoff Bennington and Brian Massumi (Minneapolis: University of Minnesota Press, 1984), xxiv.

64. Ballard, 'Introduction to *Crash*', *Re/Search*, Vol. 8, No. 9 (1984), 96.

65. See in particular Jameson, *Postmodernism* and *The Geopolitical Aesthetic*.
66. Rosemary Jackson discusses this in *Fantasy: The Literature of Subversion* (London: Methuen, 1981).
67. Stableford, Clute and Nicholls, in Clute and Nicholls (eds), *The Encyclopaedia of Science Fiction*, 2nd edition (London: Orbit Books, 1993), 159–61.
68. Sarah Lefanu, *In the Chinks of the World Machine: Feminism and Science Fiction* (London: The Women's Press, 1988), 5 and 100 respectively.
69. Joanna Russ, 'Interview', in Jeffrey D. Smith (ed.), *Khatru* (Baltimore: Phantasmicron Press, 1975), 3–4 and 47, quoted in Bukatman, *Terminal Identity*, 10.
70. Spencer, 'The Red Sun is High, the Blue Low', 37.
71. Ibid. 43.
72. Rabkin, 'Metalinguistics and Science Fiction', 81.
73. Rabkin's third category is concerned with the use of language as context, and manifests itself in the technique of self-reflexivity (or Jakobson's 'poetic function') – and is of course not peculiar to science fiction. Rabkin refers to Jorge Luis Borges, famous for his self-reflexive work, who surely speaks for many readers when he asks why we are uneasy knowing that: 'the map is within the map and the thousand and one nights are within the book *A Thousand and One Nights*? Why does it disquiet us to know that Don Quixote is a reader of *Quixote*, and Hamlet is a spectator of *Hamlet*? ... those inversions suggest that if the characters in a story can be readers or spectators, then we, their readers or spectators, can be fictitious.' In Rabkin, 'Metalinguistics and Science Fiction', 94.
74. Ibid. 87.
75. Ursula K. Le Guin, *The Left Hand of Darkness* (London: Panther, 1973), 19 and 154 respectively.
76. Rabkin, 'Metalinguistics and Science Fiction', 87.
77. Ibid. 87–8.
78. Marc Angenot, 'The Absent Paradigm: An Introduction to the Semiotics of Science Fiction', *Science Fiction Studies*, No. 6 (1979), 9.
79. Ibid. 18.

80. Myra Barnes, *Linguistics and Language in SF-Fantasy* (New York: Arno Press, 1975).

81. Thomas Cole, quoted in James Flexner, *That Wilder Image* (New York: Dover Press, 1970), 35.

82. In Aldiss and Wingrove, *Trillion Year Spree*, 446.

83. The sixth-season *Next Generation* episode 'The Chase' has Cardassians, Klingons and Romulans shadowing Picard's Enterprise, eventually discovering that all four races share the same origin. The Ancients created *Stargate*'s gate system, Ancients from an incompatible realm (dimension?) placed wormhole technology in Crichton's head in *Farscape*, and *Babylon 5* introduces us to the First Ones, and *the* First One – Lorien.

84. Aldiss and Wingrove, *Trillion Year Spree*, 446.

85. This is a familiar device in medieval literature, but this 'history' is actually a 'collection of legends, developed gradually since classical times and given form and authority by writers such as ... Geoffrey of Monmouth (11??–1154) [who] created national king-heroes like Cymbeline, Arthur and Lear, and firmly traced English origins to heroic classical times.' *Sir Gawain and the Green Knight*, introduced by Brian Stone (Harmondsworth: Penguin Books, 1959), 163

86. A modern day equivalent would perhaps be the stories of *Batman*, which exist in film, television, comic book, graphic novel and as animation. No matter what happens in one media incarnation, it can co-exist with other, radically different incarnations: the myth itself is strong enough to survive at its core.

87. Thomas Wymer, Alice Calderonello, Lowell P. Leland, Sara Jayne Steen, and R. Michael Evers, *Intersections: The Elements of Fiction in Science Fiction* (Ohio: Bowling Green State University Popular Press, 1978), 4.

88. Scholes, quoted in James, *Science Fiction in the Twentieth Century*, 101.

89. Aldiss and Wingrove, *Trillion Year Spree*, 42–44.

90. Burke, *A Philosophical Enquiry into the Origin of our Ideas of the Sublime and Beautiful*, 36–7.

91. Quoted in Robu, 'The Sublime', 25.

92. Nicholls and Robu, 'The Sense of Wonder', in Clute and Nicholls, *The Encyclopaedia of Science Fiction*, 1085.
93. Blaise Pascal, quoted in Robu, 'The Sublime', 27.
94. Robu, 'The Sublime', 27.
95. Pierre Teilhard de Chardin, quoted in Robu, 'The Sublime', 27.
96. Robu, 'The Sublime', 27.
97. Hartwell, quoted in James, *Science Fiction in the Twentieth Century*, 105.
98. Nicholls and Robu, in Clute and Nicholls, *The Encyclopaedia of Science Fiction*, 1084.

TWO: HISTORIES — THE AMERICAN WEST, TELEVISION AND TELEVISUALITY

1. In Philip French, *Westerns: Aspects of a Movie Genre* (London: Secker and Warburg, 1977), 6.
2. Scott Bukatman, 'The Artificial Infinite: On Special Effects and the Sublime', in Linda Cooke and Peter Wollen (eds), *Visual Display: Culture Beyond Appearances* (Seattle: Bay Press, 1995), 272–3.
3. Jim Kitses, *Horizons West* (London: BFI, 1970), 10.
4. Abraham Lincoln, 'Address Delivered at the Dedication of the Cemetery at Gettysburg, November 19, 1863', in *The Norton Anthology of American Literature*, Vol. 1, 2nd edition (London: W.W. Norton and Co., 1905), 1405.
5. Walt Whitman, quoted in Hellman, *American Myth and the Legacy of Vietnam*, 9.
6. Whitman, 'Passage to India', in *The Portable Walt Whitman* (Harmondsworth: Penguin Books, 1984), 278, 276, 283.
7. Hellman, *American Myth and the Legacy of Vietnam*, 10. Hellman applies his argument in relation to Vietnam specifically, and the fascination with Asian cultures which permeates American history, but the desire for union (or reunion) across the lands of the Earth with America's new man guiding the fallen of the old world, reaches beyond the tragedy of the SE Asian conflict.
8. Kitses, *Horizons West*, 9–10.

9. Frederick Jackson Turner, quoted in Roderick Nash, *Wilderness and the American Mind* (New Haven: Yale University Press, 1982), 146.

10. Alan Trachtenberg, *The Incorporation of America: Culture and Society in the Gilded Age* (New York: Hill and Wang, 1982), 17.

11. Richard Slotkin, *Regeneration Through Violence: The Mythology of the American Frontier 1600–1860* (Middletown, Connecticut: Wesleyan University Press, 1973).

12. French, *Westerns*, 24–5.

13. From classes at Clark University in 1989–1991 with Professor John Conron. See also John Conron, *American Picturesque* (Pennsylvania: Pennsylvania State University Press, 2000).

14. Trachtenburg, *The Incorporation of America*, 18.

15. Nash, *Wilderness and the American Mind*, 145.

16. John Wilmerding (ed.), *American Light: The Luminist Movement* (Washington DC: National Gallery of Art, 1980), 98.

17. Earl A. Powell, 'Luminism and the American Sublime', in Wilmerding, *American Light*, 72.

18. Ralph Waldo Emerson, 'Nature', in *The Norton Anthology*, 827.

19. Thomas Patin, 'Exhibitions and Empire: National Parks and the Performance of Manifest Destiny', *Journal of American Culture*, Vol. 22, No.1 (Spring 1999), 44.

20. Albert Boime, *The Magisterial Gaze: Manifest Destiny and American Landscape Painting, c.1830–1865* (Washington: Smithsonian Institute, 1991), 38.

21. Ibid. 20–21.

22. Ibid. 138.

23. Barbara Novak, *Nature and Culture: American Landscape and Painting 1825–1875* (New York: Oxford University Press, 1980), 18.

24. Miriam Hansen, *Babel and Babylon: Spectatorship in American Silent Film* (Cambridge, MA: Harvard University Press, 1991), 112.

25. Andrew Wilton, *Turner and the Sublime* (Chicago: University of Chicago Press, 1980), 39.

NOTES TO CHAPTER TWO

26. Bukatman, 'The Artificial Infinite', 276.
27. Novak, *Nature and Culture*, 22–3.
28. Gordon Hendricks, *Albert Bierstadt: Painter of the American West* (New York: Harry N. Abrams Inc/Amon Carter Museum of Western Art, 1974), 246.
29. Bukatman, 'The Artificial Infinite', 276.
30. Powell, 'Luminism and the American Sublime', 90.
31. Novak, *Nature and Culture*, 19.
32. Abraham Lincoln, 'Annual Address to Congress' (1 December 1862), in *The Collected Works of Abraham Lincoln*, Vol. 5, ed. R.P. Basler (New Brunswick: Rutgers University Press, 1953), 537.
33. *Star Trek*, from William Shatner's voiceover for original series. My emphasis.
34. As Scott Bukatman also notes early in *Terminal Identity*.
35. Bukatman, 'The Artificial Infinite', 272.
36. Stephen Whitfield and Gene Roddenberry, *The Making of Star Trek* (New York: Ballantine Books, 1968), 23.
37. It is odd that we place such a high value upon originality when the history of western art relies upon the *re*creation of specific art forms just as much as the ability to create afresh. See Umberto Eco, 'Innovation and Repetition: Between Modern and Post-modern Aesthetics', in *Daedalus*, 114, Part 4 (1985), 161–184.
38. For science fiction film, this is not a problem. Films are generally discrete entities and, although some films may offer open endings inviting viewer conjecture (and opening up the potential for sequels – *Planet of the Apes* (1968) for example), mostly the narrative is adequately completed. *The Empire Strikes Back* (1980) is a famous exception; it requires *Return of the Jedi* (1983) to achieve narrative wholeness – but the film is part of a trilogy and the audience arrived with awareness of this fact. In this sense, some familiarity is necessary, indeed *Aliens* (1986) works all the better for the audience having seen *Alien* (1979). As the marines encounter signs of the alien presence in the complex, the audience has more knowledge even than the 'expert' Ripley – she remained on board the Nostromo in *Alien*, only Dallas, Lambert and Kane went aboard the vessel

containing the alien eggs and witnessed other signs of the alien infestation.

39. Caldwell, *Televisuality*, 83.

40. Ibid. 6.

41. Robert C. Allen (ed.), *Channels of Discourse, Reassembled: Television and Contemporary Criticism*, 2nd edition (London: Routledge, 1992), 3.

42. Roger Silverstone, *Television and Everyday Life* (London: Routledge, 1994).

43. See especially John Ellis, *Visible Fictions* and *Seeing Things: Television in the Age of Uncertainty* (London: I.B.Tauris, 2000).

44. Stephen Heath, 'Representing Television', in Patricia Mellencamp (ed.), *Logics of Television* (Bloomington: Indiana University Press, 1990), 267.

45. Ellis, *Visible Fictions*, 128.

46. Ibid. 118.

47. Ibid. 120.

48. John Caughie, *Television Drama: Realism, Modernism and British Culture* (Oxford: Oxford University Press, 2000), 139. See also Ellis, *Visible Fictions*, Chapter 7.

49. Eco, 'Innovation and Repetition', 183–4.

50. Ibid. 162.

51. Ibid. 164.

52. Ibid. 165.

53. Caughie, *Television Drama*, 134.

54. John Tulloch and Manuel Alvarado, *Doctor Who: The Unfolding Text* (London: Macmillan, 1983), ix.

55. Ibid. x.

56. Ibid. ix.

57. David Bordwell and Kristin Thompson, *Film Art: An Introduction*, 5th edition (New York: McGraw Hill, 1997), 95.

58. The origins of the popular detective/crime story itself may be laid at the feet of serials like Wilkie Collins' *The Woman in White* (1859) and *The Moonstone* (1868), which notably also contained Gothic elements.

59. Tzvetan Todorov, *The Poetics of Prose*, translated by R. Howard (Ithaca: Cornell University Press, 1977), 47, 50–1.

60. John Fiske and John Hartley, *Reading Television* (London: Methuen, 1978), 23.

61. Ibid. 85.

62. Marshall McLuhan and Quentin Fiore, *The Medium is the Message* (New York: Bantam, 1967), 114.

63. Ibid. 63.

64. Todd Gitlin, *Inside Prime Time*, revised edition (London: Routledge, 1994), 23.

65. Quoted in Jostein Gripsrud, *The Dynasty Years: Hollywood Television and Critical Media Studies* (London: Routledge, 1995), 167.

66. Caldwell, *Televisuality*, 377n.

67. *Buck Rogers* in particular relied upon a cringe-making use (even then) of 1970s multi-coloured disco-rope lighting and frequently indulged in disco dancing itself. Meanwhile, Buck's erstwhile associate, the lovely Colonel Wilma Deering, prowled around in skin-tight lycra bodysuits which one might consider slightly incongruous for a military officer of her rank – a sharp indication of the tokenist display of women on television at the time, despite the narrative's suggested equality of gender.

68. In the UK, it ran for three revised seasons, beginning in 1969.

69. Roddenberry quoted in Roger Fulton, *The Encyclopaedia of TV Science Fiction*, 2nd edition (London: Boxtree, 2000), 543.

70. Ibid.

71. Whitfield and Roddenberry, *The Making of Star Trek*, 250.

72. Stephen Whitfield remarks upon the extraordinary numbers of letters the studio received in 1967–1968 when *Star Trek* was threatened with cancellation. Whitfield and Roddenberry, *The Making of Star Trek*, especially Part V.

73. Chris Gregory, *Star Trek: Parallel Narratives* (London: Macmillan, 2000), 39.

74. Roddenberry in Fulton, *The Encyclopaedia of TV Science Fiction*, 542.

75. Fulton, *The Encyclopaedia of TV Science Fiction*, 543.

76. See Asimov's introduction to *Soviet Science Fiction* (New York: Collier, 1962), and Jameson, 'Towards a New Awareness', 323. Asimov's stages are somewhat controversial, but they are still useful indicators of era.

77. From 'Small Screen Shooters: Four Distinguished Cinematographers Discuss the Craft of Shooting for Episodic Television', *Millimeter* (April 1988), 143, quoted in Caldwell, *Televisuality*, 83.
78. Caldwell, *Televisuality*, 88.
79. Steve Larner, ASC, 'Beauty and the Beast: God Bless the Child', in *American Cinematographer* (April 1989), quoted in Caldwell, *Televisuality*, 89.
80. Caldwell, *Televisuality*, 89.
81. Ibid. 90.
82. Ibid. 90–1.
83. Ibid. 91.
84. Ibid. 92.
85. Ibid. 377n.
86. Ibid. 92.
87. Following Roddenberry's death in 1991, Rick Berman took over the reigns of *The Next Generation* and, with Michael Piller and Jeri Taylor, expanded the franchise with *Deep Space Nine*, *Voyager* and with Brannon Braga and Chris Black, *Enterprise*. Nevertheless, the association remains very much with Roddenberry: the name has entered *Star Trek* mythology.
88. Caldwell, *Televisuality*, 13–14.
89. Ibid. 105–6. Original emphasis.
90. Darley, *Visual Digital Culture*, 139.
91. Thomas Schatz, 'The New Hollywood', in Jim Collins, Hilary Radner and Ava Preacher Collins (eds), *Film Theory Goes to the Movies* (London: Routledge, 1993), 9–10.
92. Darley, *Visual Digital Culture*, 139.
93. Ibid. 140.
94. Ibid. 140–1.
95. J. Michael Straczynski, *The Complete Book of Scriptwriting*, revised edition (London: Titan Books, 1997), 109.
96. Ibid. 110.
97. Ibid. 111.
98. He planned it for years prior to its pilot episode, wrote a majority of the episodes himself (ninety-three episodes out of 111 – including the pilot), and had input into the remainder.
99. Visual effects designer Ron Thornton, writer Larry DiTillo,

producer John Copeland and executive producer Douglas Netter had all collaborated with Straczynski on *Captain Power and the Soldiers of the Future*. See David Bassom, *Creating 'Babylon 5'* (London: Boxtree/Channel Four, 1996), 54.

100. Caldwell, *Televisuality*, 261. Caldwell goes on to point out that even shows 'like *Moonlighting* and *thirtysomething* and *Northern Exposure* – eventually became highly conscious alternative worlds after extended runs in primetime. As stardom transcended characterization and Hollywood gossip and entertainment discourse transcended the meager confines of plot, viewers came to expect stylistic volatity because of the shows' highly visible pretence and personalities.' Ibid. 262.

101. Ellis, *Seeing Things*, 63.

102. Ibid.

103. Caldwell, *Televisuality*, 26.

104. Caughie, *Television Drama*, 129.

105. Ibid. 131.

106. *Murder One*, Steve Bochco's finite series following a murder trial, attempted this, but the length was one season, and it drew on a variety of other stories along the way.

107. Caughie, *Television Drama*, 139.

108. Walter Benjamin, 'The Work of Art in the Age of Mechanical Reproduction', in Gerald Mast, Marshall Cohen and Leo Braudy (eds), *Film Theory and Criticism: Introductory Readings*, 4th edition (Oxford: Oxford University Press, 1992), 665–81.

109. Caughie, *Television Drama*, 140.

110. Ibid.

111. Ibid. 129–30.

112. This is not to detract from the earlier discussion of Eco and the importance that Neale et al., place upon repetition and difference. The science fiction genre also relies upon repetition (mostly in format), but it also combines this with originality in narrative content and imagery – a more continuous and subversive challenge than with other mundane dramas. To a great extent the mutability emerges through poetic juxtaposition.

113. Caldwell, *Televisuality*, 148.

114. Ibid. 26.

115. Ibid.

THREE: YESTERDAY'S ENTERPRISE
— REPRESENTATION, IDEOLOGY AND
LANGUAGE IN *STAR TREK*

1. J. Michael Straczynski, 'The Profession of Science Fiction, 48: Approaching Babylon', *Foundation: The Review of Science Fiction*, No. 64 (1995), 16.

2. Whitfield and Roddenberry, *The Making of Star Trek*, 128.

3. As a Borg, Seven of Nine is androgynous, but once freed from drone-hood she not only retains her strength, but is shown as highly sexual – if unaware of human niceties. The Doctor, ironically a hologram with an appalling bedside manner, spends considerable time educating her in the social graces.

4. Michèle Barrett and Duncan Barrett, *Star Trek: The Human Factor* (London: Polity Press, 2001), 184.

5. Daniel Leonard Bernardi, *Star Trek and History: Race-ing Towards a White Future* (New Jersey: Rutgers University Press, 1998).

6. Mia Consalio, *Discourses of Race in Science Fiction* (New York: Newsday, 1996).

7. Samuel Delany, quoted in Adam Roberts, *Science Fiction* (London: Routledge, 2000), 123.

8. Adam Roberts, *Science Fiction*, 130.

9. Barrett and Barrett also point out how 'white' is used in a variety of negative connotations via the deathly white of Borg Queen, and the drug used as food by the Jem'Hadar, for example. *Star Trek: The Human Factor*, 91–2.

10. Ibid. 141.

11. See Daniel Bernardi, *Star Trek and History*, and also Barrett and Barrett, *Star Trek: The Human Factor*, 142.

12. Adam Roberts, *Science Fiction*, 130–2.

13. Sigmund Freud, *The Ego and the Id*, translated by J. Strachey (New York: W.W. Norton and Co, 1960), 16.

14. Friedrich Nietzsche, *Thus Spake Zarathustra*, translated by R.J. Hollingdale (Harmondsworth: Penguin Books, 1974).

15. Hal Foster, 'Armor Fou', *October*, 56 (1991), 64–97. Foster notes that recent sf cinema 'though sometimes parodic, even critical, the armored figures of commercial culture symbolically treat fantasmatic threats to the normative social ego: for instance,

visions of cities given over to drugged minorities (e.g.,
Robocop).' Foster, 69n.

16. Stephen R.L. Clark, 'Psychopathology and Alien Ethics', in
Edward James and Farah Mendlesohn (eds), *The Parliament
of Dreams: Conferring on 'Babylon 5'* (Reading: The Science
Fiction Foundation, 1998), 156.

17. Stephen Clark discusses this point in detail. For stories
demonstrating Dickson's own thesis, Dickson's *The Final
Encyclopaedia* (London: Sphere Books, 1984), and *Chantry
Guild* (New York: Ace Books, 1988) are helpful, although most
of Dickson's *Childe* or *Dorsai* books suggest an inherently
ethical future human expansion throughout the galaxy.

18. See in particular Annette Kuhn (ed.), *Alien Zone: Cultural
Theory and Contemporary Science Fiction Cinema* (London:
Verso, 1990); and Constance Penley et al, *Close Encounters*
(Minneapolis: University of Minnesota Press, 1991).

19. Constance Penley is talking about difference in sf films such
as *The Terminator*, but I believe that her point is equally
applicable to ethnicity here. See Penley, 'Time Travel, primal
scene and the critical dystopia', in Kuhn, *Alien Zone*, 123.

20. This episode could be seen as a thinly veiled allegory on
Northern Ireland, and is an episode dropped by the BBC for
the series' first run, bizarrely, not because it showed terrorists
and the state as possibly equally culpable for violence, but
because it specifically mentioned Northern Ireland and gave
a fictional date for a diegetic 'historical' settlement. 'The High
Ground' was subsequently screened by Sky 1 and by the BBC
when the series was repeated.

21. Vic Fontaine is played by James Darren, who starred in the sf
series *Time Tunnel*.

22. Legendary to both Sisko's crew and to us, the audience, of
course.

23. Of course, copyright costs play a part here, and allusions are
considerably cheaper. Nevertheless, given the lack of even general
connections to the audience's reality, this is still a problem.

24. See Janet Murray, *Hamlet on the Holodeck: The Future of
Narrative in Cyberspace* (Cambridge, Massachusetts: MIT Press,
1997).

25. Geoff King and Tanya Krzywinska, *Science Fiction Cinema: From Outerspace to Cyberspace* (London: The Wallflower Press, 2000), 90.

26. Ibid. 92.

27. In the *Deep Space Nine* episode 'Little Green Men', the audience can understand both the Ferengi and the humans, but in-diegesis the characters cannot understand one another until the translator is mended and the assumptions lead to amusing misapprehensions. In *Enterprise*'s 'Vox Sola', the Kreetassans are deeply offended because the humans eat in public – this is seen as equivalent to having sex in public.

28. Barrett and Barrett, *Star Trek: The Human Factor*, 184–5.

29. Whitfield and Roddenberry, *The Making of Star Trek*, especially Chapters 4–8.

30. The character of 'Q', played by John de Lancie, was based upon Trelane, a pest from the original series, who appeared in 'The Squire of Gothos'. See Fulton, *The Encyclopaedia of TV Science Fiction*, 546.

31. Eric Chauvin in email interview.

32. *Voyager*'s Tom Paris and B'Elanna marry and have a child.

33. Notably, the pivotal points in the films *Star Trek II: The Wrath of Khan* (1982), *Star Trek III: The Search for Spock* (1984) and *Star Trek IV: The Voyage Home* (1986) do not lie only in the death, funeral and resurrection of Mr Spock, the Vulcan Science Officer, but rather in their parallel. The films linger respectively upon the destruction of the Enterprise at the planet Genesis, and its rebirth at Earth's starbase as the Enterprise NCC 1701A. The death and rebirth of the vessel is thus given equal dramatic weight to the death and rebirth of its First Officer.

34. See, for example, Nash, *Wilderness and the American Mind*; Yi-Fu Tuan, *Topophilia: A Study of Environmental Perception, Attitudes and Values* (Englewood Cliffs, New Jersey: Prentice-Hall, 1974); and Patricia Limerick, *The Legacy of Conquest* (New York: W.W. Norton and Co., 1987).

35. The story leads on from an occasionally visited thread in *Deep Space Nine*, where Maquis rebels have been trying to reclaim planets on which they had settled. Mostly Bajoran, but aided by various mercenaries, they continue the war with the

Cardassians after the Bajorans, now allied to the Federation, have accepted a peace treaty ceding some of the settled planets back to Cardassia. As a result, the Federation steps in to stop its own citizens and the Bajorans from continuing their guerrilla and terrorist activities. We first encounter Voyager as it sets off from Deep Space Nine in search of a particular rebel ship – commanded by Chakotay.

36. Gareth Roberts, 'The Philosophy of Balance', in James and Mendelsohn, *The Parliament of Dreams*, 49.

37. Barrett and Barrett, *Star Trek: The Human Factor*, 126.

FOUR: THE SACRIFICE OF ANGELS – MILITARY HISTORY AND IDEOLOGY

1. One of the early and impressive sfx in the series consisted of alien leader Diana (Jane Badler) 'swallowing' a live rodent.

2. A follow-up series was made in 1984–1985.

3. Susan Jeffords, *The Remasculinization of America* (Bloomington: Indiana University Press, 1989), xi.

4. Tellingly, *The Deer Hunter* and *Coming Home*, films which take very different attitudes to the war, both won Oscars – *The Deer Hunter* for Best Film and *Coming Home* for Best Screenplay (and both won awards for acting) – articulating very clearly the confusion still felt in the country even several years after the war.

5. M. Ryan and D. Kellner, *Camera Politica: The Politics and Ideology of Contemporary American Cinema* (Bloomington: Indiana University Press, 1990), 197, 197–8.

6. Ibid. 200.

7. Thank you to Sean Street for this observation.

8. To Penelope Gilliatt, 'Heavy Metal', *American Film*, XII, No. 10 (September 1987), 50–1, quoted in part in Jack Ellis, *A History of Film*, 3rd edition (New Jersey: Prentice-Hall, 1990), 370.

9. J. Hoberman, 'Vietnam: The Remake', in Kruger and Mariani (eds), *Remaking History* (Bay Press: Seattle, 1989), 177.

10. Leonard Auster and A. Quart, *How the War Was Remembered: Hollywood and Vietnam* (New York: Praeger/CBS Publishing, 1988), 33.

11. Ibid. 33–4.

12. Frances Fitzgerald, *Fire In The Lake* (New York: Vintage Books, 1989), 461.

13. Renata Adler, *A Year in the Dark* (New York: Berkeley, 1969), 199–200.

14. Auster and Quart, *How the War Was Remembered*, 178.

15. John Hellman suggests that: 'As a Green Beret, Kurtz originally sought to bring to Vietnam the American "middle landscape" represented by the "flower plantation" he saw as a young boy journeying up the Ohio river, where it appeared that "for about five miles heaven had just fallen to earth in the form of gardenias". This millennium vision of nature touched by a blessed civilisation is symbolically "all wild and overgrown now", for in Kurtz's mind Vietnam has revealed it all as a weak, naive unwillingness to see that the opposing forces of nature and civilisation can possess their full strengths only if both are followed to the extremes. Kurtz has pushed himself out onto an ultimate frontier "the edge of a straight razor" on which he says he saw a crawling snail surviving: "That's my dream, it's my nightmare." The "horror" Kurtz has become is a "ripping apart" of the contradictions in the American mythic ideal of turning away from civilisation to find the strength and virtue to redeem nature to civilisation. As a renegade Green Beret, Kurtz represents the Adamic innocence of its death-dealing heroes brought to its tragic "apocalypse" in this Asian jungle; as hard-boiled detective, and thus descendant of the western hero, Willard represents the self contemplation of that nightmarish discovery'. Hellman, *American Myth and the Legacy of Vietnam*, 200.

16. All the more astonishing, therefore, that it can indulge in such a racist depiction of the Vietnamese.

17. Larry Gross, 'Film Après Noir: Alienation in a Dark Alley', in *Film Comment*, XII, No. 4 (July/August 1976), 44.

18. Thank you to John Ellis for this observation.

19. Interviewed by Jan Johnson-Smith on 11 October 1997. All quotations from James Morrison are from this interview, unless otherwise stated.

20. Fulton, *The Encyclopaedia of TV Science Fiction*, 513.
21. Nick Joy, 'Tucker: The Man and his Dream', in *Starburst 'X-Files' Special*, No. 33 (Visual Imagination Publications, Autumn 1997), 47.
22. 'The Angriest Angel'.
23. The approach is not entirely new to sf of course; in *Deep Space Nine*, Dr Bashir is revealed to have been genetically enhanced, a fact he has keep secret for years.
24. McQueen remarks upon this in 'Dear Earth', when he resists being filmed for propaganda purposes as a 'model' In-Vitro working alongside humans in the war effort.
25. We glimpse this beside his coffee mug in 'Hostile Visit'.
26. http://www.mindspring.com/~louisep/jmdg-1.
27. Miyamoto Musashi, *The Book of Five Rings*, translated by Victor Harris (London: HarperCollins, 1995), 27.
28. *Cybervanguard* interview with James Morrison (February 1996), http://www.cybervanguard.com/interviews.morrison.html. Accessed July 1997.
29. Paula Vitaris, interview with James Morrison, reprinted from *S:AAB* Magazine (July 1997), http://www.pathcom.com/ ~nooger/flameboy/paula7.htm. Accessed October 1997.
30. Based upon Book 22, lines 260–72, in *The Iliad of Homer* translated and introduced by Richmond Lattimore (Chicago: University of Chicago Press, 1961), 442.
31. An identical Elroy unit in 'Choice or Chance' notably tortured Wang.
32. Whether one even can ascribe the word 'torture' to re-wiring what is essentially a computer with an attitude problem (a virus telling it to 'take a chance'), is a moot point since the relative implausibility of AI sentience is scarcely addressed in the series, except here when Elroy begins to make reference to the Ho Chi Minh City Treaty concerning the treatment of AI prisoners. McQueen interrupts him, telling him that it is 'nothing that means a damn in this room'. It is also addressed briefly in 'Pearly'. Here a 'male' silicate remarks that it is malfunctioning and has developed feelings for its 'female' companion unit, Felicity.
33. James Morrison, in email interview 30 June 1998.

34. Morrison adds: 'But, again, this was not a man McQueen was dealing with. It was a machine. We treat machines differently than humans when they don't work and we're frustrated. We slap or kick them. Or fix them.' Interview, 30 June 1998.

35. The limited discussion of his personal life is perhaps unnecessary – the Colonel needs to remain mysterious, enigmatic – but the nervousness surrounding the series ratings may well have encouraged this response since McQueen's role was receiving the most audience interest. McQueen's speeches in this episode are both narrative and plot-driven.

36. Musashi, 104–5.

37. Thanks to John Ellis for this observation.

38. *Cult Times*, No. 16 (January 1997), 15.

39. Morrison, interview, 11 October 1997.

FIVE: WORMHOLE X-TREME! IMAGES OF TIME AND SPACE

1. Carl Sagan, *Cosmos* (London: Abacus Books, 1991), 225.

2. Ibid. 29.

3. Laurence Krauss, *The Physics of Star Trek*, with a foreword by Stephen Hawking (London: HarperCollins/Flamingo, 1997). There are also countless books dedicated to the in-diegetic technology and science of *Star Trek*.

4. Thanks to John Ellis.

5. Nicholas Packwood, 'Engineering the Future: Speculative Technologies', in James and Mendlesohn (eds), *The Parliament of Dreams*, 100–1.

6. Rockne S. O'Bannon, who previously worked on the 1980s version of *The Twilight Zone*, created *Farscape* and worked on the various *Seaquest* adventures.

7. http://www.sci-fi.com/farscape/notes. Accessed December 2002.

8. A great many texts consider the theories of quantum mechanics, which essentially reject the absoluteness of classical mechanics and suggest that we can only predict what will *probably* happen on any occasion. A particularly user-friendly text is Richard Feynman, *Six Easy Pieces: The Fundamentals*

of Physics Explained (Harmondsworth: Penguin Books, 1998). See especially Chapters 2 and 6.

9. http://www.sci-fi.com/farscape/notes/wormholes.html. Accessed December 2002.

10. Stephen Keane, 'Time Past/Time Future: Reading Babylon Squared', in James and Mendlesohnin James and Mendlesohn (eds), *The Parliament of Dreams*, 20.

11. Ibid. 22–3. Keane refers to Roland Barthes, *Image-Music-Text*, translated by S. Heath (New York: Noonday Press, 1977), 9.

12. Darley, *Visual Digital Culture*, 104.

13. David Bordwell, Janet Staiger and Kristin Thompson, *The Classical Hollywood Cinema: Film Style and Mode of Production to 1960* (London: Routledge, 1985), 4.

14. Darley, *Visual Digital Culture*, 107.

15. Ibid. 108.

16. Ibid.

17. Ibid. 112, 113.

18. Adam Roberts, *Science Fiction*, 153

19. Ibid.

20. King and Krzywinska, *Science Fiction Cinema*, 66, 66–7

21. Christian Metz in particular writes of this dual pleasure in 'Trucage and the Film', *Critical Enquiry*, Vol. 13, No. 4 (1977), 657–75; as does Steve Neale in '"You've Got to be Fucking Kidding!": Knowledge, Belief and Judgement in Science Fiction', in Annette Kuhn (ed), *Alien Zone*, 160 80.

22. Adam Roberts, *Science Fiction*, 153–4.

23. Ebert, 'The Convergence of Post-modern Innovative Fiction and Science Fiction', 93.

24. Although a story may be written in an era deemed to be postmodern, there is no requirement for it to serve the agenda of a postmodern theorist: all forms may co-exist, one is simply likely to be dominant during a particular era. Thus 'classical mainstream' sf flourishes alongside its postmodern relatives.

25. Ebert, 'The Convergence of Post-modern Innovative Fiction and Science Fiction', 93.

SIX: *BABYLON 5*: BETWEEN THE
DARKNESS AND THE LIGHT

1. J. Michael Straczynski, 'The Profession of Science Fiction',
   5–19. Details of this are available from many other sources,
   including a posting to a fan question on 10 May 1996, available
   at http://www.midwinter.com/b5/CompuServe/cs96-05.

2. *The Next Generation*'s Borg in 'Best of Both Worlds'; *Deep
   Space Nine*'s Dominion shape-shifters through seasons 6 and
   7; *Voyager*'s Species 8472 in 'In the Flesh'; and *Stargate SG-1*'s
   Gou'ald from the start all demonstrate a firm intention to invade
   and destroy the Federations and/or Earth.

3. Pauline Archell-Thompson writes of this in detail in 'Shades
   of Darkness: Shadow and Myth', in James and Mendlesohn,
   71–9.

4. Delenn in 'Confessions and Lamentations' and Brother Theo
   in 'Passing through Gethsemane'.

5. Herbert Shu-Shun Chan, 'Space and Time Out of Joint: "War
   Without End"', in James and Mendlesohn, 29.

6. Nevertheless, when Kosh appears to save Sheridan in the 'Fall
   of Night', Lennier sees a winged Minbari figure, which he
   names 'Valeria.' Paradoxically, the Principles of the Alliance
   contains the first page of every religious book of its members,
   perhaps demonstrating how difficult it is for ideology to
   distance itself from religious morality and ethics.

7. The Vorlons are capable of 'breaking off' parts of their
   consciousness and sending them elsewhere – as Kosh does
   with Lyta and Sheridan – thus Delenn's speech suggests a kind
   of hierarchy of power within the universe as well, as if we
   evolve gradually through a variety of forms until we are at one
   with the universe itself.

8. Noel Carroll, 'Towards a Theory of Film Suspense', in
   Theorizing the Moving Image (Cambridge, Cambridge
   University Press, 1996).

9. Dukhat to Delenn in 'Atonement'. Delenn also repeats this to
   Lennier on several occasions, most notably in 'All Alone in
   the Night' and the Vorlon representative, Jack, suggests it is
   what Sheridan and Delenn face in 'Comes the Inquisitor'.

10. Straczynski plays a technician who turns off the station's lights

and departs on the final shuttle.

11. She is, of course, saved by Marcus, who uses the alien machine from 'The Quality of Mercy' to sacrifice his life force to replenish hers, in much the same as Lorien saves Sheridan with *his* life force.

12. It is worth remembering, however, that Morden is shown never to be alone, that he always has Shadow companions.

13. The Ministry of Peace – note the Orwellian overtones.

14. Gilgamesh erected the great walled great cities such as can be found at Uruk (Erech). At the height of Babylon's powers, its leader, Hammurabi, fought to create and maintain an alliance between its five rival city-states. The three-power league of Babylon, Mari and Larsa was maintained for fifteen years, waging war against the surrounding powers of Eshnunna, Elam and Assur, a war in which Babylon was finally victorious.

15. Straczynski readily acknowledges the topical horrors of war-ravaged former Yugoslavia. He drew upon the background of Yugoslavian actor Mira Furlan (Delenn) for some of 'the inner turmoil'. Straczynski, 'Profession of Science Fiction', 14.

16. This is perhaps not unlike the 'historical records' in *Galaxy Quest*.

17. Straczynski, 'Profession of Science Fiction', 15.

18. James Brown, 'Cyborgs and Symbionts: Technology, Politics and Identity', in James and Mendlesohn, 129.

19. Stephen R.L. Clark, 'Psychopathology and Alien Ethics', in James and Mendlesohn, 153.

20. Ibid. 154.

21. Kevin McCarron, 'Religion, Philosophy and the End of History,' in James and Mendlesohn, 142.

22. Clark, 'Psychopathology and Alien Ethics', 156.

23. Sinclair's initial experience is to be falsely charged with the attempted murder of Kosh, Sheridan's first action concerns a renegade Minbari cruiser, the Trigati – a horrible irony bearing in mind that he destroyed the Black Star, the Minbari flagship in the Earth-Minbari War.

24. Appropriately, given Sheridan and Delenn's engagement and attempt to unite humans and Minbari in a new alliance.

25. James and Mendlesohn, 8.

26. Lincoln's speech actually says 'the last best hope'. In *The Collected Works*, 537.

27. James and Mendlesohn, 13n.

28. 'In the Shadow of Z'ha'dum'.

29. The Vorlons are, of course, seeding planets with telepaths, playing not only at ideological manipulation, but also genetic manipulation. Notably Londo, in league with the Shadows, and from a spiritually bankrupt society, does not see anything.

30. Andy Lane, *The Babylon File*, Vol. 1 (London: Virgin, 1997), 184.

31. Marcus and Ivanova discuss the story of Valen in 'War Without End' Part 2.

32. Andy Sawyer, 'The Shadows out of Time: Lovecraftian echoes in *Babylon 5*', in James and Mendlesohn, 63.

33. Bukatman, *Terminal Identity*, 123.

34. Ibid. 126.

35. Ibid. 130.

36. See Bassom, *Creating 'Babylon 5'*.

37. Foster, 'Armor Fou', 64–97.

38. Bukatman, *Terminal Identity*, 132.

39. This experience parallels Garibaldi's efforts to find himself, after Bester has blocked his mind and turned him into an undercover operative.

40. Morden and Londo meet here in 'Chrysalis'.

41. Falling (or flying) is forever connected to Sheridan. He recalls his father telling him that if you are falling off a cliff, you might as well try to fly. Delenn offers to watch while he sleeps on the tilted Minbari-style bed and says she will catch him if he falls. Sheridan actually falls three times. Firstly, it occurs in the gentle manner of Kosh's lesson during a time of personal crisis: a bended knee, a moment of reflection and signal of acquiescence. Secondly, and more violently, it is repeated in 'The Fall of Night', when he jumps from the monorail to avoid assassination by a Centauri bomb – only to be caught by Kosh. The most violent version occurs at Z'ha'dum. As the White Star crashes through the glittering domed ceiling to deliver its deadly cargo, urged by Kosh, he jumps from the parapet into apparent oblivion. Sheridan actually falls a fourth time, but

the question must be: can a dead man fall? When he fights the second Vorlon with the help of Kosh and Lorien, Lorien must restore Sheridan.

42. *Deep Space Nine* has its Bajoran Orbs of Prophecy, but they invariably cast the seeker into a surreal past, to reconsider actions, rather than into the future – suggesting a lack of any extensive pre-planning in the series' narrative.

43. 'The Deconstruction of Falling Stars', which closes season four, takes in both. It leads us from a deceptively ordinary episode opening (the romantic return of the now-married Sheridan and Delenn to Babylon 5 for Sheridan's Presidential inauguration), into an increasingly disturbing series of visual 'historical documents', ending a million years in the future.

44. We discover in 'Atonement' that Delenn is a 'child of Valen', that she is one of his descendants. Valen is Sinclair, thus the Triluminary responds to his DNA – both in the 'future' as Sinclair encounters it, and in Valen's future, when Delenn encounters it.

45. Londo is told that he must restore the eye that does not see, not kill the one who is already dead and, at the last, surrender himself to his greatest fear, knowing that it will destroy him. Many critics have suggested that 'the eye' refers to the ancient Centauri artefact in 'Signs and Portents', but I believe it refers to G'Kar and Narn. G'Kar's eye is plucked out by Cartagia, and Londo makes a bargain with G'Kar, to restore Narn and G'Kar, if G'Kar helps him with his plot to remove Cartagia. The one who is already dead presumably refers to Sheridan, Londo's prisoner on Centauri Prime in 2277 (which we see in 'War Without End'). Londo threatens to kill him, but it later transpires that it is a show, put on for the benefit of his 'keeper', and Londo allows Sheridan and Delenn to escape. Alternatively, it could refer to Morden, who is 'dead' when he returns to Centauri Prime, and it is the destruction of the Shadow vessels and the execution of Morden which brings about the Drakh invasion. Finally, his greatest fear could be loss of control and power, originally all that he wanted, and thus allowing the Drakh keeper to take custody of him in 'The Fall of Centauri Prime' satisfies this demand. Equally, it could

be merely to surrender himself to death itself, at the hands of G'Kar – in which case he demonstrates hitherto unseen nobility in his acceptance of both. Again, without the full context for the events, which we are denied, we cannot be sure.

46. Aldiss and Wingrove, *Trillion Year Spree*, 18.

47. 'Deathwalker'.

48. Lorien reminds Ivanova that love is the greatest gift of her people – Sheridan's love for Delenn is the powerful force Lorien recognises at this time – a something worth living for. 'You should embrace that remarkable illusion,' he tells Ivanova. 'It may be the greatest gift your race has ever received.' ('Into the Fire').

49. Gareth Roberts, 'The Philosophy of Balance', 44.

50. David F. McMahon, 'The Psychological Significance of Straczynski's Universe', in James and Mendlesohn, 80.

51. Clark, 'Psychopathology and Alien Ethics', 154.

52. Neroon threatens to kill Delenn in 'Grey 17 is Missing', but saves her and sacrifices his own life in 'Moments of Transition'.

53. 'In the Beginning'.

54. Kosh #2 in 'The Hour of the Wolf'.

55. We first learn of their son, David, in 'War Without End' Part 2, when the Delenn of the future tells the time-drifting Sheridan that David, is safe. He is referred to again in 'The Deconstruction of Falling Stars' and 'Sleeping in Light'.

56. In e-mail interview.

57. McMahon, 'The Psychological Significance of Straczynski's Universe', 87.

58. According to Ron Thornton, they are actually based on garlic. From interview with Eric Reinholt.

59. Fascinatingly, the battle with the Shadow fleet is intercut with the attack on Dr Franklin and his efforts to escape from 'down below'.

60. We have already established evidence of Rabkin's other category: *Babylon 5*'s historical and generic intertextuality and self-reflexivity.

61. To Sheridan in 'A Distant Star'.

62. She finally discovers this is her answer to the inquisitor, Sebastian, in 'Comes the Inquisitor'.

63. Arthur C. Clarke, 'Who's There?', in *Of Time and Stars* (Harmondsworth: Puffin Books, 1974), 86.

64. Fred Botting, *Gothic* (London: Routledge, 1996), 164, quoted in Karen Sayer, 'Every Station Has Its Phantoms: Uncanny Effects and Hybrid Spaces', in James and Mendlesohn, 92.

65. Botting, *Gothic*, 164.

66. Thank you to Stephen Deutsch for confirming this.

67. Lane, *Babylon File*, Vol. 1, 208. Lane also makes a direct comparison to Nightwatch, and notes the odd tendency to appoint friends and family to Alliance posts in Vol. 2, 124. He comments further: 'Hmm – the Rangers as a fascist organisation who can ignore the entire judicial process in order to take their own personal revenge on those who hurt them. I hope to God this is the prelude to Straczynski's subversion of the Rangers, rather than his idea of how the perfect police force should operate. There is something terribly American about a force of do-gooders with executive authority to do anything they wish.' Lane, *Babylon File*, Vol. 2, 134.

68. Sobchack, *Screening Space*, 76.

69. Eric Chauvin in e-mail interview with the author.

70. Gareth Roberts, 'The Philosophy of Balance', 49.

71. We don't know, of course, where the sun rises on Minbar – east, west, north or south, but sunrise nevertheless signifies a new day and 'new' light.

72. 'Sleeping in Light'.

73. Used in *Star Trek: The Undiscovered Country* (1991), the phrase comes from William Shakespeare's *Hamlet*, Act III, Scene 1. Hamlet is talking of death, but perhaps in that death, resurrection.

74. Ursula K. Le Guin, 'Myth and Archetype in Science Fiction', in *Parabola* (Fall 1976), 45.

BIBLIOGRAPHY

Adler, Renata, *A Year in the Dark*, New York: Berkeley, 1969

Adorno, Theodor, and Max Horkheimer, *The Dialectic of Enlightenment*, London: Verso, 1944

Aldiss, Brian, and Brian Wingrove, *Trillion Year Spree: The History of Science Fiction*, 2nd edition, London: Victor Gollancz, 1986

Allen, Robert C. (ed.), *Channels of Discourse, Reassembled: Television and Contemporary Criticism*, 2nd edition, London: Routledge, 1992

Alloway, Lawrence, *Violent America: The Movies 1946–64*, New York: Museum of Modern Art, 1971

Angenot, Marc, 'The Absent Paradigm: An Introduction to the Semiotics of Science Fiction', *Science Fiction Studies*, 6 (1979), 9–19

Archell-Thompson, Pauline, 'Shades of Darkness: Shadow and Myth', in James and Mendlesohn (eds), *The Parliament of Dreams*

Auster, Leonard, and A. Quart, *How the War Was Remembered: Hollywood and Vietnam*, New York: Praeger/CBS Publishing, 1988

Baigell, Matthew, *Alfred Bierstadt*, New York: Watson-Guptill, 1981

Bakhtin, Mikhail M., *The Dialogic Imagination: Four Essays*, translated by Michael Holquist and Caryl Emerson, edited by Michael Holquist, Austin: University of Texas Press, 1981

Bakhtin, Mikhail M., *Rabelias and His World*, translated by Hélène Iwolsky, Bloomington: Indiana University Press, 1984

Ballard, J.G., 'Which Way to Inner Space?', *New Worlds*, 118 (May 1962), 2–3, 116–118

Ballard, J.G., *Crash*, London: Jonathan Cape, 1973

Ballard, J.G., 'Introduction to *Crash*', *Re/Search*, 8/9 (1984), 96–98

Ballard, J.G., *A User's Guide to the Millennium*, London: Flamingo Books, 1996

Barnes, Myra, *Linguistics and Language in SF-Fantasy*, New York: Arno Press, 1975

Barrett, Michèle, and Duncan Barrett, *Star Trek: The Human Factor*, London: Polity Press, 2001

Barthes, Roland, *Image-Music-Text*, translated by Stephen Heath, New York: Noonday Press, 1977

Barthes, Roland, *S/Z*, translated by Richard Miller, Oxford: Basil Blackwell, 1990

Bassom, David, *Creating 'Babylon 5'*, London: Boxtree/Channel Four, 1996

Baxter, John, *Science Fiction in the Cinema*, New York: Paperback Library, 1970

Bazin, André, *What is Cinema?*, Vols 1 and 2, translated by Hugh Gray, Berkeley: University of California Press, 1967/1972

Benjamin, Walter, 'The Work of Art in the Age of Mechanical Reproduction', in Mast, Cohen and Braudy (eds), *Film Theory and Criticism*

Beowulf, translated and introduced by Michael Alexander, Harmondsworth: Penguin Books, 1973

Bernardi, Daniel Leonard, *Star Trek and History: Race-ing Towards a White Future*, New Jersey: Rutgers University Press, 1998

Billington, R.A., *The Frontier Thesis: Valid Interpretation of American History?*, New York: Robert E. Krieger, 1977

Boime, Albert, *The Magisterial Gaze: Manifest Destiny and American Landscape Painting, c.1830–1865*, Washington: Smithsonian Institute Press, 1991

Bordwell, David, and Kristin Thompson, *Film Art: An Introduction*, 5th edition, New York: McGraw-Hill, 1997

Bordwell, David, Janet Staiger and Kristin Thompson, *The Classical Hollywood Cinema: Film Style and Mode of Production to 1960*, London: Routledge, 1985

Botting, Fred, *Gothic*, London: Routledge, 1996

Bradbury, Ray, 'A Sound of Thunder', in *The Stories of Ray Bradbury*, Vol. 1, London: Panther, 1985

Bretnor, Reginald (ed.), 'Science Fiction in the Age of Space', in *Science Fiction, Today And Tomorrow*, New York: Harper and Row, 1974

Broderick, Damien, *Reading By Starlight: Postmodern Science Fiction*, London: Routledge, 1995

Brooke-Rose, Christine, *A Rhetoric of the Unreal: Studies in Narrative and Structure, Especially of the Fantastic*, Cambridge: Cambridge University Press, 1981

Brown, James, 'Cyborgs and Symbionts: Technology, Politics and Identity', in James and Mendlesohn (eds), *The Parliament of Dreams*

Bukatman, Scott, *Terminal Identity: The Virtual Subject in Post Modern Science Fiction*, London: Duke University Press, 1993

Bukatman, Scott, 'The Artificial Infinite: On Special Effects and the Sublime', in Cooke and Wollen (eds), *Visual Display*

Burke, Edmund, *A Philosophical Enquiry Into the Origin of Our Ideas of the Sublime and Beautiful*, Oxford: Oxford University Press, 1992

Cahn, Iris, 'The Changing Landscape of Modernity: Early Film and America's Great Picture Tradition', *Wide Angle*, 18, No. 3 (1996), 85–100

Caldwell, John Thornton, *Televisuality: Style, Crisis and Authorship In American Television*, New Brunswick, New Jersey: Rutgers University Press, 1995

Carroll, Noel, *Theorizing the Moving Image*, Cambridge: Cambridge University Press, 1996

Caughie, John, 'Adorno's reproach: repetition, difference and television genre', *Screen*, 31, No. 2 (Summer 1991), 127–153

Caughie, John, *Television Drama: Realism, Modernism and British Culture*, Oxford: Oxford University Press, 2000

Clareson, Thomas D., *Many Futures, Many Worlds: Theme and Form in Science Fiction*, Ohio: Kent State University Press, 1977

Clark, Katerina, and Michael Holquist, *Mikhail Bakhtin*, Cambridge: Harvard University Press, 1984

Clark, Stephen R.L., 'Psychopathology and Alien Ethics', in James and Mendlesohn (eds), *The Parliament of Dreams*

Clarke, Arthur C., 'Who's There?', in *Of Time and Stars*, Harmondsworth: Puffin Books, 1974

Clarke, Arthur C., *Astounding Days: A Science Fiction Autobiography*, London: Victor Gollancz, 1989

Clute, John, and Peter Nicholls (eds), *The Encyclopaedia of Science Fiction*, 2nd edition, London: Orbit Books, 1993

Conron, John, *American Picturesque*, Pennsylvania: Pennsylvania State University Press, 2000

Consalio, Mia, *Discourses of Race in Science Fiction*, New York: Newsday, 1996

Cooke, Linda, and Peter Wollen (eds), *Visual Display: Culture Beyond Appearances*, Seattle: Bay Press, 1995

Cramer, Kathryn, 'On Science and Science Fiction', in Hartwell and Cramer (eds), *The Ascent of Wonder*

Culler, Jonathan, *Structuralist Poetics: Structuralism, Linguistics and the Study of Literature*, Ithaca, New York: Cornell University Press, 1975

Cult Times, Issue 16, January 1997

Darley, Andrew, *Visual Digital Culture: Surface Play and Spectacle in New Media Genres*, London: Routledge, 2000

Delany, Samuel R., *The Jewel-Hinged Jaw: Notes of the Language of Science Fiction*, Elizabethtown: Dragon Press, 1977

Delany, Samuel R., *The American Shore: Meditations on a Tale of Science Fiction by Thomas M. Disch – 'Angoulême'*, Elizabethtown: Dragon Press, 1978

Delany, Samuel R., *Starboard Wine: Some More Notes of the Language of Science Fiction*, Elizabethtown: Dragon Press, 1984

Dick, Philip K., *The Collected Short Stories of Philip K. Dick*, Vol. 1, New York: Citadel Twilight, 1990

Dick, Philip K., 'Breakfast at Twilight', in *The Collected Short Stories of Philip K. Dick*, Vol. 2, New York: Citadel Twilight, 1990

Dickson, Gordon, *The Final Encyclopaedia*, London: Sphere Books, 1984

Dickson, Gordon, *Chantry Guild*, New York: Ace Books, 1988

Donald, James, *Fantasy and the Cinema*, London: BFI, 1989

Eagleton, Terry, *Literary Theory: An Introduction*, Oxford: Basil Blackwell, 1983

Easthope, Anthony (ed.), *Contemporary Film Theory*, Longman: London, 1993

Ebert, Theresa, 'The Convergence of Post-modern Innovative Fiction and Science Fiction: An Encounter with Samuel R, Delany's Technotopia', *Poetics Today*, 1, No. 4 (1980), 91–104

Eco, Umberto, 'Innovation and Repetition: Between Modern and Post-modern Aesthetics', *Daedalus*, 114, Part 4 (1985), 161–184

Ellis, Jack, *A History of Film*, 3rd edition, New Jersey: Prentice-Hall, 1990

Ellis, John, *Visible Fictions: Cinema, Television, Video*, revised edition, London: Routledge, 1992

Ellis, John, *Seeing Things: Television in the Age of Uncertainty*, London: I.B.Tauris, 2000

Emerson, Ralph Waldo, 'Nature', in *The Norton Anthology of American Literature*, Vol. 1

Epic of Gilgamesh, The, translated and introduced by N.K. Sandars, revised edition, Harmondsworth: Penguin Books, 1972

Feynman, Richard, *Six Easy Pieces: The Fundamentals of Physics Explained*, Harmondsworth: Penguin Books, 1998

Fiske, John, and John Hartley, *Reading Television*, London: Methuen, 1978

Fitzgerald, Frances, *Fire In The Lake*, New York: Vintage Books, 1989

Flexner, James, *That Wilder Image*, New York: Dover Press, 1970

Foster, Hal, 'Armor Fou', *October*, 56 (1991), 64–97

French, Philip, *Westerns: Aspects of a Movie Genre*, London: BFI/ Secker and Warburg, 1977

Freud, Sigmund, *The Ego and the Id*, translated by James Strachey, New York: W.W. Norton and Co., 1960

Fulton, Roger, *The Encyclopaedia of TV Science Fiction*, 2nd edition, London: Boxtree, 2000

Gitlin, Todd, *Inside Prime Time*, revised edition, London: Routledge, 1994

Gregory, Chris, *Star Trek: Parallel Narratives*, London: Macmillan, 2000

Gripsrud, Jostein, *The Dynasty Years: Hollywood Television and Critical Media Studies*, London: Routledge, 1995

Gross, Larry, 'Film Après Noir: Alienation in a Dark Alley', in *Film Comment*, XII, No. 4, July/August, 1976

Guillen, Claudio, *Literature As System: Essays Towards the Theory of Literary History*, Princeton: Princeton University Press, 1971

Gunn, James, *Alternate Worlds: The Illustrated History of Science Fiction*, Englewood Cliffs, New Jersey: Prentice-Hall, 1975

Hansen, Miriam, *Babel and Babylon: Spectatorship in American Silent Film*, Cambridge: Harvard University Press, 1991

Haraway, Donna, 'A Manifesto for Cyborgs: Science, Technology and Socialist Feminism in the 1980s', *Socialist Review*, 80 (1985), 65–107

Hartwell, David (ed.), *The World Treasury of Science Fiction*, Boston: Little, Brown and Co., 1989

Hartwell, David, and Kathryn Cramer (eds) *The Ascent of Wonder: The Evolution of Hard SF*, London: Orbit Books, 1994

Heath, Stephen, 'Representing Television', in Mellencamp (ed.), *Logics of Television*

Hellman, John, *American Myth and the Legacy of Vietnam*, New York: Columbia University Press, 1986

Hendricks, Gordon, *Albert Bierstadt: Painter of the American West*, New York: Harry N. Abrams Inc/Amon Carter Museum of Western Art, 1974

Hill, John, and Pamela Church Gibson (eds), *The Oxford Guide to Film Studies*, Oxford: Oxford University Press, 1998

Hoberman, J., 'Vietnam: The Remake', in Kruger and Mariani (eds), *Remaking History*

Homer, *The Iliad/The Odyssey*, translated by E.V. Rieu, Harmondsworth: Penguin Books, 1985

Huntingdon, David, *The Landscapes of Frederic Edwin Church: Visions of an American Era*, New York: George Braziller, 1966

Jackson, Rosemary, *Fantasy: The Literature of Subversion*, London: Methuen, 1981

Jakobson, Roman, 'Closing Statement: Linguistics and Poetics', in T.A. Seboek (ed.), *Style in Language*, Cambridge: M.I.T. Press, 1960

Jakobson, Roman, 'On Realism in Art', in *Readings in Russian Poetics: Formalist and Structuralist Views*, translated and edited by Ladislav Matejka and Krystyna Pomorska, Ann Arbor: University of Michigan, 1978

James, Edward, *Science Fiction in the Twentieth Century*, Oxford: Opus Books, 1994

James, Edward, and Farah Mendlesohn (eds), *The Parliament of Dreams: Conferring on 'Babylon 5'*, Reading: Science Fiction Foundation, 1998

Jameson, Fredric, 'Towards a New Awareness of Genre', *Science Fiction Studies*, 9 (1982), 322–4

Jameson, Fredric, 'Postmodernism, or the Cultural Logic of Late Capitalism', *New Left Review*, 146 (July–August 1984), 59–92

Jameson, Fredric, *Postmodernism, or the Culture Logic of Late Capitalism*, Durham, North Carolina: Duke University Press, 1991

Jameson, Fredric, *The Geopolitical Aesthetic*, London: BFI, 1992

Jeffords, Susan, *The Remasculinization of America*, Bloomington: Indiana University Press, 1989

Johnson, William (ed.), *Focus on the Science Fiction Film*, New Jersey: Prentice-Hall,1972

Johnson-Smith, Jan, 'Of Warrior Poetics and Redemption: *Space: Above and Beyond*'s T.C. McQueen', *The Journal of American Culture*, 21, No. 3 (Fall 1998), 47–62

Joy, Nick, 'Tucker: The Man and his Dream', *Starburst 'X-Files' Special*, No. 33, Visual Imagination Publications: Autumn 1997

Kaminsky, Stuart M., *Don Siegel, Director*, New York: Curtis Books, 1974

Kant, Immanuel, *The Critique of Pure Reason*, translated and edited by Paul Guyer and Allen W. Wood, Cambridge: Cambridge University Press, 1997

Keane, Stephen, 'Time Past/Time Future: Reading Babylon Squared', in James and Mendlesohn (eds), *The Parliament of Dreams*

King, Geoff, *Spectacular Narratives: Hollywood in the Age of the Blockbuster*, London: I.B.Tauris, 2000

King, Geoff, and Tanya Krzywinska, *Science Fiction Cinema: From Outerspace to Cyberspace*, London: The Wallflower Press, 2000

Kitses, Jim, *Horizons West*, London: BFI, 1970

Krauss, Laurence, *The Physics of Star Trek*, with a foreword by Stephen Hawking, London: HarperCollins/Flamingo, 1997

Kruger, Barbara, and Phil Mariani (eds), *Remaking History*, Bay Press: Seattle, 1989

Kuhn, Annette (ed.), *Alien Zone: Cultural Theory and Contemporary Science Fiction Cinema*, London: Verso, 1990

Kuhn, Annette (ed.), *Alien Zone II: The Spaces of Science Fiction Cinema*, London: Verso, 1999

Lane, Andy, *The Babylon File*, Vol. 1, London: Virgin, 1997

Lane, Andy, *The Babylon File*, Vol. 2, London: Virgin, 1999

Lefanu, Sarah, *In the Chinks of the World Machine: Feminism and Science Fiction*, London: The Women's Press, 1988

Le Guin, Ursula K., *The Left Hand of Darkness*, London: Panther Books, 1973

Le Guin, Ursula K., 'Myth and Archetype in Science Fiction', *Parabola* (Fall 1976), 42–7

Le Guin, Ursula K., *The Earthsea Quartet*, Harmondsworth: Puffin Books, 1992

Lemon, Lee T., and Marion J. Reis (eds), *Russian Formalist Criticism: 4 Essays*, translated by Lemon and Reis, Lincoln: University of Nebraska Press, 1965

Levin, Harry, 'Science and Fiction', in Slusser, Guffey and Rose (eds), *Bridges to Science Fiction*

Limerick, Patricia, *The Legacy of Conquest*, New York: W.W. Norton and Co., 1987

Lincoln, Abraham, 'Address Delivered at the Dedication of the Cemetery at Gettysburg', in *The Norton Anthology of American Literature*, Vol. 1

Lincoln, Abraham, 'Annual Address to Congress', 1 December 1862, in *The Collected Works of Abraham Lincoln*, edited by R.P. Basler, Vol. 5, New Brunswick: Rutgers University Press, 1953

Lyotard, Jean-François, *The Postmodern Condition: A Report on Knowledge*, translated by Geoff Bennington and Brian Massumi, Minneapolis: University of Minnesota Press, 1984

MacCabe, Colin, 'Realism and the Cinema: Some Notes on Some Brechtian Theses', in Easthope (ed.), *Contemporary Film Theory*

MacHale, Brian, *Postmodernist Fiction*, London: Methuen, 1987

McCaffrey, Larry, *Across the Wounded Galaxies: Interviews with Contemporary American Science Fiction Writers*, Chicago: University of Illinois Press, 1990

McCarron, Kevin, 'Religion, Philosophy and the End of History', in James and Mendlesohn (eds), *The Parliament of Dreams*

McLuhan, Marshall, and Quentin Fiore, *The Medium is the Message*, New York: Bantam, 1967

McMahon, David F., 'The Psychological Significance of Straczynski's Universe', in James and Mendlesohn (eds), *The Parliament of Dreams*

Mast, Gerald, Marshall Cohen and Leo Braudy (eds), *Film Theory and Criticism: Introductory Readings*, 4th edition, Oxford: Oxford University Press, 1992

Matejka, Ladislav, and Krystyna Pomorska (eds), *Readings in Russian Poetics: Formalist and Structuralist Views*, Ann Arbor: University of Michigan, 1978

Mellencamp, Patricia (ed.), *Logics of Television*, Bloomington: Indiana University Press, 1990

Metz, Christian, 'Trucage and the Film', *Critical Enquiry*, Vol. 13, No. 4 (1977)

Moorcock, Michael, 'Play with Feeling', *New Worlds Science Fiction*, 129 (1963), 2–3, 123–7

Moorcock, Michael, 'New Worlds: A Personal History', *Foundation*, 15 (1979), 5–18

Murray, Janet, *Hamlet on the Holodeck: The Future of Narrative in Cyberspace*, Cambridge, Massachusetts: MIT Press, 1997

Musashi, Miyamoto, *The Book of Five Rings*, translated by Victor Harris, London: HarperCollins, 1995

Myths from Mesopotamia: The Creation, The Flood, Gilgamesh and Others, translated and edited by Stephanie Dalley, Oxford: Oxford World Classics, 1991

Nash, Roderick, *Wilderness and the American Mind*, New Haven: Yale University Press, 1982

Neale, Steve, *Genre*, London: BFI, 1980

Neale, Steve, 'Questions of Genre', *Screen*, 31, No. 1 (1990), 45–66

Neale, Steve, '"You've Got to be Fucking Kidding!": Knowledge, Belief and Judgement in Science Fiction', in Kuhn (ed.), *Alien Zone*

Neale, Steve, and Murray Smith (eds), *Contemporary Hollywood Cinema*, London: Routledge, 1998

Nicholls, Peter (ed.), *Explorations of the Marvellous*, London: Fontana, 1976

Nicholls, Peter, and Cornel Robu, 'Sense of Wonder', in Clute and Nicholls (eds), *The Encyclopaedia of Science Fiction*

Nietzsche, Friedrich, *Thus Spake Zarathustra*, translated by R.J. Hollingdale, reprint, Harmondsworth: Penguin Books, 1974

Noon, Jeff, *Vurt*, Littleborough: Ringpull Press, 1993

Norton Anthology of American Literature, The, Vol. 1, 2nd edition, London: W.W. Norton and Co., 1985

Novak, Barbara, *Nature and Culture: American Landscape and Painting, 1825–1875*, New York: Oxford University Press, 1980

Packwood, Nicholas, 'Engineering the Future: Speculative Technologies' in Edward James and Farah Mendlesohn (eds), *The Parliament of Dreams*

Parrinder, Patrick (ed.), *Science Fiction: A Critical Guide*, London: Longman, 1979

Parrinder, Patrick, *Science Fiction: Its Criticism and Teaching*, London: Methuen, 1980

Patin, Thomas, 'Exhibitions and Empire: National Parks and the Performance of Manifest Destiny', *Journal of American Culture*, 22, No. 1 (Spring 1999), 41–59

Penley, Constance, Elisabeth Lyon, Lynn Spigel and Janet Bergstrom (eds), *Close Encounters: Film, Feminism and Science Fiction*, Minneapolis: University of Minnesota Press, 1991

Poe, Edgar Allan, *The Narrative of Arthur Gordon Pym of Nantucket*, Harmondsworth: Penguin Classics, 1986

Poetic Edda, The, translated and edited by Lee M. Hollander, Austin: University of Texas, 1962

Powdermaker, Hortense, *Hollywood the Dream Factory: An Anthropologist Looks at the Movie-Makers*, London: Secker and Warburg, 1950

Powell, Earl A., 'Thomas Cole and the American Landscape Tradition', *Arts Magazine*, 52, No. 7 (1978), 110–7

Powell, Earl A., 'Luminism and the American Sublime', in Wilmerding (ed.), *American Light*

Praz, Mario, and Peter Fairclough (eds), *Three Gothic Novels*, Harmondsworth: Penguin Classics, 1986

Rabkin, Eric S., 'Metalinguistics and Science Fiction', *Critical Inquiry* (Autumn 1979), 79–97

Roberts, Adam, *Science Fiction*, London: Routledge, 2000

Roberts, Gareth, 'The Philosophy of Balance', in James and Mendlesohn (eds), *The Parliament of Dreams*

Robu, Cornel, 'A Key to Science Fiction: The Sublime', *Foundation*, 42 (1988), 21–37

Rose, Mark, *Alien Encounters*, Cambridge: Harvard University Press, 1981

Russ, Joanna, 'Interview', in Jeffrey F. Smith (ed.), *Khatru*, Baltimore: Phantasmicron Press, 1975

Russ, Joanna, *The Female Man*, New York: Bantam Books, 1975

Russ, Joanna, *Alyx*, Boston: Gregg Press, 1977

Ryan, Michael, and Douglas Kellner, *Camera Politica: The Politics and Ideology of Contemporary American Cinema*, Bloomington, Indiana University Press, 1990

Sagan, Carl, *Cosmos*, London: Abacus Books, 1991

Sawyer, Andy, 'The Shadows Out of Time: Lovecraftian echoes in *Babylon 5*', in James and Mendlesohn (eds), *The Parliament of Dreams*

Sayer, Karen, 'Every Station has its Phantoms: Uncanny Effects and Hybrid Spaces', in James and Mendlesohn (eds), *The Parliament of Dreams*

Schatz, Thomas, *Old Hollywood/New Hollywood: Ritual, Art and Industry*, Ann Arbor, Michigan: UMI Research Press, 1983

Shelley, Mary, *Frankenstein*, in *Three Gothic Novels*, edited by Mario Praz and Peter Fairclough, Harmondsworth: Penguin Classics, 1986

Shklovsky, Viktor, 'Art as technique', in *Russian Formalist Criticism: 4 Essays*, translated and edited by Lee T. Lemon and Marion J. Reis, Lincoln: University of Nebraska Press, 1965

Shu-Shun Chan, Herbert, 'Space and Time Out of Joint: War Without End', in James and Mendlesohn (eds), *The Parliament of Dreams*

Silverstone, Roger, *Television and Everyday Life*, London: Routledge, 1994

Sir Gawain and the Green Knight, introduced by Brian Stone, Harmondsworth: Penguin Books, 1959

Slotkin, Richard, *Regeneration Through Violence: The Mythology of the American Frontier, 1600–1860*, Middletown, Connecticut: Wesleyan University Press, 1973

Slusser, George E., George R. Guffey and Mark Rose (eds), *Bridges to Science Fiction*, Carbondale: University of Illinois Press, 1980

Slusser, George E., Eric S. Rabkin and Robert Scholes (eds), *Co-ordinates: Placing Science Fiction and Fantasy*, Carbondale: Southern Illinois University Press, 1983

Sobchack, Vivian, *Screening Space: The American Science Fiction Film*, 2nd enlarged edition, New Brunswick, New Jersey: Rutgers University Press, 1987

Soviet Science Fiction, introduced by Isaac Asimov, New York: Collier, 1962

Spencer, Kathleen L., '"The Red Sun is High, the Blue Low": Towards a Stylistic Description of SF', *Science Fiction Studies*, 10 (March 1983), 35–49

Stableford, Brian, John Clute and Peter Nicholls, 'Definitions of Science Fiction', in Clute and Nicholls (eds), *The Encyclopaedia of Science Fiction*

Stam, Robert, *Film Theory: An Introduction*, Oxford: Basil Blackwell, 2000

Stam, Robert, and Toby Miller (eds), *Film and Theory: An Anthology*, Oxford: Basil Blackwell, 2000

Straczynski, J. Michael, 'The Profession of Science Fiction, 48: Approaching Babylon', *Foundation: The Review of Science Fiction*, 64 (1995), 5–19

Straczynski, J. Michael, *The Complete Book of Scriptwriting*, revised edition, London: Titan Books, 1997

Stuart, Don A. [John W. Campbell], 'Who Goes There?', in Damon Knight (ed.), *Towards Infinity: Nine Science Fiction Adventures*, London: Pan Books, 1970

Suvin, Darko, 'On what is and is not an SF narration', *Science Fiction Studies*, V, No. 1 (1978), 45–57

Suvin, Darko, *Metamorphoses of Science Fiction: On the Poetics and Discourse of a Literary Genre*, London: Yale University Press, 1979

Telotte, J.P., *Science Fiction Cinema*, Cambridge: Cambridge University Press, 2001

Todorov, Tzvetan, 'Introduction', *Communication*, 11 (1968), 2–5

Todorov, Tzvetan, *The Fantastic: A Structural Approach*, translated by Richard Howard, Ithaca: Cornell University Press, 1975

Todorov, Tzvetan, *The Poetics of Prose*, translated by Richard Howard, Ithaca: Cornell University Press, 1977

Tolkien, J.R.R., *The Lord of the Rings*, London: Allen and Unwin, 1966

Trachtenberg, Alan, *The Incorporation of America: Culture and Society in the Gilded Age*, New York: Hill and Wang, 1982

Tuan, Yi-Fu, *Topophilia: A Study of Environmental Perception, Attitudes and Values*, Englewood Cliffs, New Jersey: Prentice-Hall, 1974

Tulloch, John, *Television Drama: Agency, Audience and Myth*, London: Routledge, 1990

Tulloch, John, and Manuel Alvarado, *Doctor Who: The Unfolding Text*, London: Macmillan, 1983

Tulloch, John, and Henry Jenkins, *Science Fiction Audiences: Watching Doctor Who and Star Trek*, London: Routledge, 1995

Turner, Frederick Jackson, 'The Significance of the Frontier in American History', in Billington (ed.), *The Frontier Thesis*

Tynjanov, Jurji, 'On Literary Evolution', in Matejka and Pomorska (eds), *Readings in Russian Poetics*

Verne, Jules, *Journey to the Centre of the Earth*, New York: Airmont, 1965

Verne, Jules, *Twenty Thousand Leagues Under the Sea*, London: Corgi, 1975

Whitfield, Stephen E., and Gene Roddenberry, *The Making of Star Trek*, New York: Ballantine Books, 1968

Whitman, Walt, 'Passage to India', in *The Portable Walt Whitman*, Harmondsworth: Penguin Books, 1984

Williams, Raymond, *Television: Technology and Cultural Form*, London: Fontana, 1974

Wilmerding, John (ed.), *American Light: The Luminist Movement*, Washington DC: National Gallery of Art, 1980

Wilton, Andrew, *Turner and the Sublime*, Chicago: University of Chicago Press, 1980

Wood, Robin, *Hollywood From Vietnam to Reagan*, New York: Columbia University Press, 1986

Wood, Robin, 'Aspects of ideology and narrative form in the American war film', *Screen*, 32, No. 1, 1991

Wood, Robin, 'Ideology, Genre, Auteur', in Mast, Cohen and Braudy (eds), *Film Theory and Criticism*

Wymer, Thomas, Alice Calderonello, Lowell P. Leland, Sara Jayne Steen and R. Michael Evers, *Intersections: The Elements of Fiction in Science Fiction*, Ohio: Bowling Green State University Popular Press, 1978

INTERNET

The Lurker's Guide to *Babylon 5*: http://www.midwinter.com/b5

The Lurker's Guide to *Babylon 5*: http://www.midwinter.com/lurk/universe/cast-3.html

Straczynski, J.M., post, 10 May 1996: http://www.midwinter.com/b5/CompuServe/cs96–05

Paramount's *Star Trek* site: http://www.startrek.com

APOD: http://antwrp.gsfc.nasa.gov/apod/astropix.html

Farscape: http://www.sci-fi.com

Farscape: http://www.bbc.co.uk/farscape

Space: Above and Beyond: http://www.pathcom.com/~nooger/flameboy/paula7.html

Space: Above and Beyond: http://www.cybervanguard.com/interviews.morrison.html

INDEX